Blessed are the peacemakers for they shall be called children of God.

—Matthew 5:9

Designing Conflict Management Systems

A Guide to Creating Productive and Healthy Organizations

Cathy A. Costantino

Christina Sickles Merchant

Foreword by William L. Ury

Jossey-Bass Publishers • San Francisco

Jossey-Bass books and products are available through most bookstores. To contact Jossey-Bass directly, call (888) 378-2537, fax to (800) 605-2665, or visit our website at www.josseybass.com.

Substantial discounts on bulk quantities of Jossey-Bass books are available to corporations, professional associations, and other organizations. For details and discount information, contact the special sales department at Jossey-Bass.

TCF Manufactured in the United States of America on Lyons Falls Turin Book. This paper is acid-free and 100 percent totally chlorine-free.

Library of Congress Cataloging-in-Publication Data

Costantino, Cathy A.
    Designing conflict management systems: a guide to creating
productive and healthy organizations / Cathy A. Costantino.
Christina Sickles Merchant : foreword by William L. Ury. — 1st ed.
        p.   cm.   — (The Jossey-Bass conflict resolution series)
    Includes bibliographical references (p.) and index.
    ISBN 0-7879-0162-8 (alk. paper)
    1. Conflict management.   I. Merchant, Christina Sickles.
    II. Title.   III. Series.
HD42.C68   1996   95-36410
658.4—dc20

FIRST EDITION
HB Printing 10 9 8 7 6 5

The Jossey-Bass Conflict Resolution Series

The Jossey-Bass Conflict Resolution Series addresses the growing need for guidelines in the field of conflict resolution, as broadly defined to include negotiation, mediation, alternative dispute resolution, and other forms of third-party intervention. Our books bridge theory and practice, ranging from descriptive analysis to prescriptive advice. Our goal is to provide those engaged in understanding and finding new and more effective ways to approach conflict—practitioners, researchers, teachers, and those in other professional and volunteer pursuits—with the resources to further their work and better the world in which we live.

This series is dedicated to
the life and work of
Jeffrey Z. Rubin
1941–1995

Contents

Part Three: Making the System Work

FOREWORD

Conflict today is a growth industry—in our communities, in our businesses and nonprofit organizations, in our government agencies, and among all of these. We are living today in times of intense change, and change naturally creates conflict. We cannot choose to eliminate this conflict—nor should we—but we can choose how we handle conflict. Conflict, after all, is like rainfall. Properly controlled, it can be a boon; too much at once and in the wrong place can cause a destructive flood. The challenge is to build a flood control system. The challenge with the rising flood of disputes is to create a dispute resolution system or, as this excellent book calls it, a conflict management system.

One constructive response to rising conflict has been to advocate and practice particular processes of conflict resolution such as negotiation, mediation, or arbitration. Often, however, one process is not enough to resolve a dispute; an integrated set of processes is required. If negotiation at first doesn't work, one can turn to mediation and so on. What is more, one wants to learn from each successive dispute to put into place preventive practices—ones that either prevent unnecessary disputes from arising in the first place or prevent unnecessary escalation of disputes. Finally, one wants a set of procedures in place that can deal not just with a single dispute but with the multitude of disputes that arise in any organization or in relationships between organizations. In other words, there is much value in adopting a systemic approach.

The purpose of dispute systems design is to offer the parties maximal choice and assistance in finding the best way to resolve their dispute for mutual benefit, if possible, and at the lowest cost in time, money, and relationship. The designer is, interestingly, both consultant and mediator, assisting the parties in designing their own system, one that works best for them. In this sense, the process of dispute systems design can be considered a kind of "meta-mediation," a mediation about mediation and other processes of conflict management. Dispute systems design cannot be imposed and expected to succeed; ideally it emerges from the parties themselves, often but not always assisted by a conflict resolution professional.

A number of years ago, my colleagues Jeanne Brett and Stephen Goldberg and I tried to sum up the lessons we and other practitioners had learned in our attempts to help the parties design their dispute resolution systems. We wrote a book on the subject called *Getting Disputes Resolved: Designing Systems to Cut the Costs of Conflict* (Jossey-Bass, 1988). In that book, we tried to codify certain basic principles of design, among them designing interest-based procedures, creating the motivation to engage in such procedures, designing low-cost rights and power contests, creating prevention processes, and building in a process for learning. At the same time, we recognized that the field was very much in its infancy and expressed the hope that others would develop and deepen the body of knowledge.

It is with great pleasure therefore that some years later I am able to write a foreword to a new book on the subject, one that offers a good deal of additional insight into the intricacies of designing systems to manage conflict. Cathy A. Costantino and Christina Sickles Merchant have performed the particularly valuable service of integrating into the field of designing dispute resolution systems the knowledge that has accumulated in the related field of organization development. Dispute or conflict systems are embedded after all in complex organizational systems, and a thorough understanding of their dynamics is essential. The authors have also usefully expanded on the design principle of prevention, setting out a variety of methods for heading off unnecessary disputes.

Perhaps their most interesting contribution is to apply the design principle that my coauthors and I considered most fundamental—that of focusing on the parties' interests—even more radically than we did to the process of design itself so that dispute systems design becomes, in their words, "by the stakeholder, for the stakeholder, and with the stakeholder."

The authors are well qualified to write about the subject. Each individually has a wealth of experience to share, Ms. Costantino from her work at the Federal Deposit Insurance Corporation and the Resolution Trust Corporation and Ms. Merchant from her extensive work facilitating labor-management partnerships. They have made a real contribution to advancing the field of systems design, first as practitioners, advocates, and teachers—and now as authors.

Santa Fe, New Mexico   WILLIAM L. URY
August 1995

To our parents, Carl and Jeanette, Walter and Jean, who gave us love and taught us values; to our significant others, who gave us encouragement and taught us acceptance: from Cathy to Jack; from Christina to Robert, Cheryl, and Katherine.

Preface

Conflict is like water: too much causes damage to people and property; too little creates a dry, barren landscape devoid of life and color. We need water to survive; we need an appropriate level of conflict to thrive and grow as well. How we manage our natural resources of water through dams, reservoirs, and sluices determines whether we achieve the balance necessary for life. So too with conflict management: a balance must be struck between opposing forces and competing interests.

This book is about designing effective conflict management systems within organizations. All institutions—corporations, governments, nations, families, nonprofits, hospitals, courts, universities—experience conflict, both within and with outside parties. At times, institutions are flooded with conflict. Somehow, this flood is "managed" in all systems, most frequently by denying, avoiding, controlling, or fighting it.

Increasingly, however, given today's economic, political, and *who* social realities, executives, managers, organization development (OD) consultants, human resource (HR) personnel, conflict management systems designers, and attorneys are seeking more creative and improved methods to manage conflict. They are being asked to devise processes that constructively draw conflict to the surface and channel it: these are the sluices and viaducts of effective conflict management.

Typically, organizational leaders do not view the management of conflict as systemically as they do information, human resource, and financial management systems. Rather, conflict in organizations is viewed and managed in a piecemeal, ad hoc fashion, as isolated events, which are sometimes grouped by category if the risk exposure is great enough but that are rarely examined in the aggregate to reveal patterns and systemic issues. In a sense, most organizations regard disputes as "local" events. Viewing the management of conflict systemically provides unparalleled opportunities for an organization to learn critical information about its operations, its population, and its environment—that is, to achieve a more "global" perspective.

It is our belief that the future will require executives, managers, OD consultants, HR personnel, dispute systems designers, and attorneys to have direct experience and some level of competence in the systemic management of conflict. The focus will be less on the mechanics of dispute resolution in a singular matter or a cluster of cases and more on the "big picture" of effective organizational conflict management, whether one is involved as a member of the organization or as an external advisor. Our intention here is to offer those who will be involved in "next generation" conflict management systems—by assessing, designing, creating, improving, evaluating, or managing them—a deeper understanding of the nature of conflict and the processes necessary for the effective acceptance and management of it.

Viewed systemically, conflict management presents opportunities for discovery of the core concerns of organizational stakeholders. It also offers opportunities for growth—by respecting and creatively resolving differences. *Designing Conflict Management Systems* is about accepting the current state of conflict management in an organization and assisting that organization in choosing and implementing alternative strategies on a systemic basis.

Our Background

As are many of you, we are practitioners who have experienced the frustrations and challenges of helping organizations change. We know firsthand the difficulties of dealing with fear, politics, resistance, limited resources, budgetary reductions, turf battles, lack of buy-in, and misperceptions about what we believe are healthy organizational alternatives to traditional dispute resolution. We also know the joy of working with organizations, their leadership and their stakeholders who are willing to move into the tension of examining and improving their current conflict management system. We have worked hand in hand with those who have sought and sustained substantial organizational conflict management changes, which resulted in increased satisfaction, decreased costs, and improved relationships. We wrote this book to encourage such movement toward systemic conflict management rather than ad hoc dispute resolution methods.

We offer concrete approaches to conflict management, grounded in a marriage of organization development (OD), dispute systems design (DSD), and alternative dispute resolution (ADR) principles and "best practices." We are practice oriented and therefore explore the real-life "what ifs" and "nots" of conflict management systems design, with stories, checklists, and charts as guides. Throughout the book, examples demonstrate core principles, concepts, and techniques, and case studies from three distinct settings—the government, commercial, and health care sectors—reveal diverse conflict management perspectives and applications. We welcome you as colleagues already familiar with basic organization development and management literature, principles, and practices who are specifically concerned about effective design of conflict management systems. We hope you will view us as coaches.

Underpinnings of This Book

Let us explain at the outset our own values, assumptions, and goals in writing this book. We take a value-centered approach to conflict management; in our opinion, "values" is not a word to be avoided in the hope of appearing professional or academic or neutral. Whether executive, supervisor, employee, OD consultant, HR manager, attorney, or author, we all have preferences, particularly when addressing the issue of conflict. We encourage awareness of these conflict management preferences, for we believe they influence our performance and affect, to a greater or lesser degree, the outcome of our efforts.

We believe that stakeholder participation in the conflict management design process is essential. Whether you work in the mail room or negotiate in the boardroom, organizational conflict affects you; we hold the belief that collective participation in creating conflict management processes increases the likelihood that the resulting processes will be used and preferred. With such participation, we also see the need for a sense of stewardship, for we believe that involved stakeholders are responsible and accountable for the nature and results of the changes they advocate to improve organizational functioning, particularly with regard to the manner in which conflict is handled.

Further, our experience suggests that conflict is spiral, despite the Western cultural tendency to categorize it as linear. We Westerners get uncomfortable when asked or required to tolerate ambiguity. To overcome such discomfort, many organizations try to build sequential and logical approaches to dispute resolution—first negotiate the dispute, then mediate, and if that fails, arbitrate. As practitioners, we believe that conflict is more fluid and organic that this, and we hold the value that its management starts with an evolutionary process focused on discovery, creativity, and continuous learning.

We know that we have made certain underlying assumptions about conflict in this book. To the extent that we are aware of them, we explicitly state them and encourage and welcome ongoing debate about their validity.

We assume conflict is inevitable, that it is present in every aspect of our lives—with partners, children, colleagues, landlords, neighbors, customers, managers, employees, professors, and patients. We assume that conflict is neither good nor bad—it just *is*. Conflict is a signal that someone is dissatisfied; it is an indication that a storm is approaching or that the weather is about to change. We also assume that organizations are constantly in a state of flux; they never reach permanent equilibrium or stasis. Using the phrase coined by Peter Vaill (1989), we see organizations and their participants as attempting to stay afloat in a swirl of "permanent white water," constantly changing and evolving in response to forces both internal and external.

Overview of the Contents

This book is divided into three parts. Part One offers a macro framework and looks at the "what" of conflict management. Chapter One adds more definition to a basic understanding of conflict and looks at how individuals and organizations respond to conflict. It provides a variety of information about these responses, including a discussion of "fight" and "flight" reactions, as well as denial, avoidance, and warrior stances; clues on where to look to uncover and identify organizational conflict and how to name it when it is at the core of an issue; and the potential of the Myers-Briggs Type Indicator (MBTI) for understanding various individual and possibly organization-wide responses to conflict. Chapter Two introduces the concept of conflict management as a subsystem existing within the broader organizational system. It looks at open and learning systems thinking as applied to the management

of conflict, as well as the application of other relevant OD principles to the concept that conflict management is a system. Chapter Three explores the emerging use of ADR, including an
overview of the various types of ADR; the concept of ADR as
appropriate dispute resolution; and how ADR is being used and
perhaps abused by organizations today. Chapter Four investigates
the design of interest-based conflict management systems as the
"next generation" in the evolution of systems design; it addresses
the need to involve stakeholders in the process itself and com-
pares several design models.

Part Two explores the micro or "how to" aspects of conflict
management—the elements of best practices and the mechanisms
to develop a more effective system. Chapter Five provides guidance
on particularly important entry and contracting issues as the internal or external consultant moves into conflict management systems
development work and begins the interest-based design intervention itself. Chapter Six looks at the big picture of organizational
assessment, including organizational culture—making sure that
the conflict management design fits with the larger culture—as
well as the issue of power gains and losses as the current conflict
management system changes. Chapter Seven discusses design
architecture: deciding which ADR methods to consider in developing the conflict management system and the relationship of
such methods to case selection. Chapter Eight explores training
and education issues, including methodology choices, the targeting of appropriate audiences, and the identification of recurrent
misperceptions about conflict management training. Chapter Nine
shows how to get the program launched, including tips on the use
of pilot projects and rolling out the program. Chapter Ten offers
a process for deciding if the conflict management system is really
working in terms of administration and results and identifies possible quantitative and qualitative evaluation methodologies.

Part Three explores the real-life, problem-solving, or "what if"
and "not" aspects of conflict management systems, as well as the key
concepts of acceptance and choice. Chapter Eleven addresses how
to motivate others to actually use the conflict management system
and includes a discussion of appropriate rewards and incentives and
how to tailor them to the organization's conflict management goals.
Chapter Twelve dissects the practical realities of diagnosing and
addressing both organizational and individual resistance and con-

straints. Chapter Thirteen looks at learning to live with what is—accepting the organization, its stakeholders, and practitioners as they are—and expanding the culture of conflict to offer choice.

The epilogue addresses the larger aspects of organizational conflict management in the context of individuals, groups, communities, nations, and the global village.

The resource section at the end of the book includes a list of institutions and associations that provide ADR, DSD, and OD assistance. Several selected bibliographies are also included to guide further research and to provide additional information on ADR, DSD, and OD.

It is our hope that this book will help us all to recognize that we each play a part in sustaining and managing conflict in the world around us and that we can each play our part as peacemaker.

Acknowledgments

There are many people we need to thank for their assistance and guidance in making this book a reality: our colleagues who inspired us to break new ground—Bill Ury, Marv Weisbord, Linda Singer, Michael Lewis, Marjorie Aaron, and Bob Marshak; our co-workers who explored and tested new ideas with us—Jean Savage, Ric Herrera, Charlotte Kaplow, Martha McClellan, and Pam Calloway; our colleagues in the federal government and the members of the Dispute Systems Design Working Group of the Administrative Conference of the United States who gave us feedback on our emerging ideas; and the many seminar participants who challenged those ideas and encouraged us to put them on paper.

We would also like to thank Cedric Crocker, our editor at Jossey-Bass, who so artfully and gently coached us; Cheryl Greenway, the Jossey-Bass editorial assistant who made it all somehow come together; and Gail Ross, our agent, who believed in us from the beginning and encouraged us throughout.

Finally, we are grateful to the many stakeholders and organizations we have had the privilege to work with and the honor to learn from as partners.

Arlington, Virginia
August 1995

CATHY A. COSTANTINO
CHRISTINA SICKLES MERCHANT

The Authors

CATHY A. COSTANTINO, attorney, mediator, and conflict management systems designer, is well known for her work with alternative dispute resolution (ADR) in the federal government, the legal community, and the banking industry. She was chairperson for the thirty-nation United Nations Conference on the Social Effects of Structural Change in the Banking Industry held in Geneva in November 1993. Costantino directs the nationwide ADR program at the Federal Deposit Insurance Corporation (FDIC) in Washington, D.C., and has recently been involved in designing the Office of Ombudsman at the FDIC. She is an adjunct professor at Georgetown University Law Center and a former faculty assistant for the Harvard Law School Program of Instruction for Lawyers.

A recognized expert on systems design, Costantino frequently gives seminars on creating effective organizational conflict management systems and has written numerous articles. She received both her B.A. degree and master's degree in social work from the Catholic University of America in Washington, D.C., and her J.D. degree from the University of California, Berkeley (Boalt Hall).

CHRISTINA SICKLES MERCHANT, mediator, organization development practitioner, and conflict management systems designer, is most widely known for her work in fostering sustainable partnerships between labor and management throughout the private, public, and international arenas. As a Fellow with Syracuse University's Maxwell Center for Advanced Public Management, the first director of Labor-Management Cooperation for the Federal Labor Relations Authority, and a former commissioner with the Federal Mediation and Conciliation Service, Merchant is recognized as a leader in facilitating, designing, and implementing complex and large-scale change initiatives in organizations.

In 1995, she was selected to join an international team of experts advising Hungarian representatives of enterprises, government, and trade unions on their dispute systems design for labor conflict. Also during that year, she completed her term as president of the international Society of Professionals in Dispute Resolution. Merchant received her B.S. degree from the New York State School of Industrial and Labor Relations at Cornell University and her M.S. degree, with honors, in human resource and organization development from the joint program of the American University and the NTL Institute, formerly known as the National Training Laboratory for Applied Behavioral Science.

Part One

Coping with Conflict in Organizations

Chapter One

How Organizations and Individuals Respond to Conflict

Customers complain. Co-workers bicker. Defendants dig in. Counsels advocate. Union officials demand. Organizations are rife with conflict that takes many forms and wears many faces. They can hide it, quash it, control it, fight it, deny it, or avoid it, but whatever they do, they cannot make it disappear: conflict is an organizational fact of life.

Take for example, the hypothetical Montro Corporation, a leading manufacturer of word processing software purchased by both home users and commercial businesses. Historically, its largest market has been the commercial arena. Last year, Montro introduced "Hole-In-One," a new "umbrella" software package that includes word processing, graphics, spreadsheets, and presentation applications. It is Montro's first entry into the spreadsheet and presentation software market. Recently, Montro has begun to receive complaints, particularly from home users, that the presentation package does not interface properly with the word processing package, with the result that certain categories of presentation data (particularly bar graphs and pie charts) are deleted in certain modes of operation. Yesterday, an irate home user who runs her own business called the Montro CEO, complaining about a large presentation file (and, she claims, a potential client) she lost because of this problem. The CEO, sounding annoyed, immediately called Ms. Jones, the director of the Consumer Service Department. He instructed her to meet with Mr. Tate, director of research and design, to deal with the customer, to explore the problem, and to come up with some solutions "once and for all." Ms. Jones is not looking forward to today's meeting since she and Mr. Tate have a strained working relationship based on several problems on which they have worked together in the past.

Definition of Organizational Conflict

As this story demonstrates, organizations and the individuals in roles and in groups within those organizations experience conflict both in interaction with external forces and from within. Here, there is conflict between Montro and external forces: its customers. There is also internal conflict between members of the management team: its employees. The conflict between Montro and the customer is the result of dissatisfaction and unmet expectations; the conflict between Ms. Jones and Mr. Tate stems from interpersonal dealings that have uncovered differences in the way each regards the importance of customer satisfaction. In one instance, the conflict stems from the product that Montro currently produces; in the other, from past conversations.

If conflict is an organizational fact of life, neither good nor bad, then what exactly is it? Ask any group of people and you will usually get either the characteristics of conflict or descriptions about how people feel when they experience it: conflict is uncomfortable, conflict is about disagreement, conflict means something is wrong or "out of sync." When we are unsure what something is or lack the proper word for it, we tend to describe around it.

So too with the concept of conflict.

In the organizational context, conflict is an expression of dissatisfaction or disagreement with an interaction, process, product, or service. Someone or some group is unhappy with someone else or something else. This dissatisfaction can result from multiple factors: differing expectations, competing goals, conflicting interests, confusing communications, or unsatisfactory interpersonal relations. Examples include an employee's disagreement with her performance appraisal; a manager's concern with how resources are allocated; the production department's dismay with the sales department's marketing of an important product; a contractor's displeasure with the procurement process; a customer's anger over the lack of technical support after product purchase. In the Montro example, the customer is dissatisfied with the product, the CEO may have an unmet expectation that the problem should have been raised and resolved at a lower level, and Ms. Jones is concerned that she has to deal with Mr. Tate again.

Conflict is thus a process, not a product. Organizational conflict is really an organizational indicator of dissatisfaction. By moving toward a concept of conflict as a process, we move away from the idea that conflict is a tangible "problem" that can be solved, tamed, managed, or controlled. Rather, conflict is an interaction, a signal of distress from within or outside the system. Obviously, the organization or the individuals within it may choose not to respond to the distress call (for what may be perfectly legitimate reasons), but that does not mean that the conflict ceases to exist. For example, the Montro Corporation may conclude that the problem with the Hole-in-One software is a glitch that occurs only with home customers who are not sophisticated users. Montro may choose not to redesign the product, not to refund the customer's money, or not to replace the software; this does not mean that the conflict has gone away or does not exist—it simply means that Montro has chosen to do nothing about it in this instance.

Identifying Conflict in Organizations

People frequently use the terms *dispute* and *conflict* interchangeably but they are not synonymous. Conflict is a process; a dispute may be one of several products of conflict. Conflict is the process of expressing dissatisfaction, disagreement, or unmet expectations with any organizational interchange; a dispute is one of the products of conflict. In the above example, if Montro chooses to do nothing about the conflict and the dissatisfied customer files a lawsuit, the conflict has escalated to a dispute. The conflict is the process and state of dissatisfaction; the dispute is the product of the unresolved conflict.

Whereas conflict is often ongoing, amorphous, and intangible, a dispute is tangible and concrete—it has issues, positions, and expectations for relief. Collections or clusters of disputes are simply one of the many ways that conflict manifests itself in an organization. Conflict in an organization shows up in several ways:

- *Disputes:* Grievances, disciplinary actions, complaints, lawsuits, strikes, threatened legal action, and disagreements (whether with internal parties or outside disputants) are all signs of dissatisfaction and unresolved conflict. Disputes are usually the most visible evidence of conflict; they are the by-product of conflict.

- *Competition:* Some organizational conflict manifests itself more subtly than as outright disputes. Competition, particularly within an organization or between and among subunits and individuals within an organization, may also be a sign of emerging conflict. Obviously, not all competition is a form of conflict. For example, healthy competition with other companies that produce and market the same product is normal and expected. More serious, however, may be the conflict generated by uncontrolled, aggressive competition between or among work units or colleagues within the company itself.

- *Sabotage:* This not-so-subtle manifestation of conflict can be seen in both internal and external conflicts—for example, when the customer says everything is fine and then without notice holds a press conference to announce the filing of a million-dollar lawsuit for gross negligence in the production of a product. Sabotage may also be at work when there is a "turf" battle between divisions and when innuendos about managerial competence and integrity begin to surface and spread.

- *Inefficiency/lack of productivity:* Slow work, deliberate delay, or decreased output can be evidence of conflict. Hidden conflict can lead a disgruntled yet vital employee to refuse to participate efficiently and meaningfully as part of a team effort.

- *Low morale:* Similar to inefficiency or lack of productivity, low morale is often a reaction to hidden conflict. Often, it is the result of attempting to avoid or deny conflict or of frustration with attempts to protest organizational action or inaction. Employees get weary of being retransferred, restructured, or reinvented yet again. With no mechanism for dealing with their frustration, they often lose energy, morale, and motivation.

- *Withholding knowledge:* Within many corporate cultures, knowledge is power, and withholding knowledge (information) is practiced as a form of control. Such behavior is often a sign of distrust, status hierarchies, and an "information caste system." Only certain people are entitled to know certain information; information is shared according to status (title, seniority, or office size and location). Similarly, in transactions with outside parties, withholding information may also be a sign of hidden conflict and distrust.

Organizational Responses to Conflict

Organizations have a multitude of ways to respond to conflict, choosing a particular method in light of perceived importance, context, or players. Thus, to a certain extent, organizational responses to conflict are situation- or context-specific. They may also depend on whether the individual is operating on an interpersonal, intergroup, or interorganizational level.

Moreover, organizational responses to conflict do not occur separate and apart from the organizational "culture," or the attitudes, practices, and beliefs of the system and its members. The "way we do things around here" provides the collective lens through which the organization and its key players view internal disagreement or external threat. If, for example, Montro has a reputation for playing "hardball" when it comes to litigation, it may decide to aggressively fight any lawsuit, without regard for potential harm in the marketplace and damage to its reputation.

It is easy to observe how organizational culture affects responses to conflict and leads to a variety of reactions. For example, organizations with a "warrior" mentality of "winning at all costs" usually have an evolved corporate culture that furthers that goal and that is mirrored as well in the methods employed to control and fight the threat of conflict. Thus, the initiation of a complaint or filing of a lawsuit generates an immediate and belligerent response, accompanied by threats and intimidation. Often, no efforts are made to initiate settlement discussions until both parties to the dispute are at the brink of an all-out war. Such methods of conflict management allow the organization to remain congruent with its dominant culture. The entire organizational system does not have to be "warrior-like" to have subunits within it that take on the characteristics of the warrior, either through the special skills needed in the subunit, recruitment of personnel from other warrior cultures, or subunit leader preference. For example, units of security personnel at universities, hospitals, and government agencies may develop a subset warrior culture unaffected by the more dominant cultures of learning, healing, or serving within which they operate.

Organizational responses to conflict, which are usually defined and insisted upon by the organization's culture, can be grouped into the following general categories of "fight" or "flight":

Fight responses:

• *Arrogance:* The "paternal" or "we're above it all" approach to conflict: "Well, you know how the support staff [lower-graded or lower-paid] employees are—always unhappy about something and thinking they're entitled to more. What do you expect from them?" One can identify this type of response through comments or observations that belittle the disputants themselves rather than seek to identify the root causes. Those in charge determine whether to address the issues of the less empowered and in what fashion, leading to a resolution of conflict that is *for* or *on behalf of* disputants, not *with* them.

• *Engagement:* The "bulldozer" approach to conflict, often evidenced by military words and analogies: "We're right and we always win; we fight on principle. It's a strategic decision we've made; how dare you question our tactics or suggest we did something wrong? We'll outspend, outlawyer, outgun, and outmaneuver you, so why don't you just give up now?" This approach often leads to the import of "hired guns," experts and consultants to fight the war and do the dirty work of resolving the conflict.

Flight responses:

• *Denial:* The "blanket over the head" approach to conflict: "We are one big happy family"—a dysfunctional family, perhaps, maintaining the image that all is well no matter what evidence exists to the contrary! This approach often leads to "crazymaking," or individuals within the organization thinking that they are crazy because they see and feel and experience conflict that the organizational culture denies.

• *Avoidance:* The "ostrich head in the sand" approach to conflict: "We transfer our problem employees or restructure our programs to deal with conflict, with the result that we get rid of it." This approach stems from an assumption that if you move conflict to another venue, it "goes away," but instead it often leads to programmatic and personnel "musical chairs."

- *Accommodation:* The "please don't make waves" approach to conflict: "We'll give whatever relief is necessary, but please, please don't let anyone know that we've had this problem." This approach attempts to resolve conflict by appeasing the disputants in exchange for a promise to keep the settlement terms, and the very incident of disagreement, confidential. In a sense, it is the action combination of denial and avoidance among organizational responses to conflict.

Two additional points are worth noting. First, many organizations choose not to resolve their own disputes for political reasons—their outside counsel, accountants, management consultants, and experts do that for them. These are like mercenaries; they get paid to do battle on behalf of the organization. In this way, the executives and other significant organizational players can distance themselves from the dirty work of engagement and can appear to stay congruent with the higher purposes of the organization's mission as a whole. For example, Montro might decide to have an outside law firm rather than its in-house legal department handle the lawsuit so that it does not appear to be directly taking on a customer.

Secondly, some organizations, as well as systems and individuals within that organization, may actually benefit from *unresolved* conflict and therefore may have little incentive to uncover, manage, control, or resolve it, even when conflict is counterproductive and destructive. In-house legal departments, case processing divisions, and outside counsel fall potentially into this category. Their mission—their raison d'être—is to be the point of contact and confrontation for the "cases" that surface within an adversarially based method and culture of resolving disputes. In order to continue to operate and to thrive, such units within and outside the organization have a deep economic and often philosophical commitment to seeing the warrior-like methods endure. As discussed more fully in Chapter Six, it is important to determine who will gain and who will lose from a new approach to conflict management. If, for example, Montro decides that prior to aggressively defending the lawsuit, reasonable efforts will be made to resolve the dispute internally through alternative dispute resolution procedures, outside counsel may feel threatened and left out, and consequently veto such a suggestion.

Effectiveness of Organizational Responses to Conflict

How effective are these organizational "fight or flight" responses? Ask the CEO who spends millions of dollars a year on legal fees and expenses. Ask an employee whether she thinks the organization is one big happy family. Ask the manager who has just had a problem employee transferred into his division or had his section reorganized yet again.

Measuring the effectiveness of conflict management involves looking at the results of dispute resolution efforts, the durability of the resolutions, and the impact on relationships. The effectiveness of conflict management efforts can be measured quantitatively or qualitatively; it can focus on the delivery of conflict management services or the results of conflict management interventions. Although the topic of evaluating effective conflict management systems is explored in greater detail in Chapter Ten, the issues of durability and collateral effects of solutions are applicable here. By transferring the problem employee, the immediate dispute is "resolved," but is it a durable solution? Will the employee end up being transferred again? Perhaps the company won the $50 million patent infringement suit that ate up dollars and resources for the past five years, but what happened to its reputation in the marketplace and its relationship with its customers and licensees? The bottom line is that dispute resolution may have been successful according to the traditional organizational definition in that the dispute "went away," but was the resolution an effective one? Did it actually deal with the underlying conflict? Did it address the real problem or did it just mask a symptom of even greater conflict brewing? Is it worth it if Montro eventually wins the individual lawsuit but later has to defend a class action for deceptive marketing or unfair trade practices when it surfaces that the glitch actually does exist and that Montro knew about it and did not disclose or remedy it?

Most organizational representatives, when asked about the effectiveness of their dispute resolution system, note the high cost not only in terms of dollars and time spent in resolution efforts and litigation but also in terms of the negative impact on important, ongoing relationships—both within and outside the organization—with employees and customers. Increasingly, as in the Montro example, organizations are looking to alternative methods of dispute resolution (explored in Chapter Three) and accompanying techniques to manage conflict. They are asking organization development (OD) consultants, human resource (HR) managers, attorneys, and other professionals for help in improving the effectiveness of their conflict management systems as a whole.

Individual Responses to Conflict

Individuals, in roles and in groups within organizations, also have fight or flight responses to conflict. Their response may mirror the organizational response or it may be different. At Montro, for example, Ms. Jones could decide that despite the organizational warrior culture of using litigation to resolve disputes and in light of her conviction that Mr. Tate will not be oriented toward developing a satisfactory and customer-friendly resolution, she will attempt to resolve the dispute with the customer herself through less adversarial means, such as negotiation. In this way, Ms. Jones will depart from the organizational norm and bear the full burden of the success or failure of her efforts.

An individual's attitude toward conflict, view of how change occurs, style of communication, and sense of values have a dynamic effect on how that person deals with conflict. This is as true for the individuals within the organization experiencing conflict as it is for those who work from outside the organization to improve organizational conflict management systems. The reality is that most people are uncomfortable with conflict and do not like change. The status quo often prevails because individuals accept the known more readily than the unknown. This makes the tasks of improving conflict management systems rife with resistance not only for organizational but also for individual reasons. In Chapter Twelve, we discuss the practical realities of addressing the resistance and constraints prompted by changing the way in which conflict is managed in the organization. However, the Myers-Briggs Type Indicator (MBTI) is discussed here specifically as a tool that furthers an understanding of individual—and perhaps organizational—responses to conflict and tolerance for change.

OD consultants and HR managers have long experienced the value of the MBTI as a tool for increased understanding and team building when working with individuals and groups within organizations. The MBTI is viewed here as one way to conceptualize the diversity of individual responses to conflict and hence the range of resolution methods that might address these differing needs and preferences. Use of the MBTI may even lead to enhanced acceptability of the revised conflict management system because a greater range of organizational participants' needs have been recognized and addressed. Thus, as systemic conflict management design increasingly becomes an OD and HR intervention, the MBTI has useful applications in understanding and managing conflict as well as its more common applications.

As many readers are aware, the MBTI is a measurement of individual preferences in four areas concerned primarily with information gathering and decision making. These preferences affect what people perceive in a particular situation—in a sense, what information they are inclined to look for—and how they draw conclusions about what they perceive and their preferred process for decision making. There is no right or wrong way in the MBTI, just individual preferences along a continuum. The MBTI can be helpful in seeking to understand and plan for a range of individual disputant preferences, including how processes are chosen and how they will be used. It is interesting to note that organizations themselves often exhibit a distinct MBTI preference in the aggregate, an "organizational personality type." Identification of such a preference can assist in the process of examining and improving the conflict management system as well.

As a prelude to examining the impact of MBTI preferences on individuals working with an organization's conflict management system, it is necessary to provide a brief overview of how the MBTI reveals individual inclinations in information gathering and decision making, two critical tasks in dispute identification and resolution. In the MBTI, four attitudes and preferences are measured on scales: Extraversion and Introversion, Sensing and Intuition, Thinking and Feeling, and Judging and Perceiving.

First, the Extraversion (E) or Introversion (I) preference

focuses on whether one prefers to derive energy primarily from the outer world of people, places, or things (E) or from the inner world of concepts and ideas (I). Thus, Extraverts will prefer to explore and interact with others first to generate ideas or to identify options, while Introverts will prefer to arrive at ideas and options initially through a less interactive, more internal, inner-directed process.

The Sensing (S) or Intuitive (N) preference focuses on how an individual perceives or gathers information. One person may prefer to rely primarily upon the immediate, tangible, practical, and observable information that can be received through the five senses (S) while another prefers to receive and process information through a perception of the meanings, relationships, concepts, and possibilities beyond the realm of what is immediately apparent (N).

The Thinking (T) or Feeling (F) preference is concerned with what kind of judgment one trusts first when making a decision. Either one prefers to rely primarily on analysis, logic, and objectivity (T), or one prefers to rely more on subjective, personal, or social values (F).

The Judgment (J) or Perception (P) preference focuses on what attitude is adopted in dealing with the external world. A person who prefers the J mode lives in a more decisive, planned, and orderly way, seeking to regulate and control events. One who favors the P mode lives in a more spontaneous way, seeking to understand life and to adapt to it.

Each of these four preferences is present in every individual as polar opposites on the same continuum, varying in strength and intensity. Each preference is independent of the other three, resulting in sixteen "types" or combinations denoted by the four letters of the type (for example, ENFJ, ISTP, or ENTJ). Each of the sixteen types has its own typical pattern of preferred processes, characteristics, and attitudes that are used to gather data and to make decisions. Each of these types also has different preferences, strengths, and vulnerabilities when managing conflict and when exploring the need for change in the organization's management of its conflict. Examination of the following chart (Table 1.1) yields a deeper appreciation of the range of potential and diverse expectations, preferences, and contributions among individuals with regard to

Table 1.1. Implications of MBTI for Individual Responses to Conflict and Conflict Management.

	Possible Strength	Potential Weakness
Extravert (E)	Generates high interaction within groups as leader or member; adept at idea/concept generation for problem solving	May be dominant and overpowering in interactions; tendency to overwhelm others, thus losing ideas
Introvert (I)	Generates thoughtfully clear ideas and concepts; offers studied review of problem or situation at hand	Ideas may be lost due to reluctance to expose them prematurely; tendency to become frustrated with highly interactive and verbal processes
Sensing (S)	Attends to immediate details and practical applications; tends to focus on the details of the numbers, types, and degree of disputes	May have difficulty seeing the big picture and its implications for today's actions; may have difficulty recognizing the existence of culture and trends
Intuitive (N)	Focuses on possibilities; creative and expansive data gatherer; tends to see organization as a whole, with ability to recognize culture and trends	Difficulty with "here and now" orientation; often inattentive to details; may be challenged by issues of implementation
Thinking (T)	Brings rational, objective approach to decision making; likely to see conflict as opportunity for change	May overlook impact of decisions on people—their needs, concerns, and values; tendency to focus on products first, processes second
Feeling (F)	Focuses on the fairness of how conflict and its management affects people—their sense of self, empowerment, and values	May get caught up emotionally in the process; uncomfortable with conflict, inclined to feel that conflict is "bad"
Judgment (J)	Helps focus on closure and commitment; works for a product that can be implemented and used	Uncomfortable with uncertainty; may push for closure and commitment too soon; may be controlling and "take over"
Perception (P)	Encourages options, possibilities and spontaneity; usually comfortable with prospect of a variety of choices	May have difficulty producing a final result or product or agreeing to a firm commitment

conflict and its management. Such appreciation is useful, in our view, when seeking greater effectiveness in conflict management. Moreover, such charting of preferences, in at least the MBTI's range of possibilities, illustrates the variety of individual needs and expectations that often remain unaddressed by organizational conflict management efforts. If nothing else, it enhances awareness of the challenge that practitioners, managers, and design teams face in their attempts to design improved methods of conflict resolution.

As can be seen from Table 1.1, individuals have differing preferences for and reactions to the core tasks of dealing with conflict, which are information gathering and decision making. Such differences affect the outcome of any dispute resolution effort, the ongoing management of the organization's current methods of dispute resolution, and the design of more systemic conflict management approaches. For example, an organization's main purpose might be research into concepts and ideas for application to specific and time-sensitive problems of a client population—in other words, a scientific research organization. In order to accomplish its mission, the organization will seek, attract, and employ many individuals who prefer to work in such an environment—most likely Introverted, Sensing, Thinking, Judging types (ISTJs). Because such individuals are needed to perform the organization's core mission, there may be more of these types than any other types in the system—leading to a predominant "organizational personality type" of ISTJ as well. What will be the chief characteristics of the current and preferred conflict management methods for such an organization and its participants? One might hypothesize that in a system with little face-to-face interchange, a studied yet rapid approach to the dispute at hand resulting in a final and binding decision would be preferred by the majority in the organization, including its leadership. However, what about the organization's nonresearch participants—for example, the salespeople who advertise the scientific advisory function and who acquire customers? Will such participants have the same preferences regarding disputes or organizational conflict? Based on MBTI preferences, it is unlikely that they will be satisfied by the dominant organizational preference for certain methods of handling conflict. In such instances, which occur frequently in organizations, the method preferred and employed by the majority or dominant group of organizational participants may in fact not be a satisfactory process for the remainder of the organization's participants (or their customers and suppliers). Such groups of organizational participants and stakeholders can become a source of dissatisfaction with current dispute resolution approaches (that is, the manner in which information about disputes is gathered and how decisions for resolution are reached). Such dissatisfaction can surface through the full range of individual responses to conflict noted previously: lowering of morale, decrease in productivity, or sabotage. Such symptoms of dissatisfaction are ongoing in organizations and often only generate a meaningful organizational response when they attain crisis proportions and threaten the organization in some way. At such points, organizations often call upon conflict management experts or OD practitioners to assist them—and such individuals arrive on the scene possessing an entirely different range of preferences, strengths, and vulnerabilities for dealing with conflict, as illustrated in Table 1.1, than the dominant "organizational personality type" or even other organizational participants and stakeholders. From such an example, one can picture the increasing complexity of the interaction between individuals experiencing, managing, and revising organizational conflict management systems.

Combining Organizational and Individual Responses to Conflict

Returning to our ongoing illustration of the dispute at the Montro Corporation, the application of the MBTI may illuminate the dispute further and create additional opportunities for observation and action. If Montro is inclined to make decisions from the "Thinking" orientation, it may be very rational and logical in its approach to the potential lawsuit—the bothersome home user being perceived as one of millions of customers with what is assessed to be a negligible effect on market, sales, and liability. If Montro is more inclined to make decisions from the "Feeling" orientation, it may focus on the conflict's effect on employees (Ms. Jones and Mr. Tate), customers (the irate home user), and the perception of the corporation's fairness in the marketplace. If

Montro is inclined to adopt the attitude of an "E" (or Extraverted) organization, it may be quite public about its efforts to fight the lawsuit and it may seek input and information from other companies who have faced similar lawsuits; if it is more inclined to be an "I" (or Introverted) organization, it may be more reflective and cautious in its resolution strategy, avoiding publicity whenever possible and gaining its strength and energy from within.

Of course, only broad generalizations can be drawn from the MBTI regarding whether individual responses to conflict are "in sync" with or in opposition to organizational responses to conflict. For the purpose of illustrating the variety and range of organizational and individual responses to conflict, however, the MBTI is quite useful. One possibility is that where the organizational response to conflict differs markedly from a particular individual's preferred response to the same conflict, dissonance results. For example, if Ms. Jones suggests negotiating with the customer to resolve the dispute, Montro's legal department or Mr. Tate may "dig in their heels," becoming even more adamant that Montro has done nothing wrong and that it should fight the lawsuit aggressively. Such internal disagreement as to the proper approach to the complaint at hand can lead to further conflict within the organization. Such conflict, while ever present, can be managed proactively in order to cut the human, production, and litigation costs of excessive and disruptive dissonance. The definitions of "excessive" and "disruptive" depend upon both the organizational context and the individual's tolerance for discomfort. However, in this age of leaner organizations seeking to survive in highly competitive environments, it may be in the organization's best interests (and in the best interests of those who advise such organizations) to become more acutely aware of the organization's existing conflict management system, the costs—both direct and indirect—of maintaining the status quo, and the opportunities that exist for improvements, including cost savings and heightened satisfaction.

Managers, OD consultants, and HR professionals are already abundantly familiar with chronic conflict in organizations, which is often due to internal disagreement and rivalry over how best to distribute the organization's limited resources among competing priorities and components. As a starting point in introducing a series of lenses through which conflict within and outside any organization can be viewed and understood, we have provided here a "macro" framework of conflict in organizations. In addition, we have offered information and concepts that provide a basic understanding of conflict, including individual and organizational responses to it. The ability to recognize the variety of ways in which conflict arises in organizations and how it affects individuals in roles and in groups within those organizations is an important first step toward the goal of designing conflict management systems. Keeping in mind these broad concepts will be useful now as we turn to examining conflict management as an actual and ongoing system within the larger context of the organization as a whole.

Chapter Two

Recognizing Conflict Management as a System

The design or improvement of conflict management systems derives many of its practices and principles from well-established organization development (OD) concepts and techniques. We suggest that OD can be thought of as the who, what, and why of organizational action and change, addressing how organizations, their leaders, and their members seek and sustain change: considering, planning, managing, and measuring. These core tasks are also essential to the effective design or improvement of conflict management systems. In general terms, OD is about discovering the need for change, is planned and intentional in nature, and is as durable as possible over time. We suggest that conflict management systems designers need to pursue similar goals in order to achieve a measure of effectiveness in their efforts, and that many OD principles are relevant when exploring conflict management as a system. What we offer in this chapter are not new or novel OD theories or principles but, rather, application of OD to conflict management viewed systemically.

Conflict management design extends and applies many OD concepts to the specific area of organizational conflict: the whether and how of dealing with systemic conflict in organizations. Conflict management design draws from the full range of OD theory and practice, particularly systems thinking, change intervention design, search processes, relationship building, strategic redesign and implementation, and action learning for improved conflict management systems development. Moreover, the core values associated with organization development—openness, tolerance of diversity, learning, involvement, appreciation of and management of differences, generation of valid data, and the search for feedback—are particularly critical for successful work with conflict itself and for the systemic management of it in any organization. We examine several of these OD principles, practices, and values here in more detail as they relate particularly to the design of organizational conflict management systems.

When the principles of OD (the who, what, and why) are combined with the principles of conflict management design (the whether and how), a more complete and holistic approach to effective organizational conflict management emerges. OD encourages recognition and understanding of the crucial components of organizations: purpose, structure, leadership, culture, and relationships with internal and external environments. Perhaps one of the reasons that there has been increased dissatisfaction with many of the traditional methods of resolving disputes is their frequent failure to take into account organizational dynamics: how organizations function, how they learn, how they know whether they are performing well, how they adjust to new information and the need for any change, and how they go about the business of changing. We believe that with a grounding in OD values, principles, and processes, practitioners and managers can be more effective in assisting organizations to move away from case-by-case dispute resolution programs and toward more comprehensive, even "global," identification and management of conflict in their systems.

OD is also a highly values-driven, often democratic approach to managing change and learning processes in organizations. The participatory processes of OD can yield high-quality information about the need for and the implementation of organizational decisions to change. "Success" in OD is often measured by the degree of participation in considering change and by the degree of commitment to sustaining change. If utilized with integrity, OD processes can empower the organization and its members to work and learn together, serving the ultimate goal of achieving higher performance in the face of a multitude of internal and external challenges. When applied to conflict management systems design, OD guides practitioners to design *with* stakeholders and not *for* them, yielding high-quality decisions and implementation strategies for shifting the focus from dispute resolution efforts to conflict management systems. We will illustrate how a grounding in OD values, perspectives, practices, and processes can help practitioners and managers move organizations toward a more systemic and "successful" approach to conflict management.

Whole and Open Systems Thinking

Due to the pioneering work of Emery, Trist, and others, organizations are commonly viewed today as open systems: arrangements of parts dynamically interrelated with each other and with the influences in their environment. Anyone who works with or within organizations is well aware of the following prevailing practice: organizations are structured into functional components such as production operations, sales divisions, customer service offices, human resources departments, legal departments, and the like. Each component has its distinctive purpose, population, role, and culture, and each relies to a greater or lesser extent on the other components to achieve overall organizational performance.

Further, each component of the organization is related to the whole system in a broader sense, with the need to move across or span the functional boxes or boundaries of offices, departments, and divisions in order to accomplish organizational purposes. Thus, each structural and functional component of the organization contributes to and adopts organization-wide characteristics with respect to many subsystems. Examples of such subsystems include the human system (how and which individuals are recruited, selected, mentored, and retained), the work system (how the primary mission of the organization is actually accomplished), the reward system (how the organization rewards and recognizes service and accomplishment of objectives), the financial management system (how the organization allocates and accounts for resource use), and the information system (how data is collected, managed, and disseminated within and outside the organization). What we propose is that conflict management also be viewed as a subsystem within a larger system.

A systems approach to working with organizations encourages the identification of those subsystems that make up the whole and the examination of how well they collectively interact in order to discover how to improve them. Moving this aspect of OD theory and practice into its current state, Emery and Trist (1972; see also Weisbord, 1987) pioneered the concept that improving the systemic functioning of organizations requires focusing attention on the social systems by which organizational members interact to produce results and on the technical systems that advance output and productivity in the workplace. They discovered that these "sociotechnical" aspects of the workplace and its improvement needed to be examined and improved collectively rather than segmentally, for when systems interact dynamically with each other within the core of the whole of the organization, it is difficult to identify which is cause and which is effect.

In this way, open systems thinking encourages an emphasis on the whole and the interaction of the parts, not on the parts themselves as discrete, self-supporting entities. Moreover, open systems thinking requires the organization to be receptive and responsive to external changes. Currently, organizations operate in challenging times in which shifts in product or service needs and customer or client expectations, which arise from equally dynamic political, social, economic, and technological trends in the greater environment, are a constant. Now more than ever, organizations need to gather important external information, engage in feedback, and remain flexible in order to stay competitive, viable, and alive. They and their subsystems, including their conflict management system, need to be open systems.

Conflict Management as a System

As one of the many "systems" in organizations, conflict management has been one of the last to be directly recognized and developed. It seems obvious that any organization must have a system, consciously or otherwise, by which it exposes and resolves dissatisfaction, yet this concept of conflict as a system has only recently come into focus. Even more interesting is the relatively new notion that the adequacy and effectiveness of the conflict management system has an effect on the successful operation of other systems within the organization and of the organization as a whole. Perhaps these concepts have not been recognized because organizational conflict management systems have usually been housed in discrete components (legal and human resource departments) that have the responsibility to provide conflict management services to the rest of the organization. Characteristically, these departments' specialized knowledge about the rules, processes, and techniques for handling conflict becomes a matter of job security and, as a result, is tightly held onto in order to increase the department's value to the rest of the organization. In a broader sense, the topic of conflict often makes people uneasy, and individuals, groups, and organizations will therefore conspire to avoid facing it directly. As discussed in Chapter One, boldly moving into the tension of conflict is not a common individual or organizational characteristic.

In some organizations, the resolution of inter- and intraorganizational disputes has most often been viewed as a compartmentalized staff function performed within the organization by specialists. Traditionally, dispute resolution functions have been housed in two locations within an organization: the legal department (dealing primarily with external disputes) and the human resources and/or personnel department (dealing primarily with internal disputes). Typically, separation of these functions is amplified and strengthened by mission, structure, staff qualifications, and reporting relationships separate and apart from the service, sales, or production components (the technical core) of the organization. In practice, it is often the case that the legal and human resource departments of many organizations are viewed as a necessary evil that must be tolerated to handle the conflicts that others neither like nor believe they are equipped to handle.

Looking at conflict management as but one of many systems within the larger organizational constellation permits an enhanced understanding of conflict as it arises and a sharpened recognition of the opportunities for action in managing such conflict. In this way, the OD systemic perspective aids in the process of observing how organizational units interact and produce to achieve organizational goals, including the collateral and ever-present generation and management of conflict and its costs. The adoption of OD's "helicopter perspective" allows one to metaphorically hover in the air and take a look at what is happening on the ground with respect to conflict management and how it affects other systems. The development of the ability to gain a whole systems perspective of the existing causes, costs, and resolutions of conflict is a crucial link and the common ground between OD and conflict management systems design.

Characteristics of Conflict Management Systems

As those who work with organizations experience firsthand, organizational systems operate as if they are either "open" or "closed." Put simply, open systems survive and compete through ready interchange internally and externally regarding performance, methods, resources, and feedback. To function effectively, they must stay linked with and open to influence and interdependent transactions within their domain and with the external environment (here, the concept of openness is more purposeful than the general notion of being open in communications or to the outside world). In contrast, a closed system looks almost exclusively inward for such information and influence.

Like other systems within an organization, conflict management systems have certain characteristics:

- *Boundaries.* These borders, some tangible and some intangible, separate one system from another. In the case of the conflict management system, its internal management boundaries are often clearly defined as the human resource and legal components of any organization. It is in these components that disputes arising from within or outside the organization's overall boundaries are received, processed, and resolved.
- *Purpose.* All systems have a goal or mission that is their reason for being. As long as it meets the expectations and requirements of the external environment regarding products and services, the system can continue to operate in pursuit of its purpose or goal. In the case of the conflict management system, its purpose is the resolution of various types of disputes between the organization and internal or external claimants. Explicitly or implicitly, its purpose within the larger organizational context is to reflect the dominant view of preferred responses to conflict and its resolution (for example, fight or flight).
- *Inputs.* Systems absorb multiple resources in anticipation of fulfilling their purpose: they take in ideas, people, dollars, and raw materials. The conflict management system does this as well by

staffing and otherwise funding and supporting organizational components intended to perform the multitude of conflict resolution tasks; the raw materials of the system are the disputes to be resolved.

- *Transformation.* The staff, funding, and other inputs taken into the organization from the external environment are transformed or changed in some manner by the people and technology of the system. This happens at the technical core of the organization, whether by transforming raw materials into saleable products or by providing services to clients. Typically, these core task processes, which fulfill the system's overall purpose, are accomplished by individuals, in roles, organized into groups with a defined function. Such is the case in the organizational conflict management system where staff work to transform disputes into resolutions and impasse into results through processes such as dispute and case intake, information gathering, investigation and fact finding, meetings, oral and written arguments, negotiations, litigation, and court appearances.

- *Outputs.* A system's products or services are then exported to the external environment, which, ideally, finds them useful and acceptable. The outputs of the conflict management system, which are provided internally to the organization or externally to the environment, are the "endings" of disputes, such as withdrawals of cases, decisions, agreements, and settlements.

- *Feedback.* Determining whether a system has fulfilled its purpose is accomplished through feedback. The external environment expects that the system will use feedback either to improve the products or services delivered or to revise goals and objectives in order to bring them into line with expectations. The environment, external to the subsystem (but still within the organization) or external to the organization as a whole, is thus critical to the continued viability of any open system, for it not only supplies the input of people, material, and energy, but also receives and evaluates the output. Organizational conflict management systems receive feedback from their customers, constituents, and employees regarding the adequacy, quality, cost, and perception of fairness about dispute resolutions and results.

We find that thinking of conflict management as an open system operating within a larger organizational system and within an external environment provides a useful framework for approaching conflict management system design and intervention. Unfortunately, some organizational dispute resolution programs have tended to operate as systems walled off ("closed") from the rest of the organization and the external environment, with their own culture, jargon, rules, and mission, despite the fact that conflict permeates organizational functioning and affects all phases of its operations and performance. Improving or designing conflict management systems is often an intervention centered around helping the organization and its stakeholders decide to take steps to transform a closed dispute resolution program into an open conflict management system.

Thus, an open systems perspective is another important link between OD and conflict management systems design. Operating from an open systems perspective in managing organizational conflict leads to at least two significant results: (1) identification of key areas for inquiry regarding potential change (that is, within the input, transformation, and/or output processes of the organization's current conflict management system) and (2) uncovering dissonance, dysfunction, and dissatisfaction. The conflict management system gathers this information through assessment, feedback, and other participative methods. Those who need to participate in such processes are most easily identified as internal and external "customers" and stakeholders of the organization's dispute resolution program. The assessment is done by looking at the way the organization currently deals with disputes, since that is actually its current conflict management system. Through this involvement of the entire system, both internal and external, organizations can gain a more comprehensive picture of the state of their conflict interactions, costs, and results.

Conflict Management as a Change Intervention

OD intervenors seek to develop open, empowering, and collaborative relationships with the client systems they serve. These values underlie each step of the OD process and stem from a deep concern within the profession for ethical influence and effective practice. OD practitioners have learned that from the moment they enter a system and start asking questions about the need for change, they begin to "unfreeze" the system. At a Society of Professionals in Dispute Resolution conference in San Diego in 1991, OD consultant Haywood Martin used the metaphor of sticking a spoon in a bowl of Jell-O, with the resultant jiggling of the whole mass, as a way of illustrating the effect and responsibility the change agent has once he or she enters the system. Because of these responsibilities, the OD profession encourages a values-driven and patterned approach to change, an approach that applies to change in conflict management systems as well.

Most OD intervenors are aware of and use the "self as instrument" perspective during all aspects of the change intervention process. This perspective has great significance for those who design or improve conflict management systems. (Chapter Five, "Entry and Contracting," includes a more detailed discussion of this topic.) Self-knowledge about bias, blind spots, vulnerability to certain influences, and sensitivity to conflict is of critical importance to anyone seeking to influence others and to guide change in organizational systems dealing with conflict. The open, inquiring, and participatory processes of the OD intervenor make it easy for others, including stakeholders, to see the spirit and values that underlie the basic change process. In the same way, in conflict management systems design, the practitioner or design team must often model a high level of comfort when dealing with conflict, in addition to supplying the requisite technical assistance and background.

In fact, as most OD practitioners are well aware, conflict is a regular product of organizational improvement efforts. OD practitioners often say that the system and the practitioner will experience firsthand the topic being explored. In fact, a type of projection, to use a psychological term, occurs: if the organization is resistant, the practitioner may feel resistant. This is particularly true when dealing with the fiery topic of conflict. Working successfully with conflict itself—its nature, causes, and remedies—is delicate, requiring the practitioner to coach and guide client populations more directly and supportively than perhaps at any other time. While interest-based skills such as facilitation, influencing, counseling, and coaching are often employed by practitioners in their work with change in client organizations, they may also find the development of mediation skills of particular value.

Beyond the interpersonal aspects of change interventions, OD theories and practices regarding how change occurs in organizations are as applicable to the design of conflict management systems as they are to the design of information or other organizational subsystems. We highlight here several highly relevant applications of existing OD theories and practices to the actual intervention of conflict management systems design work. As springboards, we rely on Lewin's (Marrow, 1969) pioneering work on change through problem identification and problem-solving techniques (the "unfreezing" effect of information and the use of force field analysis); Argyris's explication (1970) of the tasks of an intervenor applied to conflict management design; Emery and Trist's discovery of the existence and dynamics of sociotechnical systems (1965, 1972; see also Weisbord, 1987); Weisbord's (1992, 1987) introduction of search conferences to the United States (a method of "getting the whole system in the room"); and Senge's (1990) holistic approach to the learning organization.

As most practitioners have frequently witnessed, the status quo of any system is the result of forces driving change in opposition to forces restraining change. This balanced driving/restraining equation describes a system in its steady state at any point in time. Lewin suggested that the system's status quo can be changed by one of three methods: (1) increasing the forces driving change, (2) reducing the forces restraining change, or (3) converting restraining forces into driving forces. Common use of force field analysis in OD change efforts has revealed that focusing on the second method—reducing the forces that restrain change—often yields faster and more effective results than any other. Force field analysis is particularly useful in designing conflict management systems because it is often a series of specific restraints that operate to prevent or inhibit those with a dispute from using dispute resolution procedures. For example, in an organization where the chief dispute resolution mechanism is litigation, a manager's decision to pursue something other than litigation, perhaps some form of alternative dispute resolution (ADR), may be most strongly influenced by the number of additional "permission memos" that have to be written to justify ADR use (a restraining force). This restraining force may have a greater impact on an employee deciding whether to recommend ADR than possible recognition in the company newsletter for saving litigation costs (a driving force).

Lewin also posited that change occurs through a process of unfreezing, movement, and refreezing in response to the receipt of new information. He discovered that new and valid information, when derived freely from individuals, leads to a temporary unfreezing of current beliefs. For example, if an organization's litigation department suddenly learns that its budget is to be cut by 25 percent, previous plans to increase the number of cases handled in house or to hire new attorneys may be put on hold. Thus, the litigation department unfreezes its current actions given the impact that the new information has on underlying operational assumptions. There is then movement as the individual or institution examines the implications of the new information. This is done to revise any planned action, so it is congruent with the new information. In our example, the litigation department might, as a result of the proposed budget cut, reallocate current staff, settle cases instead of litigate, or put certain types of cases into an "inactive" status. Thus, movement is away from the current state toward a more appropriate and responsive future state in light of the new information. Finally, to relieve the tension originally generated by receipt of the new information, the individual or institution refreezes into a new set of assumptions and behaviors. Thus, in our example, there might be a permanent reconfiguration of the department and creation of a "leaner and meaner" operation where proposed actions on pending cases are more thoroughly reviewed from a cost perspective as well as a legal one. Therefore, the conflict management system has "changed" in response to new information.

It is important to note that Weisbord (1987), Peter Vaill (1989), and even Senge (1990) posit that no system has the opportunity to truly refreeze in today's climate of constant information flow, which requires continual minor and sometimes major shifts in organizational operation and design—Vaill's state of "permanent white water." Such a state requires that the organization engage in almost continuous learning, a process described by Senge in his book *The Fifth Discipline*. In conflict management systems design, breaking through the normative patterns (paradigms) that exist in the typical management of organizational conflict is often done by an assessment of just how well the system is really working. Such a breakthrough, however, may not lead to ongoing interest in continuous change: the conflict management system and its participants may favor more stability and predictability than such a step would provide them. However, the mere introduction of greater opportunities to get to the heart of disputes (usually through the use of interest-based methods) and to identify systemic forces that impede more cost-effective and satisfactory resolutions often leads to increased systemwide flexibility. Such flexibility can result in the establishment of other system corrections, which can in turn prevent the occurrence of disputes. This is done, as in other OD change interventions, through the generation of reliable information from the participants affected about what is working in the conflict management system, what is not, and what should be done to improve the system.

OD also relies heavily on the collection and feedback of valid information to drive the change intervention process. As Marrow (1969) describes, Lewin discovered the importance of such information in changing individual and collective behavior. Argyris (1970) noted as well the importance of information collection and feedback when he encouraged intervenors to accomplish three primary tasks: (1) generate valid data about issues, (2) provide opportunities for free and informed choices by system participants, and (3) encourage the internalization of commitments to action by system participants in support of the choices made. Through the studies and observations of Lewin, Argyris, and others, OD provides an understandable collection of theories, models, and processes that clarify the need for valid information and describe how change occurs in organizations, groups, and individuals. These practice theories guide "change agents" and OD intervenors in their work and are highly relevant and useful to the design of conflict management systems.

Conflict Management in the Learning Organization

A sociotechnical framework for achieving lasting improvement in organizations is useful at several levels in addressing the design of conflict management systems. As Weisbord (1987) observes regarding Emery and Trist, their critical contribution was the notion that changing and improving the technical systems associated with organizational output is inadequate unless the social systems are changed and improved as well. This discovery led to the now common practice of working to improve both systems simultaneously, for it is difficult to identify which system, the social or the technical, is most culpable in the perpetuation of an organizational problem. Further, Emery and Trist's studies revealed that the individuals directly delivering the service or the product were the most reliable source of ideas for improvement and that these individuals can also successfully implement any changes that they design. Thus, the OD field has moved away from experts solving problems for systems, and studies such as those of Emery and Trist have accelerated the movement toward working with the people directly affected by a problem in order to help them devise solutions to it. This thinking culminates in Weisbord's persuasive "learning curve," illustrated in his book *Productive Workplaces* (1987), in which he predicts that by the year 2000, OD practitioners will need to get "everybody improving whole systems." Such whole systems thinking is, we believe, the cornerstone of systemic conflict management design. Thus, it would be useful, in our view, for practitioners to incorporate explicitly into any sociotechnical work redesign effort an exploration of the existing conflict management system and its results in order to determine what role and systemic influence the management of differences has in the performance of both the social and technical aspects of the organization.

Weisbord, Emery, Trist, and others have led the way to an increased understanding of the fact that piecemeal efforts do not improve whole systems: the information is inadequate and incomplete, the urgency of the problem is not recognized, commitment is diminished, and individuals lack critical skills. Thus, the changing of a system, including a conflict management system, is like an orchestral performance, with all of the instruments playing in concert, rhythm, and harmony with each other.

Often, one of the core challenges of conflict management systems design is to achieve consensus that a business opportunity is available in tackling the issue of conflict. Some organizations seem to take for granted that high levels of ongoing conflict and their attendant costs must be tolerated until a crisis—unmanageable backlogs or successive instances of workplace violence—brings the organization's approach to managing conflict to the forefront. In such extreme instances, Weisbord's (1987) key ingredients for a successful approach to systems learning and change (including conflict management systems) might well be met: a business opportunity, some energized people, and a committed leadership. Even in less troubled organizations, the same key ingredients for change are also necessary, but the degree of opportunity perceived, the energy of participants, and the commitment of leadership may take a longer time to crystallize and mobilize. Some of these challenges to practitioners, managers, and conflict management systems design teams are addressed more thoroughly in subsequent chapters: Chapter Five, "Entry and Contracting" and Chapter Thirteen, "Changing the Culture."

The focus of OD interventions today is to encourage and assist organizations in seeking and sustaining the commitment of employees and other stakeholders to active participation in learning processes that revise and revitalize social and technical operations and performance. The focus of conflict management systems design today is to encourage and assist whole systems in recognizing and identifying conflict, learning how it operates, and actively involving management and stakeholders in designing and implementing systemic procedures that decrease dissonance and dissatisfaction and enhance achievement of the organization's goals. There is thus a correlation between OD and conflict management systems design. Throughout the chapters that follow, we will refer to the implications of OD for effective design work and to the implications of conflict management systems design for the holistic practice of OD. Our belief is that the two fields of practice have much in common and much of value to share. Taken together, they provide the framework for a systemic approach to conflict management.

Chapter Three

Managing Conflict Effectively
Alternative Dispute Resolution and Dispute Systems Design

Some organizations have moved toward more systemic approaches to conflict management. Others continue to use fight or flight methods to deal with conflict or to avoid it. In the middle are those organizations that have designed an alternative dispute resolution (ADR) approach or program to deal with particular types of disputes. These ADR programs usually grow out of a perception by management, consultants, attorneys, or the disputants themselves that traditional methods of dispute resolution are neither working as well as they should nor furthering the organization's goals. Practitioners have frequently used the principles of dispute systems design (DSD) to help organizations establish such alternative dispute resolution programs or processes for settling disputes.

The Emergence of Alternative Dispute Resolution

ADR is any method of dispute resolution other than formal adjudication such as court litigation or administrative proceedings. ADR is not a fancy, new approach but rather an alternative—characterized by common sense and flexibility. It involves the use of a wider array of approaches to resolve disputes than the traditional and often more costly methods of adversarial litigation and administrative adjudication.

Like conflict, ADR permeates our lives. Everyone engages in ADR every day: you negotiate with your co-worker about where to go to lunch, you call in your neighbor to "mediate" as you and your spouse try to reach agreement on what color to paint the living room, you arbitrate by deciding whether your son or your daughter will get the family car for the evening based on the strength of their respective arguments.

More and more corporations, businesses, individuals, groups, organizations, and courts are embracing ADR as a better way to resolve disputes. Companies such as Motorola and Aetna have ADR programs; government agencies such as the Federal Deposit Insurance Corporation, the Department of Health and Human Services, the Army Corps of Engineers, the Internal Revenue Service, and numerous other federal agencies are using ADR; local courts such as the District of Columbia Superior Court and federal appellate courts—for example, the Ninth Circuit Court of Appeals—have ADR programs; and schools such as the Fairfax County, Virginia, and District of Columbia school systems have peer mediation and ADR programs. Pick up most trade journals or newsletters and you will likely see articles on ADR and advertisements offering ADR services. Newspapers carry stories about the mediation of international conflicts, the arbitration of professional sports strikes, and the negotiation of trade agreements and treaties. Some contract disputes are arbitrated, many labor-management disputes are mediated, and, increasingly, consumer complaints are handled by ombudspersons. (We use the word "ombudsperson" here, although there is no commonly accepted version—some use ombudsman, others use ombuds or ombuds practitioner.) For those practitioners and managers who will be involved in designing and improving "next generation" conflict management systems, an understanding of ADR is essential.

Why has ADR become so popular? What are the various types of ADR and when are they appropriate? Is there a "dark side" to ADR? How is an organization development (OD) approach to conflict management systems design useful in choosing and using ADR options?

Explosion of Interest in ADR

Organizations are using it, law firms are marketing it, courts are requiring it. Why? There are a number of reasons.

Overloaded court dockets: Much has been written about the litigiousness of our society, how organizations and individuals use the courts as the "neighborhood bully" to keep people in line and to protect themselves and their reputations. As a society, we look to our courts to resolve disputes that other cultures resolve on an informal, individual, or group basis. The result of this litigation mind-set and the mountains of new laws, rules, and regulations promulgated every year has been an exponential increase in the number of cases handled by courts at the local, state, and federal level. Court dockets are backlogged; it is not uncommon for a civil case to take four to five years to actually go to trial. Court-ordered ADR programs such as the multidoor courthouse in the District of Columbia or the early neutral evaluation program in federal court in the Northern District of California are ways to clear dockets by using volunteer, court-reimbursed, or staff neutrals.

Legislation and regulations: Some recent federal laws and regulations encourage forms of ADR other than arbitration in certain disputes. For example, the Administrative Dispute Resolution Act of 1990 (5 U.S.C. section 581 *et seq.*) encourages the use of ADR by federal agencies and establishes ADR as a viable alternative procedure for the resolution of many disputes. Certain federal equal employment opportunity statutes and regulations also allow and encourage the use of ADR (29 C.F.R. section 1614); some tax regulations provide for ADR (Internal Revenue Ann. 95–2); and certain government procurement regulations provide for use of ADR (May 16, 1995 Office of Federal Procurement Policy pledge). Recent federal executive orders also promote ADR in a variety of contexts, including in federal labor-management relations (Executive Order 12871) and in the promulgation of federal regulations (Executive Order 12866). As a result of the above legislation and directives, ADR use has increased not only in the federal government sector but at the state and local levels as well.

Increasing cost and decreasing satisfaction with litigation: Many companies have grown frustrated with the cost of litigation—in dollars, in personnel time, in lost opportunities, and in the negative effect on ongoing business and employee relationships. Not only have the costs of outside counsel and experts increased but so have those of in-house counsel through overhead and support services. As a result, many corporations have embraced ADR. For example,

Motorola now requires that ADR be considered in all of its cases and has shifted the presumption by requiring its employees to demonstrate why ADR *cannot* be used (Weise, 1989). Similarly, many corporations have taken the Center for Public Resources' (CPR) "pledge" to use ADR prior to resorting to litigation with other corporations who have also taken the CPR pledge; many law firms have taken a similar CPR pledge to advise clients of ADR options. Other organizations have adopted ADR programs in an effort to curb outside counsel costs; in 1994, the Federal Deposit Insurance Corporation saved $11.5 million in estimated legal fees and expenses through the use of third-party ADR rather than litigation.

Backlash against attorneys, lawsuits, and legal costs: As a society, we love to hate lawyers; they are the brunt of endless jokes. But many are laughing all the way to the bank. Some large law firms have been known to bill $600 an hour for their services, not including the charges for the hordes of paralegals, experts, consultants, and administrative personnel needed to support them. Organizations are beginning to doubt the need for such high-priced "hired guns" to resolve their disputes. ADR is seen as a less expensive way to resolve disputes, often obviating the need for lawyers or limiting the types of disputes where they are involved.

Societal movement toward more natural and humane methods of dispute resolution: Organizations, groups, and individuals have grown tired of battering and bashing each other in the name of resolving conflict. In the last ten years, there has been an increased emphasis on communication and working together to informally resolve differences through problem solving. "Being tough" and "going for the kill" have given way to more humane dispute resolution methods, including forms of ADR in which the disputants themselves participate more actively in the resolution process. The former methods of amplifying, accelerating, and escalating conflict through litigation and other adversarial methods are in many instances no longer a good fit with evolving societal norms.

Desire to empower disputants to participate in resolving their own disputes: Self-direction and governance, total quality management, and other participatory models for employee involvement have encouraged the inclusion of disputants in the dispute resolution processes affecting them. In many of its forms, such as mediation and joint problem solving, ADR permits the disputants to craft their own solutions to disagreements. If ADR results in resolution, it is the disputants' success, not the neutral's. The disputants own and control the ADR process and often craft solutions unique to their circumstance, which they are then more committed to implement.

Increasing interest in flexible dispute resolution: There has been a growing realization that all disputes do not require the same mechanisms for resolution. For example, we currently channel many different types of disputes through the same courthouse doors: antitrust cases, commercial disputes, personal injury cases, neighborhood conflict. Increasingly, however, judges are experimenting with the "multidoor courthouse" in which certain types of cases are funneled first through ADR corridors before they are placed onto a court docket. Some disputants have become so discouraged with crowded court dockets that they hire private "rent-a-judges" or use private mediators or arbitrators instead of judges to resolve their disputes. ADR is seen as a way to introduce flexibility into the dispute resolution process—to tailor the process to the problem.

Interest in confidentiality and avoidance of publicity: Organizations and individuals alike are often reluctant to "air their dirty linen" in public. For example, mediation on the whole is a discreet process and the results can usually be kept confidential. This is often not true with court cases: the proceedings are usually open to the public and even if there is a settlement before the trial starts (or before its conclusion), some judges refuse to seal settlements, to limit public access, or to restrict disclosure. ADR can thus be used to shield disputes and settlements from public scrutiny and to prevent disclosure of repeated violations by the parties or defendants. There can, however, be potential problems with this cloak of confidentiality, as discussed below in the section "The Dark Side of ADR."

The Spectrum of ADR Options

The continuum of ADR options ranges from those that are least invasive and allow the parties the most control over the process and outcome (such as negotiation) to those that are most invasive and allow the disputants the least control over the process and outcome (such as arbitration). People sometimes mistakenly think that ADR means arbitration. However, arbitration is only one of many ADR choices. There are six broad categories of ADR options: preventive,

Figure 3.1. Dynamics of ADR Techniques.

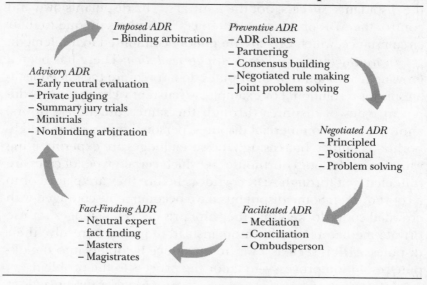

Imposed ADR
– Binding arbitration

Preventive ADR
– ADR clauses
– Partnering
– Consensus building
– Negotiated rule making
– Joint problem solving

Advisory ADR
– Early neutral evaluation
– Private judging
– Summary jury trials
– Minitrials
– Nonbinding arbitration

Negotiated ADR
– Principled
– Positional
– Problem solving

Fact-Finding ADR
– Neutral expert
  fact finding
– Masters
– Magistrates

Facilitated ADR
– Mediation
– Conciliation
– Ombudsperson

negotiated, facilitated, fact finding, advisory, and imposed (see Figure 3.1).

Preventive methods of ADR are used to attempt to preempt disputes. These dispute resolution mechanisms are decided in advance by the parties in order to govern how any disagreement or conflict will be handled. For example, many business contracts now contain specific provisions for dealing with possible future disputes: the parties will give notice of any dispute, negotiate for a certain period of time, mediate, and then submit any unresolved issues to an arbitrator. "Preventive" may be a misnomer for these ADR methods because they do not actually stop disputes from occurring; rather, they channel disagreements into a problem-solving arena early enough that escalation into full-blown disputes can often be avoided. Traditionally, most preventive clauses were arbitration clauses governed by the rules of the American Arbitration Association, but increasingly parties are adding ADR clauses, which utilize a variety of ADR methods, including arbitration. Preventive ADR can also include relationship-building methods such as partnering, consensus building, negotiated rule making ("regneg"), and training in joint problem solving. To date, relatively little attention has been focused on preventive methods of ADR, and most ADR models and charts do not even include them. As conflict management systems evolve, preventive methods of ADR will become increasingly important. Such methods recognize that conflict is inevitable and thus establish in advance mutually agreed-upon mechanisms to channel conflict when it arises.

Negotiated methods of ADR include interest-based (also known as principled, mutual gain, win-win), positional (win-lose, power-based), and problem solving (agreeing on the issues to be resolved and setting an agenda for resolving those issues, usually using principled methods). In the negotiated forms of ADR, the disputants reach their own resolution, unaided by a third-party neutral or decision maker. If they cannot come to a satisfactory resolution, the parties are free to terminate the negotiation and to pursue other forms of dispute resolution, including other ADR methods, litigation, or administrative adjudication. Some contracts may require a "cooling off" period once the dispute is identified and then good faith attempts at negotiation prior to resorting to power or rights-based resolutions.

Facilitated methods of ADR involve a third-party neutral assisting the disputants to reach a satisfactory resolution. The neutral merely helps the parties and has no authority to impose a decision or result. Examples include mediation and the use of ombudspersons. In facilitated ADR, it is the parties, *not* the neutral, who retain control of and resolve the dispute. As in the negotiated forms of ADR, if the parties do not think the proposed resolution is satisfactory, they are free to terminate the ADR proceeding and pursue other resolution options. The parties typically retain control as well over the final selection of the mediator, although some mediation programs assign neutrals to the dispute or maintain panels of neutrals from which the disputants may select. We note for clarification that there is no such thing as "binding mediation," a phrase that is occasionally heard. One can be required to participate in mediation (as in court-ordered mediation), but one cannot be required to agree to a proposed settlement derived through the mediation process. As ombudspersons do not have, by tradition, decision-making authority, they are considered another form of facilitated ADR.

Fact-finding methods of ADR may be binding or nonbinding depending upon the agreement of the parties. These methods utilize a third party or technical expert to make findings (usually on factual issues). For example, in neutral expert fact finding, the parties may use a third party to make findings of fact regarding technical issues such as asset valuation, biotechnical data, actuarial statistics, or construction specifications. The parties can agree in advance on whether or not they will be bound by the findings and whether the findings will be admissible in any subsequent proceeding. Again, the parties typically retain control over the selection of the neutral expert fact finder, who is usually a subject-matter expert and brings substantive expertise to the dispute.

In *advisory methods* of ADR, a third-party neutral (usually selected by the parties) reviews certain aspects of the dispute and renders an advisory opinion as to the likely outcome. These methods include outcome-prediction mediation (sometimes called rights-based mediation), early neutral evaluation (ENE), mini-trials, summary jury trials, and nonbinding arbitration. For example, the parties may choose to use a third-party ENE early on to provide an opinion on a legal issue in dispute, such as a contract provision or point of law, or they may decide to hold a mini-trial in which the attorneys for each side present the major aspects of their case to the clients and a presiding neutral; the neutral may then advise as to the probable outcome, working with the clients in particular to facilitate a settlement, if possible.

Imposed methods of ADR are those in which a third-party neutral makes a binding decision regarding the merits of the dispute. Most often, these methods use some form of binding arbitration—either with a single arbitrator or with several (a panel). Such arbitration is usually the result of an alleged breach of contract or agreement between the parties. Standard industry practice, regulations, or a statutory regime, as is the case with grievance arbitration in labor-management disputes, may require the use of binding arbitration as well. In these imposed forms of ADR, the parties have the least control over the process and the outcome. Binding arbitration is the method of ADR that comes closest to traditional forms of dispute resolution such as court litigation. There is a very limited right of appeal from an arbitration award, based on such extraordinary circumstances as fraud, duress, or coercion. Imposed methods of ADR, particularly where panels of arbitrators are used and the proceeding is formal and court-like, can be quite expensive and time consuming. In fact, some research suggests that certain types of arbitration are not necessarily faster or cheaper than litigation.

ADR as Appropriate Dispute Resolution

In designing and improving conflict management systems, the idea of ADR as *alternative* dispute resolution is perhaps less useful than the concept of ADR as *appropriate* dispute resolution. That is, the method of dispute resolution must be appropriate for the particular dispute or problem; there must be a fit between the process and the problem. ADR methods are not necessarily interchangeable; mediation may work in some disputes, early neutral evaluation in others, and an ombudsperson in still others. In Chapter Seven, we explore more fully the whole issue of design architecture and how to choose appropriate methods of ADR and select appropriate cases.

What is relevant here is that some organizations say that they have had bad experiences with ADR. Practitioners working in or with such organizations will hear statements such as, "We tried ADR and it just didn't work" or "ADR might work for other organizations, but it just didn't work for us because we are different." Often, the problem is not that ADR was inappropriate for the particular organization; rather, the *method* of ADR chosen was inappropriate for the particular dispute. For example, an imposed method of ADR was used when perhaps a facilitated method would have been more appropriate or congruent with the organization's mission, culture, or disputes. Unfortunately, as most practitioners know, managers and disputants rarely make this distinction, and the conclusion that is drawn (perhaps incorrectly) is that ADR as a whole does not work, not that the particular type of ADR does not work. For this reason, it is important that practitioners be familiar with the entire spectrum of ADR options so that they can accurately advise disputants and stakeholders as they design conflict management systems together.

The Dark Side of ADR

When is ADR *not* appropriate? When may traditional rather than alternative methods of dispute resolution be preferred? Once again, the link between OD principles and conflict management systems design provides guidance. Respecting the OD values of participation, openness, and feedback and using them as a backdrop allows both the practitioner and the organization to see ADR through a variety of lenses.

The use of ADR raises questions about private justice and whether only the wealthy or resource-rich can afford to buy it. Should large organizations, such as banks and securities brokerage firms, be allowed to require that everyone doing business with them resolve disputes using a particular form of ADR? So far, many courts seem to say yes, as long as the customer is informed in writing at the time the business relationship is begun and there is no fraud or coercion. Should large companies be allowed to develop their own "private law" and "private justice" through commercial arbitration? Again, so far, the answer is yes. Finally, what happens to the "little guy," the small business owner who cannot afford to pay his or her share of a panel for an ADR proceeding?

The question of whether some disputes are simply inappropriate for ADR also arises. Should domestic violence cases be kept out of court-ordered mediation on the theory that there is such an imbalance of power between the parties, even if represented by counsel, that the process is invalid and somehow flawed? Should cases raising constitutional issues, such as violations of civil rights laws or sexual discrimination laws, be deemed inappropriate for ADR and steered through the more traditional door of litigation? Should certain public policy issues, such as disposal of environmental toxins or biological research waste, be reserved for the judgment of courts or administrative bodies?

Another instance in which ADR may be inappropriate is where it is used to cover up systemic or repeated violations. For example, a hypothetical state agency may have an ADR program that makes mediation mandatory for all equal employment opportunity (EEO) disputes prior to the filing of a formal action or complaint. Ninety percent of all cases are resolved at the mediation stage, and almost all of the remaining cases settle before an actual investigation is conducted. An outside conflict management consultant notices that more than 80 percent of all cases coming through the mediation program are from two divisions in particular and that most of the complaints seem to be by Hispanic female secretaries against African American male senior supervisors and managers. When the consultant mentions this to the manager who oversees the ADR program, she comments that the agency is aware of this but that since the mediations are confidential, the public and other employees in the organization are not aware of the problem and that it is one of the reasons that the agency likes to "push" mediation to get rid of these kinds of disputes.

Here, there may be both ethical and public policy reasons to question using ADR in this fashion. Although formal processes remain available to the complainants, it appears that this agency uses mediation and negotiation to resolve these disputes in order to shield them from the public domain and scrutiny. In particular, as the agency is a publicly funded entity, it is subject to relevant state and federal laws and regulations regarding EEO. Thus, using ADR in this manner may raise serious ethical issues and violate the core principles of openness and feedback in conflict management systems design. By using ADR as a method of preventing public disclosure of statutory violations, this agency may be co-opting the process for its own organizational interests and benefit. Moreover, it may be using ADR in these cases as a means of avoiding taking remedial and preventive action in the cluster of disputes emanating from the two particular divisions. In this way, its EEO office has walled itself off from important information and feedback from its environment, acting as a "closed system." As a result, the agency runs the risk of suffering the higher ultimate costs of low morale, lowered productivity, difficulty in hiring and retaining qualified employees, and escalating litigation, with possible awards of compensatory damages resulting from its misguided efforts to use ADR to contain rather than to expose and remedy the conflict in the divisions.

It may also be inappropriate to require the disempowered to use ADR mechanisms where they have been given no choice in the matter, do not understand their rights and choices for alternative relief, or have had no hand or representation in creating the dispute resolution mechanisms in the first place. For example, this may be so in our hypothetical agency if many of the EEO complaints are filed by non-English-speaking, lower-graded employees who do not understand that being required to participate in mediation does not mean that they lose their right to pursue more formal methods of resolution. This is even more the case if these employees have not had any involvement in designing the ADR procedures, either through union representation or through representative participation on design task forces and working groups. In these circumstances, use of ADR may not only be inappropriate but also unethical under OD as well as ADR values, practices, and principles of client self-determination.

The Emergence of Dispute Systems Design

Like ADR, dispute systems design is in its infancy. DSD grew out of the ADR movement in the late 1980s as certain dispute resolvers with national and international reputations used their experiences and talents to help clients establish new forms and applications of dispute resolution methods.

Spurred by the desire to encourage less adversarial and less costly dispute resolution and guided by the principled, interest-based negotiation techniques of *Getting to Yes* (Fisher and Ury, 1981), these individuals worked separately to develop new methods and procedures to resolve disputes. They ran into a host of different challenges: what should the new systems look like; who should be able to use them; what types of alternatives should be offered; how should the procedures be structured; what factors determined whether people used the new methods; and what motivation, skills, and knowledge did people need to use the new alternatives? Other dispute resolvers who were facing similar challenges came forward and a new interest group appeared within the practice of ADR: the dispute systems designers. In 1990, the central theme of the conference of the Society of Professionals in Dispute Resolution was "Designing Dispute Resolution Systems."

At about the same time, the first book on DSD was published: *Getting Disputes Resolved* (Ury, Brett, and Goldberg, 1988). Subtitled "Designing Systems to Cut the Costs of Conflict," this text was revolutionary: it provided for the first time (through a case study of the authors' actual experience working with coal miners, their union, and management) a systematic way of looking at dispute resolution procedures. It set forth a classic DSD model composed of three primary dispute resolution methods, six principles for setting up dispute resolution procedures, and four stages of dispute systems design. An understanding of these methods, principles, and stages is essential for the conflict management practitioner, so we briefly review them here.

Power, Rights, and Interests

Power-based methods rely on who has more power, as illustrated by violence, war, and strikes. Today, strikes are perhaps the only form of true power-based resolutions seen in organizations in the United States. In a distressed dispute resolution system, many disputes are resolved through power; in an effective system, few (if any) disputes are resolved through power. An example of the result of years of power-based dispute resolution practices is, for example, a plant closure where the intractability of labor and management disputes has led to a "lose-lose" lack of confidence in company, employee, and product reliability by customers and financial backers.

Rights-based methods are grounded in fixed rules or principles: they impose a determination based upon entitlements, merits, credibility, and positions. Examples include litigation and binding arbitration. Third parties such as arbitrators and judges determine who is right in a given dispute, as measured against the contract, the accepted practice, or the law. In rights-based methods, questions of equity and justice are resolved through determinations devoid of power contests.

Interest-based methods are those in which the parties identify their concerns, needs, and desires as a starting point in addressing the issues in dispute. They indicate the "why" of a problem or issue and then use methods grounded in such principles to arrive at resolutions that are mutually acceptable and satisfactory. These resolutions take into account all of the parties' interests. Such methods include mediation, facilitation, and interest-based problem solving. In an effective dispute resolution system, most disputes are resolved on the basis of the interests of the different parties involved.

The DSD model posits that interest-based methods of dispute resolution are less costly (in overall terms, not just dollars) and more satisfactory (addressing more of the disputants' concerns) than rights-based methods, which are in turn less costly and more satisfactory than power-based methods of resolution. The overall prescription for improved dispute resolution encourages parties to resolve their dispute first by using interest-based methods and then by using low-cost rights-based methods where necessary. Interest-based methods are considered better methods of dispute resolution because they result in lower transaction costs, greater satisfaction with outcomes, less strain on the parties' relationship, and lower recurrence of disputes.

Six Principles

The DSD model also sets forth six practical principles to guide those who design dispute resolution mechanisms:

1. Put the focus on interests (encourage the use of interest-based methods such as negotiation and mediation).
2. Provide "loop-backs" (make procedures available that allow the parties to return to a lower-cost method, such as negotiation).
3. Provide low-cost rights and power "backups" (offer low-cost alternatives such as arbitration if interest-based procedures fail).
4. Build in consultation before and feedback after (notify and consult before taking any action and provide postdispute feedback to prevent similar disputes in the future).
5. Arrange the procedures in low-to-high cost sequence (encourage negotiation before mediation, then mediation before arbitration).
6. Provide the motivation, skills, and resources necessary (ensure that the procedures are supported and therefore used).

Four Stages

Finally, the DSD model advocates four stages (strikingly similar to basic OD tasks) to guide dispute systems designers in their work: (1) diagnosis; (2) design; (3) implementation; and (4) exit, evaluation, and diffusion. The designer performs the necessary tasks at each stage, makes recommendations, and, assuming client approval, moves on to the next stage, thus completing the design for the organization or institution.

The Dark Side of DSD

The DSD model was revolutionary, and it has provided critical guidance for those who design and improve conflict management systems. However, as practitioners (and OD practitioners in particular) have used the DSD model, certain loopholes have emerged when the model is applied in an organizational context.

First, the classic DSD model tends to cast the designer in the role of "expert" in the diagnosis, design, implementation, and evaluation stages of revising an existing dispute resolution system. The designer personally assumes the burden of identifying the root causes of dissatisfaction with the existing system and of redesigning it to build in more interest-based options and opportunities (such as problem-solving negotiation and cooling-off periods). Although the model advocates establishing a "design committee," participation as a value put into action is not paramount in all stages of the intervention. Rather, in the DSD model, ultimate responsibility for success appears to lie with the designer instead of the stakeholders themselves. As Weisbord, Senge, and others have cautioned OD practitioners and managers, an "expert" approach does not result in the organization (and its members) collecting information and learning about itself, determining as a whole how to remedy what is unacceptable in the face of organizational and environmental factors, and committing itself to seeking and sustaining change. In addition, the model suggests medical attributes, with the designer diagnosing the dispute resolution program, pronouncing it ill, prescribing a cure, administering the medicine, and determining whether the prescription has worked.

Second, the classic DSD model takes a somewhat linear, mechanistic approach toward building dispute resolution systems, seen most clearly through its focus on matter-specific and single disputes (or clusters of disputes) rather than on conflict as a whole. The DSD model works with disputes and builds dispute resolution mechanisms; it does not accept conflict or view disputes as a byproduct of underlying conflict nor does it address larger systemic conflict management issues such as organizational and individual responses to conflict and the "fit" among organizational mission, culture, and conflict management.

Third, the classic DSD model does not rely heavily on prevention as a necessary aspect of dispute resolution programs. As noted previously, interest-based methods such as conciliation, consensus building, and facilitation can be used in advance to prevent disputes before they happen, as can inclusion of dispute resolution clauses in contracts and agreements, teaching communication skills, and instituting certain forms of predispute negotiation.

Finally, and perhaps most troubling for practitioners who have worked with it, the classic DSD model fails to adequately consider organizational dynamics. It discusses the need for participants to develop knowledge, skill, and motivation to use a newly imposed dispute resolution system and acknowledges as well that the organization operates in a larger environmental and cultural context. However, the DSD model fails to address critical organization dynamics that have a direct impact on effective implementation, including organizational culture, resistance to change, and incentive and reward structures.

The Continued Evolution of Resolution

Taken together, OD, DSD, and the interest-based concepts of ADR provide the necessary ingredients to create effective conflict management systems. We call this synthesis of "best practices" from OD, DSD, and ADR *interest-based conflict management systems design*. We have illuminated some aspects of the negative aspects of both ADR and DSD for the express purpose of encouraging the evolution of this synthesis in the most principled manner possible.

As the history of conflict management systems, processes, and techniques evolves, we believe organizations and individuals will become more aware of their fight and flight responses to conflict and choose to adopt more systemic approaches to the management of such conflict. Moreover, stakeholders will seek an ever greater involvement in the process of designing conflict management systems. As a result, we believe that practitioners will be pressured to discover and utilize increasingly sophisticated interest-based design practices in order to create conflict management systems *with* stakeholders, not *for* them.

Chapter Four

Involving the Stakeholders
Interest-Based Conflict Management Systems

Practitioners who actually design dispute resolution systems, including alternative dispute resolution programs, have relied on a variety of practices and techniques to guide them in their interventions. Some of these practices are grounded in organization development (OD) principles, others derive from alternative dispute resolution (ADR) techniques, and still others stem from dispute systems design (DSD) principles. As societal, political, and economic forces nudge organizations toward more systemic conflict management models, however, we believe that practitioners will also be expected to integrate systems-oriented and participatory practices into their design interventions. They will be expected to design interest-based systems *with* stakeholders, not *for* them. If *you* build it, they may or may not use it. On the other hand, if *they* build it, they will use it, refine it, tell their friends about it, and make it their own.

We suggest that this is a "next generation" approach to design interventions and call it *interest-based conflict management systems design*. We see this model of organizational conflict management systems design as a commonsense evolution and synthesis of OD, ADR, and DSD "best practices."

The Evolution of Resolution

As practitioners have probably already recognized, interest-based conflict management systems design is neither radical nor revolutionary. It is simply further movement along the continuum of the historical development of dispute resolution and conflict management. We see this "evolution of resolution" continuum (Figure 4.1, below) as having four "quadrants," which represent how organizations have historically developed their approaches to managing conflict (Table 4.1, below). We see organizations moving increasingly into Quadrant IV as the next generation of conflict management: interest-based methods of dispute resolution created through interest-based processes of conflict management systems design.

The evolution of resolution continuum shows the journey taken by most U.S. organizations in seeking improved conflict management capability and how the DSD principles of power, rights, and interests have been utilized historically in the design process. It also illustrates the developmental attempts by organizations to design ("what") and implement ("how") systems for managing conflict, suggesting that organizations are now moving toward a conflict management model where there is greater congruency, once again, between the dispute resolution *methods* and the conflict management design *process,* with the congruency based upon interests.

In Quadrant I, organizations are dominated by the belief that they must fight for survival against their workers, their competitors,

Figure 4.1. Evolution of Resolution Continuum.

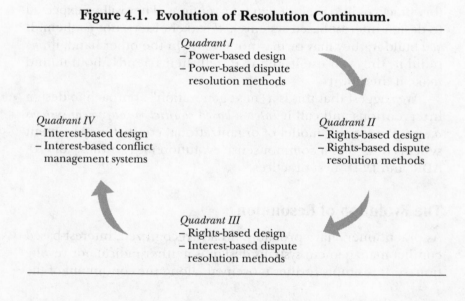

Quadrant I
– Power-based design
– Power-based dispute resolution methods

Quadrant IV
– Interest-based design
– Interest-based conflict management systems

Quadrant II
– Rights-based design
– Rights-based dispute resolution methods

Quadrant III
– Rights-based design
– Interest-based dispute resolution methods

Table 4.1. Comparison of Method and Design Characteristics in Conflict Management Systems.

	What: Method	How: Design
Quadrant I	Power-Based Methods	Power-Based Design
Quadrant II	Rights-Based Methods	Rights-Based Design
Quadrant III	Interest-Based Methods	Rights-Based Design
Quadrant IV	Interest-Based Methods	Interest-Based Design

and their environment. The rewards of risking capital to organize a company can lead to beliefs that the owners are in charge and are entitled to dominate all facets of their milieu (the robber baron mentality). In this environment, disputes are seen as highly threatening. Historically, the rise of the U.S. labor movement and the relations between companies and their workers from the late 1800s into the 1930s illustrates this type of dispute resolution system. There was an explosion of strikes involving property damage, the use of force, violence, and death: power-based methods of dispute resolution through power-based design.

In Quadrant II, the focus is on rights and entitlements, which are imposed. In this stage of dispute resolution systems development, organizations and interest groups usually take their disputes "off the streets" because the cost is deemed to be too high to institutions, groups, individuals, and society. The usual pattern is to provide legislative frameworks for determining who is right and then to pursue such rights through litigation and the courts. These rights-based methods are imposed through rights-based designs, which relieve the system of the high costs associated with violence and other power-based contests. Gradually, the system and its organizational players experience patterns of case law development, which provide precedent and guidance in sorting through the daily need for dispute resolution. Organizational players conform to these patterns and the system settles down for a while. This procedure is visible in the historical development of labor relations in the United States, where the Wagner Act of 1935 established basic rights for workers to form unions and to bargain collectively with their employers. Several decades of case law and further amendments to the Wagner Act settled most of the critical questions for organizations dealing with labor unions—that is, what was permissible and what was prohibited in dealing with employees organized by a union. Historically, one can also point to the civil rights cases and legislation of the 1950s and 1960s as examples of Quadrant II dispute systems design: rights-based methods imposed through rights-based processes (courts and legislation).

In Quadrant III, organizations use interest-based methods of dispute resolution but design them in a rights-based manner: the organization uses ADR but imposes the ADR mechanisms on the disputants without identifying their concerns or preferences and without involving them in the design process. Those with a stake in the resulting system are left out of the process—the organization designs and decides *for* them, not *with* them, frequently with the advice of ADR "experts." This is where most organizations are today, particularly in their use of ADR. Examples include mandatory, court-ordered ADR and mandatory employee dispute mediation programs. Confronted with the high costs of using the rights-based forums and dissatisfied with the resulting "win-lose" impact on ongoing relationships, organizational leaders have flocked to ADR courses to learn the newer and perhaps more enlightened methods of resolving disputes. The problem, however, is that these interest-based methods are often imposed or required through rights-based designs, with little or no input from institutional or individual stakeholders. The resistance that practitioners encounter to the acceptance and use of interest-based methods of ADR often stems from this incongruity. Resistance may also be a by-product of the disputants' lack of information about the change and how it will affect their dispute or may result from a lack of skills needed to pursue and use interest-based resolution processes. Disputants may also be concerned that the new system has been devised as a smokescreen to dilute their mandated rights. All of these factors diminish incentives to use an imposed system of interest-based resolution methods: interest-based methods through right-based design.

Quadrant IV is the direction in which many organizations are heading today; it is the next generation of conflict management, moving beyond imposed ADR regimes. Using interest-based conflict management systems design principles to create interest-based dispute resolution methods adds a congruency to the equation that has been historically absent. Such congruency makes the system more stable, more satisfactory, and more likely to be used by disputants. Here, the stakeholders have an active and integral role in creating and renewing the systems they use. This model has both a broader and a more customized focus than the other quadrants in that it admits and addresses the reality and inevitability of conflict within the organization itself, not just singular disputes with external entities. One of the most recent examples of the encouragement of the interest-based design of interest-based dispute resolution methods is Executive Order 12871, Labor-Management Partnerships, which developed from the Clinton administration's National Performance Review (NPR). Focused on "creating a government that works better and costs less," the Report of the National Performance Review (Gore, 1993) sought to encourage the reinvention and streamlining of the federal government by eliminating red tape, focusing on customers, empowering employees, and returning to basics. With respect to Executive Order 12871, while one can claim that a presidential executive order is clearly a mandate or power-based design, which executive branch managers, including military leaders, ignore at their peril, the language of the order itself is strikingly interest based. In the preamble to the executive order, federal managers are instructed to create partnerships with their counterpart unions to identify problems and craft collaborative solutions to problems arising in the reinvention and redesign of the federal workplace. The result of Executive Order 12871 and the National Performance Review has been the birth of a national structure and framework for the creation and support of agency "partnership councils," including the joint education and training of management and labor representatives in the use of ADR and the application of consensual methods of dispute resolution to issues of reinvention and workplace disputes. While mixed to date, the responses to the order have constituted a historical leap forward in the encouragement of interest-based dispute resolution methods through interest-based conflict management systems design principles. This has been accomplished by the example of the executive order as a vehicle for encouraging radical change in dispute identification and resolution processes, by the scale of the application (the entire federal executive branch population), and by the nature of the imprimatur (direct involvement of key stake-holders in the creation and operation of joint councils in which the identification and resolution of issues will proceed).

Quadrant IV participative design processes usually lead to an understanding that conflict management systems, rather than dispute resolution programs, yield optimal results and are more durable. It is an approach to design that leads to greater understanding and awareness among system participants that the causes of conflict are systemic, integrally connected to and in concert with the operation of other systems in the organization. It encourages the remedy of conflict systemically as well, building the capacity of the organization to learn about itself through the ongoing development of areas of disagreement and dissonance. Further, it allows system participants the opportunity to practice interest-based skills and joint problem-solving techniques, which stakeholders will need in order to *use* the system with satisfaction and empowerment. Lastly, designing interest-based methods through interest-based processes is both a partnering and a problem-solving process. When the system's stakeholders are involved collaboratively in the design process, they become true partners in identifying, understanding, and managing their disputes—and have a more vested responsibility for the successful operation of the conflict management system.

Table 4.2. Comparison of Conflict Management Systems.

	Quadrant I	Quadrants II, III	Quadrant IV
Identity of Designer	Authority-Reactive	Expert-Imposed	Stakeholder-Derived
Attitude Toward Conflict	Avoidance of Disagreements	Accommodation of Disputes	Acceptance of Conflict
Analysis of Conflict	Random	Rational	Realistic
Method to Manage Conflict	Control	Criteria	Collaborate
Focus of Efforts	Institution	Individual Cases	Interest Groups
Key Players	Power Figures	Providers	Partners

Comparison of Conflict Management Systems

The distinctions among the four quadrants in the evolution of resolution continuum are perhaps best understood by comparison, as seen in Table 4.2.

Identity of the Designer: In an *authority-reactive* system, dispute resolution is dictated by those in charge within the organization. They decide how disputes will be handled and impose their decisions on the disputants. This method of designing dispute resolution programs is most common in Quadrant I systems, where power and rights-based approaches to conflict management dominate. In *expert-imposed* systems, consultants (usually from outside the organization) diagnose the disputes, design a new system based on what they think is best for the organization, and recommend that their design be adopted. Design is thus a product, not a process. This method of design is usually found in Quadrant II and III systems, where, for example, management makes the decision (rights-based design) that mediation (interest-based method) will be offered. Many of today's ADR programs fall within this category. In Quadrant IV, *stakeholder-derived* systems, the stakeholders actively participate in the design, which is a process, not a product. Stakeholders may be guided by an expert or specialist, but the design is done *by* the stakeholders and *with* the stakeholders, not *for* them.

Attitude Toward Conflict: This category explains how the organization views conflict in its many forms. In Quadrant I systems, the preferred method of conflict management is *avoidance of disagreements;* conflict is seen as signaling a challenge to authority and thus the proper response is assertion of control. This is the "how dare they challenge us" approach—"they" being contractor, employee, customer, or claimant. Alternatively, the system equates disagreement with unhappiness and has a low tolerance for it. In such an organization, denying or avoiding disagreement produces the least discomfort and the most control. In Quadrants II and III, there is a recognition and validation of the existence of singular or clusters of disputes but not of conflict as a broad concept. Disputes occur that must be "fitted" to the courts, legislation, case law, or other standardized attempts to manage conflict; thus, disputes are *accommodated.* An organizational attitude such as this admits that disputes exist but does not see or admit the existence of conflict. This type of organization usually channels disputes into a predetermined format, perhaps preferring, in a sense, the use of the Myers-Briggs Type Indicator (MBTI) "Thinking" preference for decision making based on logic and objectivity (discussed in Chapter One). There is little, if any, effort to anticipate conflict or disputes, to use preventive interventions, or to be concerned about the effect of conflict on people. Often, such organizations have great difficulty with disputes that are deeply imbedded in personalities, organizational culture, or systemwide practices because such disputes do not fit the existing framework or are resistant to standardized resolution attempts. Quadrant IV systems sharply contrast with all of the others in that there is an *acceptance of conflict* as inevitable and natural: conflict is seen as an opportunity, not an obstacle. These organizations design flexible conflict management approaches that accept the organization as it is at the present time, facilitate disputants' participation in the system, and provide a range of options for the settlement of disputes. In Quadrant IV, attention is given as well to the prevention of disputes and to the development of skills so that system participants will experience the greatest range of choice in their problem-solving efforts.

Analysis of Conflict: Here we see that Quadrant I systems are *random* in the way they handle disputes, dealing with them on an ad hoc basis as they arise, with a reactive rather than a proactive posture. In Quadrant II and III systems, there is a *rational* approach to disputes—organizations can study them, classify them, categorize them, and, eventually, predict and stabilize them. This linear, Western method of categorizing disputes requires that disputes fit into a standard category, which practitioners note is increasingly rare. The Quadrant IV system provides a sharp contrast once more with its *realistic* (and dynamic/spiral) approach toward conflict—appreciation of conflict's ever changing nature, its inherent polarities, and its ongoing responsiveness to changing demographics, culture, and markets. In such a system, conflict yields critical and valued information and feedback about organizational performance, thus serving as one more means of improving it.

Methods to Manage Conflict: In Quadrant I systems, organizations attempt to *control* conflict—avoid it, rename it, eradicate it, limit it, and deny it. The system's unstated fear is loss of control;

its challenge is to control conflict by any means, even if it results in higher overall costs to the institution and individuals. In Quadrant II and III systems, organizations develop *criteria* for dealing with conflict, often linear and logic-based processes and procedures for handling disputes. Here, the assumption is that conflict lends itself to prediction, identification, and standardization. By contrast, Quadrant IV organizations *collaborate* with stakeholders about how to manage conflict and how to create conflict management systems that honor and enact the principles of participation, openness, and feedback. Embracing these values generates conflict management systems characterized by flexible approaches to resolution, appreciative inquiry into the pattern of disputes, and substantial efforts to address and eradicate systemic causes of conflict.

Focus of Efforts: This category identifies who and what is the target of the organizational dispute system design effort. In Quadrant I systems, it is the *institution* or organization itself that is the all-important target. The state of the organization must be preserved at all costs and must be protected from the implied threat of conflict. In Quadrant II and III systems, the focus is on the ad hoc treatment of *individual* categories of disputes—events, cases, or dissatisfactions resolvable in isolation from each other. Quadrant IV systems focus instead on the *interest groups* (stakeholders: institutional, group, and individual) in the system as the target. Collective learning and feedback—from a variety of perspectives—about how well the organization is doing in its management of conflict as it relates to these interest groups is valued. By tapping into the whole system, both internal and external, organizational participants discover valuable information not only for adjustment and revision but also for creativity and growth. Thus, the target focus for the conflict management design effort in Quadrant IV systems is comprehensive and inclusive.

Key Players: In Quadrant I systems, these are the *power figures* in the organization: they control the questions and they decide the answers. In Quadrant II and III systems, it is usually the *providers*—experts and consultants—who decide what is wrong, figure out how to fix it, and then impart their specialized (and often "superior") wisdom and knowledge. In contrast, Quadrant IV conflict management systems identify both the organization and its stakeholders as *partners* in joint problem solving and in the design process, each with rights and responsibilities for the ongoing vitality and overall health of the organization.

It may seem apparent that we are most supportive of the development of Quadrant IV conflict management systems. However, creation of Quadrant IV systems is certainly not the only answer for all organizations, nor even a possibility for many. As with any model or construct, it is just that—a model that must be adapted to the context and the circumstance of particular organizational systems. However, it operates from a set of assumptions and limitations that are well worth examining. For example, Quadrant IV assumes the existence of organizations and individuals capable of recognizing the crucial role conflict management plays in organizational performance and results. It assumes the wisdom and willingness of organizational leaders to loosen their perceived obligation to control and unilaterally determine organizational operations in favor of involving those with a stake in organizational conflict. It assumes a willingness to recognize the value and importance of ongoing openness, flexibility, learning, evaluation, and modification of any conflict management system.

However, in spite of the above preference, we along with countless managers, design teams, and practitioners know only too well that one must take the organization as one finds it: closed, poorly led, resistant, dysfunctional, frightened, in disarray, in crisis, in reorganization. We recognize these limitations and address some of the constraints posed by such eventualities on conflict management systems design later in the book (Chapter Twelve, "Resistance and Constraints: Having Tea with Your Demons" and Chapter Thirteen, "Changing the Culture: Accepting Conflict and Encouraging Choice"). We also recognize that there is no magic in Quadrant IV thinking; it is hard work for everyone involved, from organizational leaders and members, to other stakeholders and consultants, to practitioners and design teams. However, we think that Quadrant IV perspectives and approaches make good common sense in dealing with the scale and scope of organizational strife in today's turbulent environment. If organizations today make it an objective to utilize some if not all elements of Quadrant IV, that will increase the likelihood that tomorrow's conflict management systems will stand the tests of accessibility, fairness, durability, and effectiveness.

DSD Principles in Action

Interest-based conflict management systems design takes the basic DSD principles of power, rights, and interests and applies them in an organizational context. Rather than focusing primarily on dispute resolution methods, interest-based design applies DSD principles to the design intervention itself. This results in balancing and congruity: interest-based methods created through interest-based design is, in a sense, "walking the talk." Let us briefly examine the relevance of the six principles of the classic DSD model to the interest-based conflict management systems design context. For example, at the hypothetical SunSystem Consulting Company, which provides training and educational services, the six principles are relevant in the context of a dispute with a state government agency dissatisfied with the quality of software training manuals received from SunSystem pursuant to an ongoing contract.

The first principle, putting the focus on interests, really means that the starting point in organizational conflict management becomes the statement, clarification, and illumination of the issue at hand from the perspective of the needs and concerns from the interest groups. In other words, rather than initially seeking various means to cover up the core concerns that give rise to the dispute through positions (one party's idea of a solution) and other strategies to mask the real problem or concern, the conflict management system is designed to provide processes at the outset that promote and support the identification of such core concerns. In our hypothetical case, this means that the contract administrator for the state agency deals directly with the project manager at SunSystem, identifying the problem and the concerns it raises as soon as they occur. It may also involve designing some preventive mechanisms for measuring satisfaction with the product during the process rather than solely at the end.

The second principle, providing "loop-backs," means that the organizational conflict management system is designed to encourage a flexible return, if needed, to other interest-based methods, such as prevention or negotiation or fact finding, when the current process is unsuccessful in resolving the dispute. Such looping back to the full range of the ADR spectrum is cyclical and provides additional opportunities short of amplification of the dispute to glean additional information or insight into the problem at hand. For example, at SunSystem, this may involve some type of negotiation between the contracting officer and the project manager, followed by presentation of the dispute to some neutral evaluator. If new information is uncovered by the evaluator, the parties may choose to "de-escalate" the dispute and resume interest-based negotiations.

The third principle, providing low-cost rights and power back-ups, means that the conflict management system includes in its design the realistic awareness that initial efforts will not always be successful and that reasonable alternatives are necessary to provide for continued low-cost efforts to reach satisfactory resolutions. Often, the availability of these backups can serve as leverage: some disputants may be more willing to explore the unfamiliar and unpracticed world of interest-based problem solving knowing that if it fails, there is always arbitration of the dispute (low-cost rights backup). At SunSystem, for example, the dispute resolution procedures spelled out in the contract (mediation, then arbitration) give the parties a backup, which allows them to engage in good-faith negotiation efforts.

The fourth principle, building in consultation before and feedback after, suggests that the conflict management system be designed to encourage discussion about the nature of the dispute and optimal ways of resolving it before resolution efforts begin. Then, once resolved, the system requires that an evaluation process occur so the results of the resolution process can be assessed and a determination made of the need for system modification. In this way, the conflict management system is encouraged to be one that is more intentional, open, and engaged in an ongoing learning process to allow system adjustment and encourage dispute prevention. At SunSystem, ideally the parties themselves (the project manager for the state and the contracting officer for SunSystem) would have been involved in face-to-face negotiation of the initial contract so that they could have achieved a mutual understanding of the scope of the project, as well as expectations and potential areas of disagreement. Once the current dispute is resolved, they would again sit down face to face and evaluate their satisfaction with the conflict management system, making any necessary modifications to benefit the ongoing contract.

The fifth principle, arranging the procedures in low-to-high cost sequence, encourages the resolution of disputes, in the first instance, at the lowest level and by the least adversarial means possible. The progression is typically one of discussion and exploration of whether there is a dispute, to negotiation of the apparent differences, and then to some appropriate form of ADR. In this way, the disputants remain in control of the process for as long as possible. In addition, the choice to resolve the dispute and in what manner remains with the disputants themselves for as long as possible, and all the costs of the process are kept as low as possible for as long as possible. As noted above, at SunSystem, the backup of a final, binding, imposed resolution method allows the parties to engage in negotiation and other appropriate methods of ADR without fear of impasse or litigation.

The sixth and last principle—providing motivation, skills, and necessary resources—focuses on those factors that enable the other five principles to succeed. Here, the conflict management system is geared toward participation of stakeholders and the empowerment of disputants to resolve their differences themselves with the least escalation of costs and minimal third-party intervention. For this to occur, resources must be expended early on to a broader community within the organizational system in order to build greater knowledge and understanding of conflict itself, resolution options, and processes. All of this provides greater motivation to system participants to use a revised system. Further, in a systemic organizational conflict management design, a wider universe of system participants are trained in the skills necessary to achieve the goal of more local and interest-based resolutions of disputes. In addition, by the very act of supporting the effort to institute alternative dispute resolution methods, organizational leadership signals that a new age of conflict management has arrived. That in itself is a powerful motivator in any system intervention. At SunSystem, for example, this might mean an organizational shift at the state agency toward involving project managers (rather than just contract officers) in early contract negotiations in order to communicate expectations and identify potential problem areas that will require management support. This may also mean training project managers in contract procedures and explicit assurance to contracting officers that they are not being replaced or "cut out of the picture."

OD Values in Action

As mentioned above, many organizations today are operating from a Quadrant III framework when it comes to conflict management: using interest-based methods of ADR but designing these methods in rights-based ways. For example, the hypothetical Aztec Corporation might become alarmed at the number of complaints surfacing that are related to allegedly disparate promotions in certain departments and might as a result choose to require (rights-based design) that these internal concerns be channeled to the Office of the Ombudsperson (an interest-based method) before an employee is allowed to file any formal complaint with the Human Resources Department. If the new procedure is mandated by Aztec management without any input from employees or their representatives, it may be viewed as an attempt to co-opt those who file complaints and may be resisted to the point of public protest. Interest-based conflict management systems design, on the other hand, would create any new procedures by identifying first what the nature of the problem is with the active participation of those affected and interested. Only with such clarification and involvement would a representative design effort proceed to research, discover, and institutionalize appropriate resolution processes. With the OD values of participation, openness, and feedback honored and enacted throughout the design intervention itself, the result is greater acceptance of the problem at hand and the need for action.

By maximizing the ideas and input of all relevant participants, the resultant output—a conflict management system rather than a dispute resolution program—has greater potential to be durable, satisfactory, and actually used. Similar to the theory that there is a higher level of compliance with mediated rather than imposed resolutions because the parties have been an integral part of the process and have "owned" both the process and the resolution, so too with interest-based as opposed to imposed design. As practitioners have witnessed time and time again in organizational settings, stakeholders are more likely to use systems in which they feel they have a stake or have had a hand in creating. The notion of participation in this context is in the design process itself, not merely in the resulting, predetermined dispute resolution product.

For example, using an interest-based conflict management systems design model, employees or their representatives at the Aztec Corporation would actively participate in identifying the perceived problem, designing appropriate modifications to the existing complaint procedure and presenting those recommendations to Aztec's senior officials. In other words, Aztec stakeholders would actually be involved in "shuffling the deck" and would not simply be dealt a new hand.

As discussed in Chapter One, "arrogant" organizational responses to conflict tend to look down on certain classes of disputants, believing that the organization must do things for them since they cannot do for themselves. One manifestation of this has been the tendency of some organizations to design dispute resolutions systems *for* classes of disputants, not *with* them, and to refuse to ascertain disputants' needs, preferences, or concerns as a starting point for the design. In particular, organizations have tended to design *for* the disempowered—those who have fewer resources or muted voices. At Aztec, this may manifest itself as a task force, formed to study the problem, composed entirely of division directors and section managers.

Participation: Participation in interest-based design means involvement of all organizational levels in designing the conflict management systems that affect them. Each part of the organization has a purpose, population, and product that gives rise to disputes. By tapping into the entire system and its parts, an interest-based design process has the potential to address more disputes from a variety of perspectives. At Aztec, for example, getting input from employees as well supervisors may reveal that the problem is actually not disparate treatment regarding promotions themselves but rather disparate assignment of tasks or responsibilities with higher promotion potential.

Openness: Interest-based conflict management design requires an openness by all stakeholders to dialogue and to possible change; a mutual willingness on the part of both the organization and its stakeholders to explore interests and dissatisfactions directly, honestly, and in a true spirit of partnering; joint problem solving; and stewardship. As practitioners know, openness can be difficult in organizations. Past practices of rewarding constructive criticism with reprisal and contribution with ostracism are common. To create openness, preliminary work often needs to be done to establish a safe environment. This might occur at Aztec, for example, by having organizational leaders express their preference for (and belief in) initiating a dialogue about possible changes to existing complaint procedures related to promotions and by establishing representative focus groups to raise concerns and then a representative task force to explore the issue and make recommendations. Openness in the interest-based design process is really a matter of how people give and receive communication in the organizational context about the issue of conflict management.

Feedback: Giving and receiving constructive feedback about dispute resolution practices and processes is integral to the learning and evolution of the organization's conflict management system. Feedback is a corollary concept to openness, to open systems thinking, and to the principles of interest-based conflict management systems design. It represents a willingness on the part of the stakeholders to *offer* useful comment and critique as well as a willingness on the part of the organization to *consider* valid comment and critique.

Feedback as it relates to interest-based conflict management systems design requires both the ability and the willingness to ask how well things are working, to learn about what is not working, and to pursue making changes where necessary. In interest-based conflict management systems design, providing feedback is a right with corresponding responsibilities. Drawing forth comment or criticism is the first step. However, one cannot simply criticize or complain. One must also take part in the re-creation of the system; one has the responsibility to couple a complaint with a request for change. Under this model, for example, the representative Aztec task force would do more than merely conclude that the existing procedures are not working; as organizational stewards with responsibilities to the system as a whole, the task force would generate options for possible change strategies and feed these options back to appropriate organizational stakeholders, such as Aztec management and Aztec co-workers.

Interest-based conflict management design has one further characteristic that links it to OD and sets it apart from the classic DSD model and ADR approaches. Instead of assuming stability and predictability in the management of conflict and disputes, it assumes almost continual change and progression. The model sees conflict management as an open system; there is a recycling, a renewal process that makes the design evolutionary, dynamic, and spiral in nature. This continuous improvement of the system through reevaluation and reflection ensures that it addresses the interests and needs of both the organization and its stakeholders. Interest-based conflict management systems design is thus not a one-time process where you do it once, put it on paper, and move on to the next project. Rather, this model of design maintains an openness to constant feedback in order to acquire information and opportunities for action. In this sense, interest-based conflict management systems design is never done or complete. Some practitioners and, to use the MBTI once more, some "Judging"-type organizations prefer closure and may find this concept of design as an ongoing process disconcerting and uncomfortable. Nevertheless, interest-based conflict management design is about staying open and dynamic.

Lastly, interest-based conflict management systems design honors the OD value of stewardship by all stakeholders, who assume responsibility for the health and continued vitality of the organization. There is a mutuality or partnership in such a design process: stakeholders are responsible for offering valid, constructive feedback with suggestions for change; the organization is responsible for encouraging and considering such feedback.

ADR Practices in Action

Many design practitioners are also mediators or are familiar with mediation as a dispute resolution technique. In significant respects, interest-based conflict management systems design is really the mediation of an entire system. It is the designer acting as a facilitator, providing processes, and otherwise assisting the organization and its stakeholders to work together to fashion their own conflict management system. It is the designer questioning whether system stakeholders and other necessary parties are "at the table," are involved meaningfully in the design process from the beginning. Similarly, just as a mediator has no power to impose a decision on the parties, neither does a designer impose a conflict management system on an organization and its stakeholders. However, as in mediation, an interest-based designer can assist an entire system in understanding and accepting its conflict, can guide it through the highly participatory process of discovering consensus about resolution potentials, and, by not imposing a decision, can empower system participants to accept and manage their own conflict not only now but in the future. Just as disputants are more likely to comply with a resolution reached through mediation because they were integral to the process, so too are stakeholders more likely to use and be satisfied with a conflict management system that they have helped to design.

In the ensuing chapters of Part Two, we will explore the "how to" of each of these specific tasks of interest-based conflict management systems design and look at the practical steps in creating Quadrant IV conflict management systems.

Part Two

Designing and Improving Conflict Management Systems

Chapter Five

Entry and Contracting
Starting the Systems Design Effort

The challenge for practitioners is how to apply the principles and values of interest-based conflict management systems design to the technical and practical aspects of their design work. Here, most design efforts are initially concerned with the questions of who should be involved in the design, whether to proceed, and how to begin. This chapter focuses on the very beginning stage of conflict management systems design work in an organization and provides practical ideas for this start-up phase. We use hypothetical examples in this chapter (and throughout Part Two) from three settings: a federal government agency, a community hospital, and a national food products company. We start from the premise that the manner in which the design effort is started—the initial definition of the problem, the use of internal and external staff and/or expert resources, the creation of collaborative relationships between designers and organizational leadership, and the decision as to how interest-based practices will be honored in the organizational system—is crucial to the ultimate outcome of the intervention and change effort.

Dispute Resolution Problems and Opportunities

As practitioners know, there must be both a *presenting problem* and a *perceived opportunity* in order for an organization to initiate change in any of its systems. The same is true with regard to any change in the way an organization manages its conflict. Organization leadership, stakeholders, and constituents need to have a sense that something is amiss in the system and that a different way might be better—cheaper, faster, more lasting, more satisfactory. Otherwise, the organization has little or no motivation to address the need for change through the commitment of time, energy, and resources.

The *presenting problem* is one that is perceived by critical organizational players as requiring attention and needing possible change. With regard to disputes, this attention may come from a variety of sources. For example, has the XYZ Company been embarrassed by news coverage about a defective product or a failure to satisfy customers? Is it well known in the industry that the ABC Agency is rife with employee disputes? Is there ongoing, expensive litigation at the DEF Nonprofit Corporation regarding allegations of sexual harassment or misuse of funds? Often, disputes such as these simmer beneath the surface of organizations while the organizations go through a variety of quiet contortions to deal with them. Then, all of a sudden, the disputes explode and come to the public's attention, perhaps through a sensational court settlement or newspaper exposure. Examples include toxic waste sites and their environmental and community impact, labor disputes and resulting strikes, and class action suits on issues such as product liability and medical malpractice.

For the organizational participants concerned about the effect of these disputes on the continued viability of the organization, once they have recognized the presenting problem, questions about *perceived opportunity* arise:

- How can we minimize the visibility or change the public perception of how our organization handles these disputes?
- How can we reduce our financial exposure?
- How can we prevent future disputes of this type?
- How can we improve our relations with customers, employees, or the community so that we will be known as a good organization for which to work or with which to conduct business?

These questions may arise any time an organization's dispute resolution is costly, unsuccessful, or unsatisfying. Further, in this age of the "quality" movement in organizational management and service, questions such as these are being asked more frequently as organizations attempt to satisfy their customers and promote a healthy and productive workplace. In addition, practitioners are more frequently asked to become involved in these change efforts.

The Federal Securities Management Agency

The Federal Securities Management Agency (FSMA), a hypothetical government agency, is responsible for regulating all securities transactions and brokers in the United States; for liquidating mutual funds that are unsafe, unsound, or insolvent; and for protecting the public from fraudulent securities practices. It is an "appropriated fund" agency that receives its funding directly from Congress, with its headquarters office in Washington, D.C., and five field offices around the country. FSMA is overseen by a five-member board of directors: the chairman of FSMA, a Treasury Department representative, a member of the New York Stock Exchange, a member of the public, and an academic selected by the White House.

Recently, FSMA has come under congressional scrutiny and public attack for two reasons: allegations that FSMA operates a "hostile work environment" for female professionals in at least two of its field offices; and allegations that it has taken too long to pay out investors and liquidate the Red River Fund, which was deemed insolvent more than two years ago. At least three congressional committees have indicated they intend to hold hearings on these matters after the next recess. Yesterday, the general counsel, Susan Jason, told her dispute resolution specialist, Larry Terrence (appointed under the Administrative Dispute Resolution Act), to look into both of these situations and report back to her in two weeks with findings and recommendations.

At FSMA, the presenting problem is already public: both the internal disputants (female professionals) and external disputants (dissatisfied investors) have aired their complaints outside the agency, probably to the press and to congressional staff. Although neither set of disputes has yet erupted into formal litigation, that possibility looms large in addition to the formal hearings scheduled in Congress. As Larry Terrence begins his investigation, however, he will need additional information about the nature of the presenting problems, gained internally and externally from some of the disputants themselves. General Counsel Susan Jason—to focus on the immediate client—may have a range of motives in seeking Larry's help. What is most clear, however, is that the FSMA is in "hot water" because these two disputes have gone public. In a sense, the presenting problem is akin to a crisis and therefore provides Larry with an unparalleled opportunity to demonstrate the effectiveness of interest-based processes as an alternative to litigation. Given his possible marginal position as the lone dispute resolution specialist in the functional organizational unit of the general counsel's office (the agency's legal department) and the fact that the general counsel has dropped these "hot" disputes in his lap, there is also great risk that Larry will fail in his efforts to introduce alternative dispute resolution within a highly rights-oriented culture of a regulatory agency. Thus, Larry's work in the next two weeks with the perceived opportunity and the presenting problem is challenging. At the outset, he must formulate a plan for inquiry and entry into the two ongoing disputes that generates sufficient information about the viability of using alternative procedures in either or both disputes. Such information must come, discreetly at first, from those with a stake in the outcomes of any resolution efforts. At the same time, he will have to assess and build the level of internal concern, commitment, and support from FSMA's leadership for creative responses to the problems at hand. He must take care throughout his initial inquiry to maintain an exploratory attitude rather than an advocacy stance toward the appropriateness or applicability of alternative dispute resolution (ADR) to the two dispute arenas. His best approach is to make exploratory inquiries of the various disputants and respondents to ascertain the fit between the disputes and alternative approaches and the willingness of the key participants to search for less costly, more satisfactory, and more durable options to dispute resolution. The remainder of this chapter suggests how Larry might proceed in the ensuing weeks to appropriately enter this situation in an interest-based fashion and contract with key constituencies to optimize the results of any ADR applications to which they agree.

In this respect, Larry is aided by the pressing nature of both presenting problems. FSMA has at least the following opportunities, which arise from the disputes at hand:

- To improve its image with the public and Congress
- To develop new dispute resolution systems if it is determined that the current systems are not working effectively

- To reduce the risk and cost of litigation, as well as possible awards of relief by a court
- To develop systems to handle similar types of disputes in the future
- To increase the level of employee satisfaction and productivity

If Larry can help organizational stakeholders to see that there are important business and organizational improvement opportunities in the manner in which the disputes are approached and resolved, his efforts will be more fully supported, for such a focus on the future energizes rather than discourages the individuals involved. In this way, the presenting problem and the perceived opportunity can be joined to summon sufficient energy, commitment, and creativity to sustain a change effort at FSMA.

The Internal Specialist

In order to gather more information so they can consider whether to act and what to do, most organizations usually assign someone on the existing staff to investigate possible opportunities and options to resolve the perceived presenting problem. Whether it is someone from the legal staff, the human resources staff, or a special collateral duty assignment for another staff member, this individual is usually given the task of gathering information about alternative dispute resolution options and determining what other organizations have done to resolve disputes similar in nature.

Sources for information abound in the alternative dispute resolution community (see the resources at the end of this book). There are ADR books, journal articles, and magazines. ADR personnel from other organizations can be contacted, and there are professional and service organizations, both public and private, willing to share information and resources. Once connected with these resources and aware (perhaps for the first time) of alternative methods to resolve disputes, internal dispute resolution specialists often get highly energized by the range of commonsense ADR choices available to change the way the organization resolves disputes. They may confer with others within the organization and begin to build a network to discuss how and where to begin changing the dispute resolution system.

This overflow of enthusiasm and excitement about the possibilities for changing the dispute resolution system often leads to early (and usually premature) efforts to introduce ADR. Because ADR appears to make such good sense, the internal specialists communicate all they have learned about ADR to organizational leadership and make recommendations for adoption of certain ADR procedures—for example, a mandate that all cases of a certain type must be mediated or that an ombudsperson's office be established. Often, their enthusiasm about change in the status quo generates suspicion, fear, and resistance because it is not grounded in a sound and thorough assessment of any presenting problem. Rather, the specialists tend to present only their own perceived opportunity for solution based on an assumption that the system needs to be changed. Numerous outside consultants (particularly those who have been called in to deal with the aftermath) have seen internal specialists who get caught in this dilemma and the effect that such an assumption can have on any subsequent change intervention.

Experienced practitioners have learned to anticipate that there will be resistance to any change effort in an organization's conflict management system. The practice of anticipating that proposed changes will lead to concern and resistance in initial stages of conflict management systems design efforts is useful, particularly for the internal dispute resolution specialist who can get caught up in the energy of the moment. In addition, internal specialists often need to learn to go slowly. The first challenge is to expand the number of organizational participants involved and to share with them all the available information about possible ADR options, refraining from making specific recommendations at this early stage. Rather, the organizational participants are encouraged to focus on what problems there are, if any, and then to identify any likely opportunities for change. Whether this is done with the assistance of an external consultant or internally, this step of widening the scope of organizational members involved in the design effort is critical.

The External Consultant

The first interventions into an ongoing system by an external consultant, particularly around the issue of conflict, cast a long shadow on the ultimate outcome. In fact, entry is often the key element in determining whether any change effort will be undertaken.

At this stage, it may be useful for the organization to employ the services of an experienced external conflict management consultant or designer, for a number of reasons:

- Internal organizational participants often listen more attentively to and accord more credibility to the advice of an "outside expert."
- External designers bring expertise and experience from their work with other organizations to the technical and practical aspects of design work and may be viewed as less threatening.
- The objectivity and independence of the external designer may facilitate the surfacing of sensitive organizational issues without the same peer pressures and cultural and career limitations experienced by internal specialists.
- External designers may add a "big picture" perspective to the various components of the design effort.

In addition, the inclusion of an external consultant in the conflict management design may be an incremental process. That is, some consultants may be invited into the organization for a specific task, such as training or assessment, which may eventually grow into a systemic design intervention. We readily admit that few organizations are prepared to make sweeping changes in their conflict management systems at once, or to embrace all aspects of interest-based design initially. Moving toward interest-based conflict management systems design is often an incremental process that starts where the organization is at the time. Perhaps the organization is at a point where it can consider change in one limited aspect of its conflict management system.

In essence, designers, whether internal or external, are not merely substantive experts; they are also (and perhaps more importantly) system intervenors. The decision to invite an external designer into the organization is in many cases the first intervention into the ongoing system. It may require the internal specialist to persuade key organizational leadership that necessary resources should be expended to obtain external assistance with the assessment and design process. Often, the internal specialist, either alone or in conjunction with leadership, will interview potential designers to determine and recommend which consultant is not only affordable but also provides the best match of experience and practice with the host organization. Such interviews usually include questions about not only the experience and expertise of the external designer but also values, philosophy, and style. Does the individual have an understanding of organizational principles and intervention techniques? Specifically, are participation, openness, feedback, and organizational self-determination hallmarks of the designer's intervention model? Is this person familiar with core dispute systems design principles? Does he or she have actual design experience, not simply experience as a neutral (a mediator or arbitrator), including previous involvement with other organizational interventions and change efforts?

Once an external designer is selected, the next step is for the internal specialist and organizational leadership to negotiate a collaborative design contract with the external consultant. This negotiation helps clarify the respective roles and expectations of the two design specialists and leadership and frames the subsequent intervention and working relationships.

The Design Contract

Whether the primary responsibility for entry to explore the redesign of the current dispute resolution system belongs to the internal specialist or an external systems designer, the initial entry stage in interest-based conflict management systems design includes the following steps:

- Engage critical stakeholders in generating information about how the organization is managing its disputes.
- Provide an opportunity for these same stakeholders to determine whether such information indicates a need for any change in the dispute resolution system.
- Educate stakeholders about the critical ingredients for a successful design effort.

At this entry stage, organizational leaders may need to be educated about an interest-based approach to conflict management systems design and its reliance on participation, openness, and feedback mechanisms at every stage. In other words, there is often an unwritten (although many practitioners have found it a good idea to put it in writing) yet clear contract between the designers and the organizational leadership regarding guiding principles and processes: what the design process will look like and how it will be conducted. Some practitioners have been frustrated in their design intervention efforts because there was no "meeting of the minds": organizational leadership had a different idea of what the intervention would be and how it would work. If neither the internal specialist nor the external designer can achieve an understanding and agreement with organizational leadership on the design principles, values, and scope of the intervention, the chance of effective and lasting change is dramatically lowered.

Thus, even before the "real" work begins, the critical leadership group and the designers must reach agreement on how the process of exploring potential change in the dispute resolution system will unfold. The reason for clarifying these core principles at this stage of the intervention is that to start off on the wrong foot broadcasts a message to the rest of the organization that this is just another gimmick, another "imposition" by experts and authority. As practitioners know, one does not get all-important buy-in and commitment *after* the design process is completed; buy-in is an *ongoing* process of gaining trust and must be cultivated and nurtured from the very beginning, with meaningful participation and influence from the top down, the bottom up, and sideways.

The contract also ensures that critical factors in the ultimate implementation of the design within the organization are not overlooked. If there is no clear understanding with organizational leadership about how the design process will be conducted and the importance of involving key stakeholders in the design tasks, organizational leadership may increasingly demand recommendations from and shift responsibility for the change effort to the designer "expert." This makes the design not a process but a product—by the designer, imposed by leadership on the stakeholders—and can lead to serious if not insurmountable problems in the implementation phase. This is one reason why it is advisable that critical leadership and key stakeholders "own" the design process from the beginning: it increases the likelihood of successful implementation and decreases the potential for sabotage (usually by disenfranchised stakeholders, those threatened with power loss, or other critical constituencies).

In many instances, entry is the most delicate part of the change effort because organizational leaders may not understand *how* lasting change occurs in any organization. As a result, apart from the design process itself, the designers may have to educate organizational leadership on how change occurs in an organization and how it is sustained. Thus, the key elements contained in the design contract are the following:

- Initial identification of the key stakeholders in a dispute system revision (end-users, customers, labor unions, and others)
- Commitment that these stakeholders will be actively involved in the assessment, design, implementation, and evaluation stages
- Understanding and acceptance of basic change and design principles, including the possibility that there may be no need for change in the existing dispute resolution system
- Acceptance of and commitment to the need for evaluation and feedback at every stage of assessment, design, implementation, and evaluation, with an understanding of the fluid nature of conflict management
- Willingness of designers, stakeholders, and leadership to actively "partner" in a collaborative problem identification and resolution process and mutual expression of what that might look like
- Agreement on who (individual, committee, or collective consensus) will make the final determination of whether a revised system will be adopted, upon what criteria, and how that decision will be implemented

By reaching this understanding in advance, the designers and organizational leadership establish a collaborative relationship as a model for the process to follow. Moreover, practitioners have discovered that the very act of designing, through its processes of participation, openness, and feedback, often builds and improves organizational relationships among stakeholders as a collateral effect to the technical aspects of changing the existing dispute resolution system.

If the designer is clear about his or her values and philosophy at the outset, the organization and its stakeholders then have the opportunity to explicitly decide—not by mere silence, omission, or lack of decision—whether they will accept and affirm these values as operating principles to guide the design process. If they do, their commitment will need support, coaching, and guidance from the designer throughout the design process. Conversely, the invitation to affirm these values is also the invitation to decline them, and the designer must be ready to accept that decision if the organization and its stakeholders decide accordingly.

Hopevale Hospital Center

Hopevale Hospital Center (a hypothetical organization) is a for-profit non-teaching hospital and medical center located in a mid-sized community in the Northeast. Until ten years ago, it was the only hospital in the area and prided itself on being part of the community. It now competes with a newly constructed high-tech facility, Mainline Hospital and Medical Center, which is a teaching hospital and part of a large national health maintenance organization chain. Mainline has recently been drawing patients from Hopevale, particularly in the specialty areas of cardiac and pulmonary treatment (it has several nationally known physicians who practice in these departments). The nurses at Hopevale are unionized; recent attempts to organize the cafeteria workers have been unsuccessful.

Hopevale's revenues decreased substantially last year, due to a large malpractice judgment, competition from Mainline, and uncollected patient accounts (particularly from emergency room visits). Staff morale has declined at Hopevale, overall wages are lower than at Mainline (except for the nurses), and the hospital is still involved in one medical malpractice lawsuit with over $20 million in exposure and one lawsuit with a pharmaceutical supply firm regarding a $100,000 payment allegedly due. Plans to enlarge the Emergency Department and renovate the Cardiac Care Unit were put on hold last week by the board of directors, much to the displeasure of several community action groups.

Six months ago, the Hopevale board of directors brought in a new CEO, John Kernan, who is an experienced hospital administrator and is interested in maintaining Hopevale's reputation as a comprehensive community-based service facility while retaining its financial viability. When asked at last week's board meeting to identify the hospital's disputes he is most concerned with, he identified three: declining staff morale and deteriorating relationships among doctors and nurses, declining reputation and support in the community, and increasing litigation costs and exposure. The board directed him to make recommendations for dealing with these matters.

Yesterday, John designated his assistant, Sheila Downey, as the "dispute resolution specialist" to look into these three matters and to hire an external consultant to assist them in making recommendations to the board.

Here, as the "internal specialist," Sheila might be tempted to begin her efforts by focusing on one of the three arenas of dispute (staff morale and relationships, outstanding lawsuits, or community dissatisfaction), gathering information on her own, and contacting other hospitals to determine how they have handled similar situations. In addition, she may be tempted to explore ADR opportunities in one of the dispute arenas, such as the potential use of arbitration in the pending lawsuit with the pharmaceutical company, and make recommendations back to the CEO.

By using an interest-based participative design approach instead, her role at this early stage of the intervention would be to engage other organizational players that have information about these three dispute arenas—the medical director and other doctors, union representatives for the nurses, employee representatives for other nonunionized hospital workers, the Legal Department regarding the lawsuits, managers and employees in the Cardiac Care Unit and Emergency Department, and members of the community who are dissatisfied. It is appropriate for her to gather information about ADR alternatives in each of these three dispute areas but only as examples of possible options to be shared with other organizational participants.

The selection and hiring of the external consultant may be the task around which Sheila can organize the various and diverse stakeholders. While the task before her is the hiring of an external consultant, Sheila may first want to gather a group of stakeholders (doctors, union representatives, employees, representatives from the Legal Department, and members of the community) and raise the board's and the CEO's concerns. At this early stage, she can enlist the support of these groups and assess their degree of interest in the opportunity for improvement that faces them (perceived opportunity and presenting problem). Sheila may also ask the interested stakeholder groups about their preferences regarding external expert consultation. The stakeholders may then choose to commit to organizing themselves into a representative task force to work with Sheila and any outside consultant. With an exploration and clarification of such a group's ongoing purpose and role, Sheila would then be in a position to work with the group on all three of the dispute matters at hand. Sheila and the stakeholder group could thus begin to gather more information about the three dispute arenas and accomplish the initial task of bringing in an outside consultant. Sheila could probably hold screening interviews with several consultants, preparing a recommendation to the CEO that two or three of the candidates be invited back for further interviews with the stakeholder group. In looking for an external conflict management designer, Hopevale probably will seek someone who has experience in a health care setting and understands the culture and operation of hospitals. In addition, it needs someone who can work well with a variety of participants (including the board of directors, the CEO, lawyers and the Legal Department, doctors and nurses, the union, and community leaders) and has a diverse track record of conflict management interventions from a variety of settings and applications. Given the scope of the intervention and the diversity of the stakeholders, Hopevale would probably not want to hire an inexperienced designer nor one who is uncomfortable with large-scale, high-involvement change efforts.

Let us assume that Hopevale eventually hires Jeff Linton from Conflict Consultants. Here, the design contract with Conflict Consultants needs to be quite explicit given the nature and expense of the planned intervention. Hopevale would want to have a clear understanding of Conflict Consultants' philosophy and practices and some sense of the timetable of the intervention. Indeed, Hopevale might want to have Conflict Consultants present a "conflict management systems design proposal" to the board of directors to let the board know of the approach planned to address each of the three dispute arenas and to explore the level of commitment to such an approach. Conflict Consultants in turn needs to clarify what the working relationship will be with Sheila as the internal consultant in order to ensure that it has access to both internal and external stakeholders, to know who will make the ultimate decision regarding any changes in the three dispute arenas, and to have an organizational commitment to ongoing learning about conflict management efforts through feedback and evaluation processes.

Designer/Intervenor Roles

Not only in the entry phase but also in subsequent phases of design interventions, designers are asked to wear many hats and take many roles. Although designers are not responsible for the creation and implementation of the system, they are clearly accountable for the nature and effect of their intervention and work products. Thus, how designers act in their many roles raises questions of values, integrity, and effectiveness. In the last chapter, we noted that interest-based design is similar to the mediation of a system, and we noted that many of the tasks in the mediation process are similar to the tasks of interest-based design. In the same way, the roles of the designer are similar to those of a mediator.

The designer as *catalyst* triggers movement in the system without becoming part of the reaction. The designer lends energy and excitement to the change effort—suggesting, encouraging, guiding, affirming, questioning, not deciding or imposing. In Hopevale, this will be the role of Conflict Consultants—to coax, to coach, to stay "global," to encourage the hospital and its many stakeholders to make necessary changes in the conflict management system, but not to decide for them nor to get caught up in any local disagreements by taking sides.

The designer as *educator* teaches the organization and its stakeholders about conflict and change and makes them aware of communication styles and techniques. The designer also educates about how organizations function and how they change, as well as about possible design strategies, ADR options, evaluation methodologies, and training techniques. At Hopevale, this may take the form of Jeff Linton and Sheila Downey educating various groups, including employees and community representatives, about appropriate ADR options and training programs. They may also seek to inform and perhaps educate the board of directors or the CEO about successful conflict management in other hospital settings and about how to lead their institution in a change process, as well as to point out the obstacles that Hopevale may face in the three dispute arenas.

The designer as *facilitator* assists the organizational and individual stakeholders to work together as a group, identifying their interests and creating options for a more effective conflict management system. This involves allowing the stakeholders to proceed at their own pace and to negotiate their own agenda—again, to facilitate, not direct or impose. At Hopevale, this may mean that Sheila needs to facilitate the stakeholder group's exploration of why the board of directors is pursuing such a strategy at this juncture and what questions need to be asked of an external design consultant about how a conflict management change intervention takes place. In other words, throughout her activities, Sheila needs to facilitate system members' learning about conflict choices.

The designer as *translator* interprets ADR ideas and options to the various stakeholders and constituencies, explaining their nuances. This involves translating only what has been explicitly stated and not interpreting a particular concept or idea in a way that favors a preconceived conclusion or result. At Hopevale, for example, this may require Jeff Linton, as an external consultant, to translate to community members that Hopevale is willing to work with them to create options concerning continued Emergency Department services, without suggesting how or committing to a particular approach or combination of options. At this stage, Jeff's goal is to signal the hospital's willingness to find appropriate solutions through approaches that will involve customers as well as hospital management, doctors, nurses, and others.

Finally, the designer is *an agent of reality*, identifying those areas where change may be difficult, where stakeholders may resist, where organizational structures or practices may create constraints, or where knowledge and skills are lacking. This is more than simply being a prophet of doom or a troubleshooter: it involves identifying ownership of potential problems and developing collaborative efforts with and among stakeholders to craft solutions. At Hopevale, Jeff Linton may have to become an agent of reality, explaining that based on his inquiries, the medical malpractice lawsuit with $20 million in exposure is not likely to be dropped. He may suggest that a more informed and realistic, less wishful approach to preserving and enhancing the hospital's financial viability is needed for further efforts to resolve that dispute. For example, he may discover that the lawsuit arose because the aggrieved patient and his family could not get access to the hospital's legal and medical staff to have their questions answered and to satisfactorily investigate the problem. Frustrated with this inattention and especially with the Legal Department's challenge to "file a lawsuit if you think you are so smart about medical matters," the patient and his family did just that, Jeff might discover. He might indicate that efforts can continue to be made to resolve the lawsuit as favorably as possible but also suggest that key stakeholders may wish to explore what measures need to be considered to prevent future lack of access of this type from occurring.

Given these multiple roles that the designer plays, questions arise as to what background, experience, and training is relevant for conflict management systems designers. We believe that an important characteristic of an effective systems designer is a belief in and ability to honor and enact the values of participation, openness, and feedback. In addition, it is helpful to have a working understanding of organization development (OD) practices, dispute systems design (DSD) principles, and ADR processes and a practiced repertoire of communication, facilitation, mediation, and negotiation skills. However, like most dispute resolution skills, conflict management systems design is both an art and a science— the "science," based on principles and techniques, can be taught and modeled, but the "art" of orchestrating such high-involvement processes in a topically sensitive area can only be accomplished through experience and practice. It is the art portion of conflict management systems design that comes from within the designer personally; it is a measure of one's ability to express oneself and use one's gifts in the creation of a design intervention that reflects core principles and values.

The Self as Instrument

Most choices to act in the service of interest-based design values, both in the entry phase and later stages of the intervention, require courage on the part of the designer—courage to promote organizational and stakeholder self-determination in the design process; courage to resist when powerful players insist on manipulation of the designer for their own ends; courage to stay humble in the dispensable nature of the facilitating role; and courage to let the system fail, if need be, so that it can learn about achieving its own path to success. Funches (1989) captures this spirit of the work of conflict management design. Concerned about the effective use of self in change processes, she notes three gifts practitioners can provide to client populations:

- Discernment: The ability to distinguish between work and nonwork in client behavior and to frame activities that enable clients to understand their behavior better and to make choices for goal achievement
- Presence: The ability to be "here and now" in the client system, as well as the ability to use one's ways of doing, being, and seeing the world as a method of teaching the client system to grow and learn
- Heart: The ability to attune and connect oneself to the client system with compassion, grace, and passion for the work of change

These "gifts of self" are the art portion of conflict management systems design. The "who" of the designer affects the "how" of the process. How designers share these gifts, how they conduct themselves, whether they honor core values and principles, whether they "walk the talk"—these aspects of self are crucial to the entry phase and all subsequent phases of the design intervention. OD practitioners, so often well schooled in understanding and using the self as instrument, may find further development of their level of comfort with conflict through their systems design work. This comfort and confidence in applying conflict resolution processes during a change intervention can enhance one's effectiveness and help minimize the stress that often surrounds conflict management systems design work.

The Designer as Role Model

By using the self as instrument, the designer serves as a role model for the organization and its stakeholders. That is, the behaviors modeled by the designer during the entry phase—participation, openness, feedback, respect for differences, comfort with conflict, direct communication, collaboration—are the very values and skills that the organization and its stakeholders will use to develop enhanced conflict management capacity and capability. To a certain extent, the stakeholders look to the designer for cues regarding how the conflict management system and ADR processes will operate. Will procedures be imposed or derived? Will differences be respected, tolerated, or quashed? Will decisions be collaborative or conspiratorial? Will conflict be perceived as good, bad, or value-neutral?

Most effective designers practice what they preach: they use interest-based participative techniques in their dealings with client populations during the entry phase and throughout the intervention. They live the values of participation, openness, and feedback; they do not just state them or expect others to adopt them. By being self-reflective, and perhaps self-effacing where appropriate, effective designers are able to put aside preconceived notions of what the organization needs, who should be involved, or what will work best.

The Chompist Company

The (hypothetical) Chompist Company is a mid-sized food products manufacturing company located in the Midwest. It started out as a family-run business fifty years ago and has gradually grown and taken a place in the national market. Chompist is a privately held company; the majority shareholder and president is Daniel Teznicki, grandson of the founder. Chompist produces frozen foods, which are distributed to large restaurant chains and other wholesale customers. Within the past two years, Chompist has also moved into the consumer retail market, particularly the upscale market of healthy, low-fat, easy-to-prepare gourmet frozen dinners geared toward young professionals and two-income families.

Currently, Chompist is facing disputes in three areas. Last month, the state in which the Chompist production plant is located indicated its intent to propose new regulations governing the handling of meat and meat by-products, including frozen food production. If passed, these regulations will be a financial and production burden to Chompist, as well as to several other frozen food companies in the state. In addition, employees on the production line have begun to complain to supervisors that the machinery is old and needs updating; they claim it is unsafe and jeopardizes their health and have threatened to contact the Occupational Safety and Health Administration. Finally, ten retail consumers from the West Coast have contacted the Customer Service Department in the last two days alleging that they became ill after eating the Chompist Scandinavian Soufflé frozen dinner; one of them indicated that she intended to contact the local newspaper. This morning, Teznicki hired Anne Logan, an external conflict management consultant, to handle these three matters.

Designers' Traps and Pitfalls

Because designers use themselves as instruments extensively not only during the entry phase but throughout the entire design process, and because the organization and its stakeholders usually have high expectations of a designer's ability to assist them, there are several common traps and pitfalls to which designers can fall prey. These traps can cast long-lasting shadows on the design intervention. If the designer stays alert, these traps and pitfalls can be dealt with directly and honestly in ways that actually further and complement the design process. There are four common pitfalls that can affect both the designer personally and the design itself:

Enabling

The organization and its stakeholders may become dependent on the designer for approval, for feedback, for options, for guidance, for making their need to learn about themselves "go away," and for resolution of disputes that arise in the course of the design. Particularly in organizations that tend to avoid or deny conflict, it is easy for both the institution and some individuals to become dependent upon the designer. This relieves them of the responsibility of dealing with difficult and time-consuming design processes, such as assessment. It is thus not uncommon for designers to become "codependent," "enabling" the system to depend upon them rather than encouraging it to take responsibility for its own learning and discovery.

Dependency manifests itself when, for example, an organizational leader or a particular interest group asks the designer to convince an office or division of the need to move in a particular direction or to correct a difference of opinion about a certain element of design. In its most dependent form, stakeholders or leadership may attempt to "hook" the designer into doing their work by insisting that the designer is the expert and should thus decide a certain matter for them. In addition, dependency may also precipitate the designer getting caught in the crossfire of personality clashes, warring divisions, or jurisdictional turf battles. Often, this trap can be avoided by refusing to engage and reminding the stakeholders and leadership that it is *their* system, not the designer's.

At the Chompist Company, for example, Anne Logan as the external design consultant might be asked by Daniel Teznicki to intervene with the line workers directly and convince them that the equipment is safe, or she may be asked to intervene in a disagreement that has erupted in the Customer Service Department over how to handle the ten consumer complaints. In each of these situations, Anne needs to remember that she is a facilitator, not a decision maker; she is not there to convince stakeholders but rather to collaboratively work with them and with organizational leadership to identify, plan, manage, and implement needed changes in the current conflict management system.

Being the Bad Guy

This tactic is sometimes used by management or executives who have already placed limitations on the conflict management system but have not articulated or shared them for fear of being the bearer of bad news or perceived as closed minded. As a result, they rely on the designer to relay, on their behalf, what is not possible and what is not negotiable. This ploy is particularly dangerous because if the designer takes the bait, his or her credibility with the rest of the organization's stakeholders can be seriously and perhaps permanently compromised and damaged. It is a variation of the "designer as translator" theme but used in the service of someone else's (often a manager's) agenda and someone else's translation. Often, this trap emerges during the entry or assessment phases.

Here, it is often useful for the designer to simply refuse to play this type of game and to offer instead to mediate or facilitate a discussion between organizational leadership and stakeholders about any restrictions or limitations, their origin, and their intended purpose. This is an illustration of the conflict resolution practice of moving into the tension that can be a significant learning experience for those involved, including the designer, where critical information about the culture of the organization and the dominant preference for managing conflict in the system can emerge. Moreover, handling such an attempt to make the designer the "bad guy" can model alternative methods for problem solving and illustrate communication skills that may need to be learned as integral components to the effective implementation of any revisions to the conflict management system.

At the Chompist Company, Anne might be asked to contact the dissatisfied consumer and talk her out of going to the press. As an external consultant, this is not her role. She could, however, offer to act as a coach to any company representative who is assigned this role, suggesting conflict management approaches to the forthcoming conversation, which would further the ultimate objective of signaling to the consumer that the company is concerned about her problems and is willing to remedy the matter in collaboration with her.

Playing the Savior

Unless designers are aware of their own needs, it is easy to fall into the trap of thinking that they are indispensable and can control the ultimate success or failure of the systems design. Designers are particularly vulnerable to this pitfall when organizational members lavish them with praise and positive feedback. It is possible that system players are covertly hoping to hold the designer personally responsible for the success (or more likely the failure) of the system. Given these influences, it is easy for designers, consciously or unconsciously, to indeed believe that they are responsible for the success or failure of the system and in this way abrogate the core values of interest-based design in order to force or ensure success as it is defined in the particular organizational context.

While there are instances where it is appropriate for the designer to influence the development of appropriate conflict management systems, there are few, if any, circumstances in which designers should control the design. Where designers are feeling vulnerable to stakeholders or to leadership's desperation to have the designer control the process, they may want to withdraw and reflect, perhaps "going to the balcony"—standing back and taking an objective look at the situation as an observer—as Bill Ury recommends in his book *Getting Past No.* This allows designers to reaffirm their own boundaries, values, and "contract" with the organization. Also, if there is a design team or codesigner working with the organization, designers may want to consult with them as a reality check about what is occurring. Some designers working solo have successfully used "shadow consultation"—that is, informally sought advice—with uninvolved, impartial colleagues in order to gain another perspective, get a reality check, and discover if there is something they may not have noticed. It may seem obvious but is important to note nonetheless that professional and ethical standards, such as confidentiality, must be respected in any shadow consultation, whether formal or informal.

At the Chompist Company, Anne may become convinced that she has to save the line employees from poor working conditions. She may find herself getting caught up in the merits of the allegations rather than in dealing with the underlying conflict. If she is unable to facilitate a meaningful dialogue between management and production personnel on this topic, the employees may blame her and she may feel that she has failed them.

Letting It Fail

There may come a time in the entry phase, or even later in the process, when the organization decides not to continue to pursue redesigning the conflict management system. Here, the tendency of the designer is often to attempt a "fix," to encourage leadership to proceed with the design or to encourage the stakeholders to reconcile and avoid "divorce" by staying together for the sake of the system or the success of the change effort. Sometimes, the designer may be tempted to intervene directly with the necessary players, stakeholders, or constituents in order to fix it. Although many practitioners have the mediation and negotiation skills necessary to facilitate in such interventions, engaging in such actions nevertheless undermines the core value of organizational and stakeholder self-determination. Although it may be personally difficult for the designer to do, it is sometimes wise to allow the system to fail. In some situations, this is the best intervention possible. It signals clearly and directly that the designer respects the principle of self-determination, truly believes that the conflict management system belongs to the organization and its stakeholders, and can stay constant in the face of stakeholder-derived decisions *not* to act.

An even more important result of an organizational decision not to pursue a change effort may be that it often leads stakeholders to make subsequent decisions that remedy what was missing and to reengage in conflict management systems design at a later time. It may have been that the time, conditions, or resources were not ripe for a revised conflict management effort. Accepting that fact and being sensitized to the preferred conditions for an effective design effort may position stakeholders and leadership to find a better opportunity in the future. Thus, allowing the system to fail if necessary is not a failure on the part of the designer. Rather, it is a part of the organizational learning process that the designer is attempting to encourage. The designer should take heart, at least, in the notion that the organization and its stakeholders learned about their current conflict management system, assessed its viability, and determined as a result that conditions did not favor a change.

At the Chompist Company, management may decide to investigate the consumer complaints internally but publicly take the position that the complaints are frivolous. Despite Anne's consultation with the company encouraging an open dialogue with consumers or the adoption of some form of ADR, the management may choose to ignore her suggestion. The result *may* lead to expensive lawsuits and adverse publicity. As a result, Chompist may decide to let the system fail in this regard and undertake the risk of fighting the litigation and suffering the adverse publicity. Depending on the outcome of such approaches, the company may learn firsthand why revised consumer complaint procedures might be an important business opportunity and later seek further assistance in implementing such procedures.

To Proceed or Not to Proceed

Through a planned, focused, and inclusive entry—one in which key constituencies map the scope and the style of design work—designers (whether internal or external) reach agreement with their organizational counterparts and thus fulfill Argyris's primary tasks of intervenors (1970): to assist affected organizational members' generation of valid data, to provide for free and informed choices in light of such data, and thus to inspire an internal commitment to act from organizational members.

But what if organizational leadership is not committed to action? What if leadership will not buy into the interest-based process? What if there is no agreement on a contract? While this chapter outlines the key ingredients of an ideal entry and contracting intervention, often such explorations with the organization's leadership do *not* result in total agreement about the scope and manner of the design work nor affirmation of interest-based principles. Depending upon which and how many of the critical factors for effective entry discussed in this chapter are missing, the designers must determine whether there is sufficient energy to proceed and sufficient commitment to core principles to succeed.

As practitioners know, many design efforts lead to useful change even when optimal entry conditions are missing. It is a basic OD principle that there are many routes to a worthy result. In fact, there is always *something* missing: lack of access to all the necessary stakeholders, reluctance of leadership to consider feedback, unwillingness of leadership or stakeholders to collaborate in a design effort. In such cases, it is useful to remember that the designer can start from where the particular organization is and engage it in a process of learning as it proceeds. The designer may need to help leadership explore their concerns about revising the conflict management system, their reasons for not wanting stakeholders involved in the design process, or their fear of feedback. It may also be helpful to use examples of other organizations or competitors who have successfully redesigned their conflict management systems. Publicizing such successes may build sufficient critical mass for the organization to consciously engage in appropriate design processes or at least to consider change. Often, a review of these examples from similarly situated organizations will reveal that the forces driving the change in other organizations were not totally interest based but were partially driven by pragmatic organizational concerns. Examples include organizational survival ("the bad publicity from these disputes is killing us") or the existence of a highly positioned and politically persuasive champion for such change ("as CEO, I am committed to leading this company into the twenty-first century, and we are going to start with our conflicted relationships with regulators, consumers, and employees").

At FSMA, for example, Larry Terrence's exploration of the hostile work environment claims may involve looking at other agencies who have faced similar allegations: what was the nature of the claims, was there adverse publicity, what was the cost of litigation related to the claims, were there repercussions with congressional oversight committees or congressional funding? Larry may conclude that the potential adverse publicity and repercussions to the agency are so great that they are an incentive for FSMA to take a proactive stance in actively involving employees in designing a revised conflict management system to handle such complaints. The general counsel may decide that she is going to take a leadership role in this area by championing the right of employees to work in a nonhostile workplace.

What if there is still no commitment to interest-based design processes? From the designer's perspective, there is another aspect to a design contract that must not be overlooked: when to walk away from the proposed project. Most practitioners have faced this dilemma at one point or another in their work with organizations.

There are differing motivations that drive organizations to change their methods of managing conflict, as noted in previous chapters. For example, the designer may discover that the introduction of ADR is intended to cover up systemic abuses in organizational programs, such as developing a mediation program where

EEO complaints are resolved internally and confidentially so that practices are not public or reported to shareholders. Similarly, the organization's definition of success may be to co-opt those having disputes with it by using a particular resolution method for containing conflict.

Where the organizational motivation to change the conflict management system is contrary to the core values of participation, openness, and feedback, the designer may have to decide whether to proceed as part of the change process—to be "used" as an instrument of change in order to educate and inform organizational leadership about the wisdom and integrity of their intention. In some instances, the designer may decide to walk away from the effort, deciding that the system is not ripe for change, that it is impossible to work effectively while restricted from seeking input from stakeholders within the organization or constituents outside the organization, or that the motivations behind the creation of the conflict management system are unethical.

Individuals, groups, and organizations are uncomfortable with conflict; it is natural that introducing the principles of participation, openness, and feedback into conflict management processes will cause discomfort and resistance. Most practitioners have come to anticipate such a response. In these instances, education and information about the flexible use of appropriate dispute resolution mechanisms can be useful and may be sufficient to allow the negotiation of a mutually acceptable design contract. However, if the designer becomes convinced that the motivation and integrity of the client organization are suspect and that core design principles will not be respected, a decision to walk away from the design may be in the best interests of the designer, the stakeholders, and ultimately the system itself. At some point in the future, the organization may decide that it is ready to provide the necessary resources and commitment to proceed, contacting the designer to begin anew.

In sum, effective entry into the system is an intervention by itself and the result of a "contract" between organizational and design leadership. The organization is clear about what it expects from the designer, and the designer has clearly established his or her expectations with regard to role, values, and assumptions. In addition, the organization and designer are in agreement about the scope of the work to be performed, who needs to be involved, how the work will proceed, and the time frame. This early work in the entry phase sets the tone for the design process. It is in this phase that the designer communicates and models, often for the first time, the spirit with which the work will proceed, by helping to create a partnership of collaboration with the organizational leadership and membership. In this way, the work of organizational assessment can begin.

Chapter Six

Organizational Assessment
Looking at the Big Picture

With the benefit of a contract between the design team and the organizational leadership, the focus of the design effort shifts to assessment: of the organization itself, of the nature and number of disputes, of resolution methods, and of results.* In some instances, this may be the first time that the organization and its members have collected and examined dispute resolution information. Here, the design team encourages and guides the system in taking time out from the daily grind of dispute resolution to move "above the fray," where it can look at the larger organizational issue of systemic conflict management. This assessment focuses on the macro perspective: that is, what is happening in the system as a whole. The participative, open process used to conduct the assessment and solicit feedback continues to set the tone for the design effort.

Several obvious questions come to mind at this point: Why spend so much time and so many resources doing an organizational assessment? Why involve the stakeholders in the assessment at all? Why not just have the designers do the assessment, report to management, have management make the decision to change the dispute resolution process, and then announce what the new process will be? In many organizations, the answer to these questions determines whether there will be buy-in for a revised system and whether the revised system will actually be used. During the

---

* In many instances, there will be only one designer, either an internal specialist or an external consultant, but for the rest of Part Two, we will use the term *design team.*

assessment, critical answers about organizational mission and culture are uncovered, and sources of organizational power are identified, allowing for the development of a design that is congruent with and tailored to the specific organization and its stakeholders.

An organization does not initiate interest-based design merely in order to be seen as "kinder and gentler"; there has to be something in it for all the stakeholders—for the organization itself, for leadership, for employees, for customers, for disputants. This is the "WII-FM" (what's in it for me?) of conflict management systems design. As practitioners know, if stakeholders or constituents cannot answer the WII-FM question to their own satisfaction, they are unlikely to actively engage in change efforts.

We freely admit that interest-based design takes longer than traditional rights-based design. It has been our experience, however, and that of many of our colleagues and fellow practitioners, that a conflict management system that is the result of a participative process has fewer implementation and compliance problems than one that is not.

In addition, it is worth clarifying here that assessment is just that—assessment. As practitioners know, it is not a conclusion that something is wrong with the system; that is why we do not use the term *diagnosis* to describe this stage of the design process. "Diagnosis" is a medical term that connotes an illness. In assessment, the design team members (particularly those from within the organization) may have to resist the temptation to make and communicate assumptions about whether the current system needs to be changed. At this stage, the task is simply to assess and to do so as a coach or guide rather than as an expert.

The Organization

The assessment begins with the organization taking a look at itself and identifying several key components. What is the organizational mission? What does the organization do and why does it do it? Is there a shared understanding, both within and outside the organization, of what the organization does? In organizations where there are dissonant views of the mission, there are usually differing views of how conflict should be managed and of what is "successful" conflict management. Thus, within an organization whose dominant mission is regulation of other industries, there will be a substantial component that engages in enforcement efforts, typically focusing on litigation or administrative adjudication such as cease and desist proceedings. At the same time and in the same organization, there may also be a component whose purpose is to encourage compliance with regulations through education and training of industry representatives. The differing technologies by which the two important mission-related components do their work—litigation in one and education and training in the other— will drive the dominant view of how conflict within the organization should be handled. Perhaps the litigation and adjudication component will prefer imposed methods of resolution, while the education and training component will prefer negotiated or facilitated methods to uncover concerns and possible avenues to resolution. In addition, how an organization defines its mission often determines how it measures its success. In order for there to be a "fit," the conflict management system must somehow further the organizational mission and promote the success of the organization by enabling it to do its business better, whether that means faster, cheaper, or more efficiently.

The assessment also explores the "culture of conflict" at the organization: how the organization views conflict and how it makes decisions about conflict. Does the organization avoid conflict? Deny it? Fight it? Control it? Is conflict seen as a sign of failure? How does the organization make decisions: is it risk-aversive, decision-avoiding, hierarchical? What is the attitude toward change? What would the typical response be to a suggestion for change in dispute resolution practices? Answers to these questions provide clues as to possible barriers to introduction of a revised conflict management system, point out possible areas of resistance, and are pivotal in fashioning effective implementation strategies that consciously reduce such barriers and restraints (Chapter Twelve, "Resistance and Constraints," addresses such issues in greater depth).

The organization's "customers" also need to be identified. Do they receive a product or a service? Are they constant, or are they an ever changing population? Are there both internal customers and external customers? What is the relationship of the organization to its customers? How does the organization know if its customers are satisfied? Such information helps clarify the organizational mission and provides a snapshot of the needs and interests of one interest group, usually a key stakeholder in the dispute resolution system.

At our hypothetical Chompist Company, the mission is to make money by selling frozen food products. Complying with regulations, satisfying customers, and employing productive workers are all tangential to this mission. The fact that the company is for-profit and manufactures a product affects the type of conflict management system that it uses. A "congruent" conflict management system at the Chompist Company promotes the efficient manufacture and sale of its product in the target markets. If the conflict management system enables Chompist to manufacture frozen food more efficiently and more cheaply, resulting in increased sales and satisfied customers, the system fits with Chompist's organizational mission. In particular, Chompist probably wants a conflict management system that decreases the visibility and publicity of any customer disputes, promotes its image as a law-abiding and safety-conscious (responsible) company, and helps ensure a steady and productive workforce.

With regard to its culture of conflict, the Chompist Company is a family-run business. It is likely that many employees have been with the company for years and know the company president, Daniel Teznicki, personally, given both the size of the company and the size of the town. Thus, there may be a desire to handle internal disputes more informally and on a more personal basis. However, because it is a smaller company, there may also be a top-heavy and patriarchal dispute resolution structure and process, with senior management making most of the decisions about how disputes will be resolved (the "I'm the boss around here" approach) and with little involvement from lower-level supervisors or line employees.

As for Chompist's customers, there are apt to be a large percentage of repeat and long-term ones among the retail and wholesale populations and thus customer relationships and satisfaction will be a driving aspect of Chompist's conflict management system. Such customers will be sensitive to any change in product line, so they are likely to expect stability and familiarity in the conflict management system as well. An inquiry may reveal that there are already a multitude of fragmented and highly individualized alternative resolution procedures informally in place between company sales representatives and wholesale customers as well as between wholesalers and their large retail customers, such as supermarkets.

The Disputes

In order to frame the investigation and assessment from the outset, the design team asks itself and others, "What are the various *types* of disputes in our system?" There are disputes among employees, supervisors, and organizational subcomponents, and there are the inevitable disputes between the organization and its customers and constituents. The types of disputes vary accordingly, from grievances over work performance and evaluation, to dissatisfaction with products or services, to disputes with contractors and vendors. Here, many practitioners have found it useful to first paint a broad picture of the current state of the organization's disputes, followed by a more detailed study of those disputes that generate the most distress for the organization, its members, and its stakeholders.

Information about what disputes exist can most readily be acquired by contacting the organization's personnel officers, labor relations and union officials, contracting and procurement specialists, and legal counsel. From these specialized points of contact, general categories of disputes can usually be identified.

At the end of this initial stage, the design team hopes to have a list of the different types of disputes occurring both within the organization and with elements of its external environment. With this information in hand, the team turns to assessing the nature of the disputes—the issues involved, the tenor and/or tone, and the effect on the organization and ongoing relationships. All disputes are costly for an organization, whether in terms of time, money, lost opportunity, resources, or relationship with customers, employees, and stakeholders. The design team identifies and accumulates these costs, since they will be among the key forces driving any eventual change effort, be it incremental or systemwide.

The next step is to assess the *number* of disputes. How many disputes are there of each type? Has the number increased or decreased over the last several years? Why? What is the anticipated volume of disputes for the future? What factors will influence whether the number of disputes increases or decreases? Although numbers alone are not a sufficient indicator of the state of a dispute resolution system, they are one measure of the level of distress in the organization. Anticipating trends that may give rise to future disputes allows the design to be tailored to the direction and perceived needs of the organization over time and to create a conflict management system that is most responsive to new and evolving concerns.

At the Federal Securities Management Agency (FSMA), the agency's dispute resolution specialist, Larry Terrence, will have to gather information about the type, number, and nature of disputes—both internally with regard to hostile work environment claims and externally with regard to investors involved in the Red River Fund. Information about the type and number of formal hostile work environment disputes can probably be obtained from the agency's Office of Human Resources, the Office of Personnel Management, or the Office of Equal Employment Opportunity. It will be much more difficult, if not impossible, for Larry to get information about informal, unfiled complaints, but if separate discussions with supervisors and employees can be arranged, such information may be revealed provided that participants feel it is safe to tell Larry (who is affiliated with the General Counsel's Office) about these incidents. As for the Red River claims, this information can be obtained from trading records, accounts and ledgers, or other documentation to which the agency would have access as a result of its regulatory role with the Red River Fund.

Having explored the types and numbers of disputes, Larry would then turn to an investigation of their specific nature—the issues, the tenor of the disputes, and the effect the disputes have on FSMA. It may be that FSMA has responded to the hostile work environment allegations by transferring the women to other sections (perhaps resulting in workplace disruption and workload disparity), by denying them promotions and recognition, or by giving them less interesting or visible matters to handle (resulting in additional personnel grievances). The allegations may also have adversely affected the promotion potential of the supervisors involved or created a disruptive workplace environment for other employees. Larry may also find that a small group of women are responsible for a disproportionate number of the allegations. With regard to other disputes under investigation, the Red River claimants' issues may not only be for the repayment of their investment but also for the manner in which they were treated by FSMA and for alleged posttakeover mishandling and negligence of their claims by agency employees.

The Resolution Methods

By talking to various organizational participants and disputants from both within and outside the organization, design teams often find it relatively simple to ascertain the existing dispute resolution mechanisms for various types of disputes and the roles performed by individuals in dispute resolution investigation and resolution. At this stage, the design team is first concerned with what dispute resolution processes are currently available. Are most disputes resolved informally without resort to court or administrative remedies? Are there any preventive or negotiated mechanisms in place to resolve disputes? If disputes are resolved formally, what methods of dispute resolution are used (court, arbitration)? The design team will also want to collect any written dispute resolution processes and procedures utilized throughout the organization.

At FSMA, for example, there is probably an informal, precomplaint counseling mechanism in place for hostile work environment disputes whereby employees can request a meeting with an equal employment opportunity counselor or a joint meeting with their supervisor and a representative from the EEO Office. The procedures probably escalate fairly quickly after that, beginning with the filing of a formal complaint, conduct of a formal investigation, referral to the Equal Employment Opportunity Commission, and eventually litigation. For the Red River claimants, FSMA probably has an internal administrative remedy that the claimants must exhaust before they can get their money, with formal litigation following the administrative procedure.

The corollary to determining what procedures to use is determining who chooses the method of dispute resolution and who has authority to resolve disputes. In some organizations, particularly those that are linear, vertical, or bureaucratic, the method of dispute resolution is predetermined by a policy or procedure, and stakeholders have little or no control over it. In other organizations, the method is chosen by someone "up the ladder" who is relatively unaffected or disinterested in the dispute yet has the authority to impose a resolution or method on the disputants. In other settings, the person with "line responsibility" for the dispute may be able to recommend or even choose a form of dispute resolution. In a very few organizations, disputants have substantial control over the dispute resolution method chosen.

It is important to note that the person who chooses the dispute resolution mechanism may not be the same person who has actual authority to settle the dispute. This lack of continuity and responsibility creates challenges. For example, a staff attorney in the legal division may be able to make the decision to file a lawsuit *or* to use ADR, but regardless of the size or nature of the case, that attorney may have to go up through the hierarchical chain of command to settle a case, regardless of the process chosen.

Understanding the "who" is often an indication of where the power lies within the organization's conflict management system. In many organizations, the people who control selection of the dispute resolution process and the resolution of disputes have both power (the ability to influence) and authority (the ability to decide). As a result, they may have a personal stake in preserving the status quo dispute resolution process and may be potential sources of resistance to any change effort. It is wise to identify these people early on in the assessment phase, to solicit their input and concerns, and to involve them in the decision and commitment to change if any decision to change is made.

At FSMA, the procedures for resolving hostile work environment claims are probably inflexible. While the aggrieved employee is the one who decides whether to escalate to the next level by filing a formal complaint or pursuing litigation, the accused supervisor has little or no say over whether the agency will settle the dispute and on what terms. Such decisions are made by a manager or attorney in the EEO Office or the Legal Division, in consultation with the Chairperson's Office. With regard to the Red River claimants, they must follow the prescribed procedures to exhaust their administrative remedies, although there may be a window of opportunity during that process to engage in negotiation with an FSMA claims specialist or FSMA fund manager. Once the claimant files litigation, it is likely that FSMA attorneys, not the claims

specialists, will play a larger role in determining any eventual settlement, again seeking ultimate approval from those higher up in
the organization.

It is not enough to inventory the official methods used to
resolve disputes and to catalogue who has the power to choose a
method and authority to resolve a dispute. The follow-up question
must be posed: *why* does the organization use the dispute resolution methods it does? The decision may be driven by mission, culture, time, cost, history, or the organizational structure itself. Each
of these factors has a different yet powerful impact on any eventual
change effort. For successful implementation, it is critical that the
design team unearth the "why" behind the "what" and the "who."

At FSMA, the agency probably handles its hostile work environment allegations in the manner it does because of government-
wide regulations and traditional practices. For the Red River
claims, the exhaustion of administrative remedies is probably also
required by statute and may be seen by the agency as a way to discourage frivolous claims.

The Results

Finally, the design team looks at the results of the resolution
processes. Are disputes actually resolved? How long does it take?
How much does it cost? Do the resolutions stick? Are the disputants satisfied with the resolutions? What effect do the results
have on ongoing relationships? On the organizational mission?

As practitioners know, this involves looking not only at tangible results (money collected, money paid out, promotions, rein-
statements, and others) but also intangible effects: how the results
affect the organization and its stakeholders (bad publicity, nasty
interdivisional bickering, or turf wars). It is often these intangible
effects that cause the most distress to the organization and its stakeholders.

At FSMA, there are both tangible and intangible results of dispute resolution efforts, which Larry will need to explore. For example, he will need to look at the remedies adopted in hostile work
environment disputes: does FSMA pay monetary damages, give
retroactive promotions, transfer aggrieved employees, take most
cases to litigation? What are the results, actual and perceived, of

each of these on the employee, on the supervisor, and on the work-load of the agency? How much time do supervisors spend on these matters as related to time spent on other, substantive agency business? How much time and effort in the EEO Office, Office of Personnel Management, or Legal Division is being devoted to these disputes? What is FSMA's reputation in the government community with regard to these types of disputes? If possible, it is useful for an internal conflict management systems designer such as Larry to quantify some of these costs in dollars, in hours, and in productivity. With regard to the Red River claims, he will also look at dollars, time, and reputation. How much money does FSMA spend to defend these claims, using either in-house legal resources or outside counsel? What are the FSMA personnel costs in terms of claims specialists, case managers, attorneys? If an investor's claim is disallowed, how much will FSMA spend to defend the matter in court, how long does it take, what is the average cost of an award in those cases where FSMA loses, and what is the effect of these claims on its relationships with other investors, with other government agencies, with the regulated industry, and with Congress?

The Assessment

In the assessment phase, as with entry and contracting, the design team needs to be clear about its process. In this regard, Chris Argyris's (1970) three tasks of any intervenor are well worth recalling. Initially, the design team concerns itself with generating valid data. The term *valid* here refers to collecting information about the nature and state of the organization's disputes from the appropriate stakeholders. The inquiry starts with *who* are the individuals (managers, supervisors, technicians, employees, union representatives, and customers, both external and internal) in a variety of roles (complainant, respondent, case intake officer, investigator, advocate, decision maker) currently involved in identifying, investigating, and resolving these various types of disputes? To do an accurate and meaningful organizational assessment, the design team should ideally have access to all of these individuals and be able to assure them that there will be no reprisal for participating, offering information, or making suggestions. Unfortunately, this is often not the case and ultimately practitioners have to take the organization as they find it with the resources, support, and level of safety that the organization is willing and able to provide. In particular, however, it is advisable for the design team to talk to actual disputants (both within and outside the organization) and the organization's dispute resolvers to get their input as to what is working and what is not working in the conflict management system's current practices, based on these participants' unique experience with it.

Next, the design team determines what types of information it needs from these individuals. Generally, interviews can be conducted or a questionnaire developed that asks the following critical questions:

- How are these particular disputes handled?
- To your knowledge, why are disputes handled this way?
- How many of these disputes occur and what are the costs, both direct and indirect, of handling them?
- From your perspective, what is working well with respect to the handling of disputes?
- From your perspective, what is *not* working well?
- If you could change the current dispute resolution process, where would you focus your efforts and what would you do?
- If the process is changed, what problems and resistance do you anticipate?
- If the process is changed, who will gain power and who will lose power?

Interviews of short duration are the preferable process for acquiring the above information from relevant stakeholders. In face-to-face interviews, the design team has the opportunity to ask clarifying questions. In addition, interviewees often volunteer important information about unwritten rules and practices and the informal fashion in which the disputes are actually processed and resolved. To maximize the potential for an open and frank discussion, however, it is helpful if assurance can be given that the interview or survey results will be reported without attribution and that the organizational leadership has agreed to support the inquiry through a guarantee of no reprisal.

In a hospital intervention such as we have described at Hopevale, Conflict Consultants will want to conduct one-on-one interviews to obtain information from the various groups of stakeholders: employees, union representatives, doctors, Cardiac Care Unit and Emergency Department managers and employees, attorneys from the Legal Department, and community representatives. During these interviews, Conflict Consultants will first need to explain who they are and why they have been brought into Hopevale. They will also want to guarantee the participants that the interviews are confidential and that comments will not be offered with attribution to the hospital administration. It may be necessary to design a short survey to circulate to those individuals (for example, some doctors and nurses) who will be difficult to access for interviews given schedules and time constraints. Many of the questions listed above will need to be addressed in these interviews and surveys: How are staff disputes handled at Hopevale and why? What could be done to improve relationships between doctors and nurses? What are the costs of defending malpractice litigation and lawsuits with vendors such as pharmaceutical companies? What is working well with the way Hopevale handles disputes with outside parties? What needs to be changed? How can Hopevale be responsive to the concerns of the community? What is the greatest impediment to a more effective conflict management system at Hopevale?

After the interviews are concluded or surveys completed, the design team gathers the results into a manageable and identifiable series of observations about the current state of the dispute system (working well, not working well, number and nature of disputes and their costs, history of resolution processes, and opportunities to improve). It is important that the design team not overwhelm the groups receiving the data (leadership, employees, stakeholders) with too much detail or too much information, such as voluminous reports or statistical treatises. Rather, the information should be loosely grouped into the above eight areas of questioning, with some tentative observations about what the interviewees said (as a whole, not by reference to specific individuals). These data and conclusions are then presented to as many system participants and stakeholders as is possible for confirmation, clarification, or revision.

One method of conducting the "report-back" is through the use of focus groups, a tool that organization development (OD) practitioners have used for a long time. Once the information is gathered and organized, separate focus groups of relevant stake-holders can be constituted for brief feedback sessions, facilitated by design team members. The overall objective of these sessions is to share what has been learned, to validate the data, to discuss the implications of such information, and to make tentative recom-mendations for action, if necessary. This stage of the assessment is the feedback of information to the stakeholders involved. It poises the system participants to receive and validate the data and to make a free and informed choice (Argyris's second task of inter-venors) about whether the information gathered is true, indicates a need for change, and if so, of what nature.

The feedback of information through focus groups allows the key organizational players in a particular dispute processing arena to gather, often for the first time, and to analyze together the suc-cess of or need for improvement in their operation. Through such discussion, and with the data objectively presented by design team members, the stakeholders have an opportunity to honestly appraise their work and to identify reasons for concern and areas for change, if any.

It is also useful to feed the information back to outside stake-holders such as customers or those who have disputes with the organization. This can also be done through focus groups but in actual practice is most often done through interviews or surveys. Although it may seem odd to ask for feedback from the "opposi-tion," it is worth remembering and reminding the organization that there are two parties (and often more) to the dispute equa-tion and that a successful change effort requires buy-in and use by organizational disputants as well as any external disputants. In addition, the outside disputants often bring observations and sug-gestions that those within the organization are not aware of or have not considered.

Beyond the opportunity to uncover outside stakeholders' dis-satisfaction, however, there are other reasons for soliciting feed-back. The focus group, with the assistance of facilitators, can talk freely about the interests and needs being met by the current sys-tem. For example, are some interests being served at the cost of the interests of others in the system? Does the system impose res-olutions on the disenfranchised or less powerful? What are the results of such power imbalances? The group can also explore some of the incentives and disincentives for using the current conflict management system. These observations provide clues for possible action to improve dispute resolution procedures, utilization, and satisfaction with results.

In addition, facilitators can encourage the group to discuss the origins of the current dispute resolution procedures. This allows for linkage of current procedures to relevant policies, procedures, laws, and regulations; to organizational mission and goals; to organizational history and culture; and to organizational attitude toward conflict and change. It informs all those with a role in the system of the "why" of the current dispute resolution process; it can also serve to educate system participants about key considerations in any contemplated redesign. In addition, it gives the design team some sense of the interests of particular groups and the "who" served by the status quo. Understanding the who helps highlight incentives and disincentives for modifying the existing system and identifies possible locations of either resistance or support.

The next task of any focus group is the identification of specific areas of concern with regard to the current dispute resolution procedures and results. For example, it could be that in the labor-management dispute arena, one of the hidden costs of the grievance procedure is that the constant escalation and elevation of disputes away from the point of origin (which might, for example, be an employee and her supervisor) does nothing to resolve or repair the relationship between these individuals. Instead, the current procedure may leave the relationship frustrated by delay and loss of control over outcomes as more and higher levels of both internal and external officials become involved in the investigation and advocacy of the management and employee rights involved in the dispute. The indirect costs of such dispute resolution procedures may be a deterioration of morale and productivity and an increase in workplace stress and potential for violence. Frequently, this part of any focus group's discussion leads to the identification of many previously unknown costs to the organization: dollars, management and staff time, employee morale, workplace disturbance and sabotage, adverse publicity, diminished reputation in the marketplace, and recurrence of disputes. With the surfacing of such information, the focus groups identify the need for change and possible areas to target for improvement. The design team records and memorializes these target areas, especially if the assessment involves the examination of a multiplicity of dispute resolution procedures and focus groups.

At Hopevale, it will be particularly important for Conflict Consultants to rely on focus groups to validate and organize the information obtained from interviews and surveys. Given the typical culture and structure of most hospital settings (highly separated by functional specialty, by locus of activity), Conflict Consultants will probably seek to organize multiple cross-functional focus groups around several hospital-wide issues. Nurses, union representatives, doctors, management, and patients might comprise a focus group to study the management of conflict between doctors and nurses; another focus group, including community representatives, doctors, nurses, financial management representatives, and management officials, might study hospital-community relations. Human resources personnel and hospital attorneys, as available, may also be included as staff subject-matter experts. Such an approach produces higher-quality information (that is, information from a variety of perspectives and experience) about the issues under review. Conflict Consultants will probably note that such diverse, relatively conflicted groups as these will require facilitators experienced in conflict management techniques. Moreover, Conflict Consultants will likely encourage the key leadership of the various interest groups involved to convene the focus groups, stating the hope they have for an objective and meaningful assessment of the issues under discussion and the manner in which these issues are currently being handled. Further, and lastly, Conflict Consultants will probably provide highly structured tasks for the focus groups to perform with respect to the information needed. Thus, the focus groups will review the numbers, nature, and types of disputes and identify the what, who, and why of current resolution methods. The pursuit of this information by the focus groups themselves will have the collateral effect of allowing the members of the focus groups to wrestle together about how they have come to be in the present situation (*presenting problem*); group participants will become fully apprised of the issues and opportunities presented in their respective areas of focus. Conflict Consultants may then suggest that the focus groups go through part of an interest-based problem-solving process, where members identify the interests of those affected by the issue and creatively brainstorm together possible options for revising the current conflict management system to address such divergent interests on the presenting dispute arena (*perceived opportunity*).

Usually, an organizational assessment generates feedback that certain disputes are of greater concern than others. Some disputes may be causing more distress, costing more, taking more time, or damaging customer or employee relationships. These perceptions are invaluable to the design team: they provide guidance about where initial efforts to improve the organization's conflict management system *could* (not should) begin. They also illuminate once again the organization's culture of conflict management—the way key stakeholders view various types of disputes and their perception about appropriate and acceptable methods for their resolution.

The design team takes note of those parts of the dispute resolution system that have generated the most concern. Which disputes are most costly, in what ways, and what is the effect on the organizational mission? The team then looks to the "why" to see if it is a force that can drive (and sustain) change in the particular organizational setting. For example, if "doing more with less" is an organizational driving force, can the direct and indirect costs of conflict be quantified? Are such costs being incurred in an area of increasing importance to the organization—and hence, will any potential change to improve the conflict management system provide an identifiable benefit?

Usually by this point a valid picture of the organization's current state of dispute resolution practice has emerged. The next challenge is to identify for organizational leaders and stakeholders possible areas that are ripe for change, leading to Argyris's third task: gaining internal commitments to act.

The Proposal

With its enhanced knowledge of the organizational culture, mission, and conflict management system, the design team can now present its discoveries and proposals for any change to the organizational leadership. Here, the team prepares and presents a focused and well-reasoned strategy that addresses the need for change but does not violate the normative culture of the organization's conflict management practices. At this stage, as practitioners know, the design team must not only deal with the facts of the presenting problem and the perceived opportunity for change but must also anticipate, admit, and address the real-life political dynamics of any change effort. There will be gains and loss in perceived power as a result of any change; there will be resistance and constraints to overcome.

The drastic approach—"what you now have is dead (or outmoded or unfashionable) and we must change everything and everyone in your current system who is handling x types of disputes"—is inadvisable. Similarly, the "we must create something new (a new structure, a new office, a new division, a new box on the organizational chart) to have an effective system" tactic is also inadvisable. Rather, it is much more useful to make specific observations about the parts of the system where the apparent interests (cost, time, durability of and satisfaction with outcomes) of the organization and its disputants are not being met. Here, the objective is to outline clearly for the organization the opportunities for improvement in parts or the whole of its conflict management system as linked to organizational goals. This allows the organization to choose to approach interest-based conflict management systems design incrementally or experimentally, if need be, by making changes in one particular area as a start. We know that this is not necessarily the result that many practitioners like to see today. However, we have seen many worthy systemwide efforts start and grow from high-quality, high-results, limited, pilot ADR initiatives. For some reason, conflict systems management change seems very difficult to initiate on a systemwide basis. This may emanate from our Western cultural belief that it is "better to fight than to switch" our methods, processes, or the very culture of engaging in conflict.

With regard to strategy, the conflict management systems design proposal addresses the unmet needs of the organization and its stakeholders and points out how the revised system will further the organizational mission. Thus, the presentation can be in the form of a pro-and-con analysis of various applications of interest-based resolution processes to the issues presented. Practitioners have also found it useful to share the ADR experience, including any measurable results, of other organizations confronted with similar presenting problems.

The design team must also be able to answer the WII-FM question described above for each of the stakeholders (the organization, leadership, employees, disputants, customers) as it relates to the recommendation for a revised system. If the answer is "nothing" for any of the key stakeholders, the change effort, even if successfully implemented, will not be sustained. It is thus advisable for the design team to explicitly note "what's in it" for each component of the organizational system: leadership, managers, employees, stakeholders, customers, the public.

The presentation can also identify possible pitfalls and resistance. Of particular concern to leadership will be the disruption that change is likely to cause. The unspoken question in such strategic discussions is who will gain power and who will lose power if the conflict management system is altered. Successful strategic introductions of ADR into ongoing systems require that the design team anticipate these and other questions leaders will have and provide either expertise, testimony, or other persuasive information about the impact of the proposed redesign on the organization's existing political, cultural, structural, human resource, and symbolic systems, both formal and informal.

By having involved stakeholders both within and outside the organization who have a role in dispute resolution, the design team increases the likelihood that its recommendations will be accurate and well founded. Needless to say, the stakeholders, perhaps in their respective focus groups, can always be asked to meet with the organizational leadership and to clarify questions about what is going on in a given part of the system (assuming there is no fear of reprisal), thereby supporting the analysis and recommendations of the design team.

The creation of a critical mass of key supporters and champions for change is critical at this juncture. The objective of this final stage of assessment is to get the organization's leaders to tentatively buy in to both the arena for change (the what) and the basic map and scope of the effort (the how). In other words, if the arena identified is avoidance of litigation and its attendant costs, the design team should be prepared to identify the causes that give rise to the concern as well as to demonstrate how ADR processes alleviate those concerns. As we will discuss further in Chapter Nine, the key implementation strategy will usually be an experimental, pilot approach, which addresses leadership concerns and measures the effectiveness of the revised system. Thus, it may help during a presentation of a proposal for change to emphasize the experimental or pilot nature of any initial change, as well as the openness to modification inherent in any attempt to revise the existing conflict management system; the design team is thus encouraging an open and learning systems perspective.

At Hopevale, Conflict Consultants' presentation to the board of directors is critical. If possible, Jeff Linton will want to canvass the directors in advance to find out their particular concerns about the three dispute areas, any specific topics they would like addressed in the presentation, and any experience or expertise they have with conflict management or alternative dispute resolution (for example, some of the directors may be attorneys, others may serve on the board of directors of community groups, still others may have past involvement with labor-management relations). Ideally, the presentation should be made collectively, with participation by members from as many of the involved interest groups as possible (the nurses' union, doctors, in-house attorneys, employees, patients, and community representatives).

Initially, Jeff will give a brief overview of the state of each of the three dispute areas, with descriptions and examples of current disputes and how they are handled (here, stories or anecdotes are of great benefit). He might then summarize the findings of the surveys, interviews, and focus groups, outlining the process used and revealing some of the suggested approaches. For example, the focus groups might have suggested any of the following: more joint in-service training for doctors and nurses; a physician-nurse practice council; regular meetings between the nurses' union and hospital managers to discuss hospital-wide issues and developments; inclusion of an ADR clause in vendor contracts; ADR training for in-house Hopevale attorneys, managers, and union stewards; arbitration of the pending medical malpractice suit; or creation of a hospital-community coalition to involve members of the community and hospital representatives in addressing matters of mutual concern. Jeff might then outline the anticipated costs and effects of each of the suggestions and explain how the proposed ADR approaches may resolve some of the current disputes, prevent others from developing, and further the hospital's purpose and objectives. In this culmination of the assessment stage, he will also need to address the WII-FM question for hospital management and its key constituencies with regard to why the current approach to dispute resolution needs to be revised. Finally, he will note any anticipated resistance and constraints (continued competition from the high-tech hospital, Mainline; possible continued community dissatisfaction; deeply embedded resentment between doctors and nurses; resistance to ADR from external parties) and seek the organizational leadership's support for reducing such restraints wherever possible.

The Decision to Act

At this point, deciding to move ahead with a revised conflict management system is usually natural and nonthreatening. In most cases, reliable information about costs and concerns generated by the system's own members results in an organizational decision to change in *some* way, although perhaps not in the way that stakeholders hoped or expected. As with entry and contracting, the decision to change is a conscious commitment by both leadership and stakeholders. The decision is more easily made when the design team supports, educates, and coaches decision makers about the need for and the road map to achieving sustainable improvements in the organization's management of conflict.

The design team, however, must also anticipate and be prepared for an organizational decision *not to change* or, as is more usually the case, a decision *not to decide*. Difficult as it may be for the design team to accept, this can be a perfectly valid exercise of organizational self-determination—a free and informed choice that must be respected. An organizational decision not to change or indecision is not a failure on the part of the design team; their efforts have been a success if the organization has been supported in learning about its conflict management systems through stakeholder involvement. Also, as practitioners know, the design team's assessment intervention itself—through its respect for openness, participation, and valid feedback—has already changed the system in some way.

If the organizational leadership decides to move forward to introduce change in its conflict management system, several tasks must be accomplished. From the take-off point of buy-in by organizational leaders and members, the design team must ensure that it has the necessary authority and support to begin developing and implementing a revised conflict management system, and it must identify the specific resources that will be necessary to implement the change effort. Any championing or marketing efforts expected of top leadership must also be expressly pursued and, it is hoped, agreed to at the conclusion of the organizational assessment.

With an organizational assessment in hand and a decision and commitment to change from organizational leadership and stakeholders, the design team is now ready to turn to the more micro, technical, and architectural aspects of the conflict management systems design.

Chapter Seven

Design Architecture
Constructing Conflict Management Models

In contrast to organizational assessment, which looks at the big picture and the "macro" aspects of the design effort, architectural construction focuses on disputes themselves and methods of resolution, which is the "micro" part of managing conflict. Organizational assessment is concerned with the why, what, and who of the current dispute resolution system; design architecture looks at the whether, when, and how of any new conflict management system.

In exploring design architecture, we focus on alternative dispute resolution (ADR) as one possible enrichment of an organization's capacity to manage conflict in its system. More specifically, we look at architectural considerations: whether, when, and how to use ADR. In exploring each of these issues, we offer six key principles to guide the design architecture process. The first two principles address "whether," the next two focus on "when," and the last two concern "how."

Of all the tasks of creating a conflict management system, design architecture has perhaps the greatest potential to become mechanistic and linear; it is the task that probably lends itself most easily to a rights-based, expert-imposed approach. As practitioners, we are tempted to simply choose types of disputes within an organization to which we can apply ADR processes; it is easier, faster, and less burdensome than interest-based design architecture. However, as many practitioners have discovered, choosing ADR methods for the organization can have its own drawbacks: disputants do not understand ADR or they fear it is taking away their rights, so they do not use it; disputants work against the implementation because they were left out of the design.

For these reasons, we encourage participation, openness, and feedback in the architectural design process, as elsewhere. Only after the organization and its stakeholders understand where they are can they agree on where to go. With a comprehensive organizational assessment and the identification of "hot spots" of dissatisfaction with the current structures, processes, and results, the organization can begin to make collaborative choices about what aspects of its conflict management system and dispute resolution mechanisms need attention and perhaps change. By clarifying what is missing and by exploring concerns, the organization and its stakeholders can then, with the coaching and guidance of the design team (who are the "design architects" at this stage), evaluate appropriate dispute resolution alternatives.

Whether, When, How

The first question of design architecture is whether to use ADR at all. Perhaps it is not better, cheaper, faster, more durable. Perhaps the current methods of dispute resolution are working just fine, and there is no need for change. Here, the design architects, the organization and its stakeholders ask the following questions in determining whether to use ADR:

- What, if anything, is missing in these disputes?
- Do stakeholders express dissatisfaction and frustration with all or only part of existing dispute resolution processes?
- How do stakeholders express this dissatisfaction?
- Is an ADR process a possible and appropriate way to address the concerns expressed?
- If so, what type(s) of ADR is/are appropriate?
- Would such ADR steps or processes be a good "fit" with the goals of the organization (mission) and the technology of doing its work (culture)?

If it is decided that ADR is appropriate, the next inquiry for the design team, the organization, and the stakeholders is when to use ADR:

- At what stage of the dispute is there a gap or complaint?
- Can an interest-based process be introduced at that point in the existing procedure?
- Would such an addition address the concern expressed?
- If an ADR step is introduced at that time, what is the likely effect on subsequent stages of the existing dispute resolution system? Would ADR enhance or diminish the possibility of satisfactory resolution?
- Have preventive forms of ADR (such as partnering, ADR clauses, joint problem solving) been attempted with regard to these disputes—before they arise?
- For both prevention and new ADR steps, will disputants have the necessary skills and knowledge to use ADR effectively to resolve the disputes at that stage?

The *how* stage of design architecture is then a blend of the answers to the above questions (whether and when) with the spectrum of ADR options, a continuum from preventive to imposed methods, as illustrated in Chapter Three (see Figure 3.1, "Dynamics of ADR Techniques," p. 38).

Here, the design architects educate themselves about where the problem is, whether ADR can address the concern, when it could be introduced to maximize benefit and minimize harm, and which ADR options would most clearly suit the case. In addition to consultation with individual and institutional stakeholders, discussions with other organizations regarding their experience with ADR applications is invaluable throughout all stages of the design architecture process.

In applying the whether, when, how analysis to our hypothetical case, the Chompist Company, external design consultant Anne Logan might first look at disputant dissatisfaction: Chompist's concern with the proposed statewide regulations, employees' dissatisfaction with working conditions and machinery, and consumer dissatisfaction with Scandinavian Soufflé Dinners and with Chompist's handling of their complaints. In looking at whether ADR is an appropriate response to any of these disputes and concerns, Anne might suggest that Chompist participate in a negotiated rule making ("reg-neg") for the proposed regulations, joint forum creation and problem solving for the working condition disputes, and mediation for the consumer complaints. Given the company's mission (to make products efficiently and sell them at a profit) and its informal approach to conflict resolution, these methods would fit well with the organizational culture, whereas there may be resistance to more imposed and adversarial methods of ADR such as arbitration or even a mini-trial.

Use of reg-neg will depend on the state's willingness to engage in this process and on Chompist's ability to garner support for this approach from other affected parties. As time is of the essence here with the regulations to be proposed shortly, Anne will probably want to raise the reg-neg option with Chompist management immediately. With regard to the employees' working conditions, Anne may suggest that a joint labor-management safety committee be established to provide a permanent forum for joint problem identification and solving of safety issues for the workers. Such a forum may not only have a problem-solving role but may also be a joint locus of control and direction for training and education of the workforce on safe operation of equipment (a preventive ADR application). As with the others, the consumer complaints need immediate attention, particularly given Chompist's concern about its reputation in the marketplace. Taking a similarly preventive approach, Chompist may determine that the establishment of an ombudsperson's office is needed to explore and resolve consumer complaints. Usually, an ombudsperson assists in resolving a dispute or acts as a facilitator to make sure that a complaint or dispute gets to the right person or department for resolution, following up to ascertain that the dispute has been handled. (In some organizations, such facilitators are given the authority to recommend how the dispute should be resolved.) For each of these interventions, Anne will need to provide guidance to Chompist on how to encourage the development, by employees and consumers, of the necessary skills and knowledge to use these methods.

Six Principles

The whether, when, how paradigm for design architecture can be translated into practical guiding principles that can help frame any design architecture effort:

1. Develop guidelines for whether ADR is appropriate.
2. Tailor the ADR process to the particular problem.
3. Build in preventive methods of ADR.
4. Make sure that disputants have the necessary knowledge and skill to choose and use ADR.
5. Create ADR systems that are simple to use and easy to access and that resolve disputes early, at the lowest organizational level, with the least bureaucracy.
6. Allow disputants to retain maximum control over choice of ADR method and selection of neutral wherever possible.

Whether to Use ADR

PRINCIPLE 1: Develop guidelines for whether ADR is appropriate.

Although ADR is an acronym for alternative dispute resolution, many practitioners engaging in design architecture find it useful to think of ADR as "appropriate" dispute resolution, as discussed in Chapter Three: is ADR appropriate for this *type of conflict,* and if so, what *type of ADR?* This involves helping the organization choose the dispute resolution mechanism that is most tailored to the particular stage or category of dispute—the least costly, most timely, most satisfactory, and most durable methods to employ in seeking resolution. ADR is not an off-the-shelf, one-size-fits-all product. Many organizations have discovered this the hard way by taking some ADR procedure that was marketed to them or an ADR process that worked at another organization and importing it wholesale into their operation, without regard for the unique characteristics of their own milieu. ADR is like a box of ingredients waiting to be mixed, a process to be tailored to the particular organization with its particular context and culture.

Organizations are made up of people, culture, technology, and mission, and it is important to ensure that the ADR design is congruent with all of these. Based on an organizational assessment, design architects (as a team or as individuals) critically evaluate whether ADR is understood and viewed as useful by employees and disputants, whether it could further the organization's mission, and whether it fits with the organization's culture. For example, an organization that has a "warrior" culture—a preference for adversarial methods of resolution—may be more likely to accept and use imposed methods of ADR (binding arbitration) than to relinquish disputes to facilitated methods (mediation). The same may be true of organizations whose mission is to enforce some regulatory scheme or ensure compliance with a particular set of standards. Conversely, an organization whose mission is to foster international or community relations may be more prone to use facilitated methods of ADR, such as negotiation and consensus building.

One might say that the "technology" an organization uses to fulfill its mission—negotiating, advocating, educating, analyzing—is a clue to which particular ADR methods might be most suitable. Through the use of the organization's preferred methods, ADR can make sense to organizations and their members. Many practitioners have discovered that those ADR methods that are congruent with the organization's characteristics are more likely to be identifiable to disputants and used by them recurrently.

In some cases, however, ADR may not be appropriate at all. For example, where an organization wants to establish a rights-based precedent that can be used in other cases, the court system, rather than ADR, may be the most appropriate forum for resolution. Similarly, if the government has a significant policy that it wants to test, it may be inappropriate to use ADR. In fact, the Administrative Dispute Resolution Act of 1990 provides that an agency should consider *not* using ADR if one of the following six factors is present: the need to establish precedent; a question of significant public policy that requires additional procedures before a final resolution can be made; the desire to create an established body of policy and decision; the necessity for a public record, which cannot be provided by ADR; the need to maintain ongoing supervision or jurisdiction for compliance, and ADR would interfere with that requirement; or the matter significantly affects absent persons or organizations who are not parties to the ADR process. The considerations for determining whether ADR is appropriate are applicable to the private and nonprofit sectors as well. For example, a company may decide that it wants to push the edge of the law in a particular area, such as patent infringement or the use of no-compete clauses. A nonprofit organization bringing a class action suit on behalf of disabled students in a school district may decide that it needs ongoing supervision by the court to monitor and enforce any consent decree. Even here, it may still be possible to reach a resolution through some form of ADR, such as mediation, if the parties can petition the court at a later date to enforce the settlement or appoint a master.

The working assumption in many organizations, however, is that ADR *is* appropriate. Motorola, for example, developed an in-house ADR program in which ADR is considered on an ongoing basis throughout the life of a dispute. Motorola shifted the burden to its organizational managers, supervisors, and line personnel to demonstrate to leadership why ADR *cannot* be used (Weise, 1989).

Practitioners frequently assist organizations in analyzing the particular circumstances in which ADR is clearly inappropriate and in developing guidelines setting forth these instances. Such guidelines are developed jointly between the organization and its stakeholders, and organizational participants are then informed and educated about the analysis necessary to support a conclusion or recommendation that ADR is inappropriate.

At Federal Securities Management Agency (FSMA), one of our hypothetical organizations, Larry Terrence will need to work with stakeholders and FSMA management to make an initial determination whether ADR is appropriate in the hostile work environment and investor claims cases. This could be done by talking to actual disputants to see whether they are interested in using ADR (the dispute may have become so entrenched that they are determined to go to litigation) and to management to see if they are willing to engage in good-faith ADR. Even if these particular disputants are not interested in ADR, it may be worthwhile for FSMA to jointly develop ADR procedures as a preventive mechanism for future cases. Given current federal statutes and regulations, some form of ADR is probably appropriate in hostile work environment cases; the issue is to determine what type of ADR. As for the investor claims, absent any statutory or regulatory requirements, the question is whether ADR will further FSMA's mission and save costs. Even if the answer to these questions is yes, FSMA may decide that it wants to litigate some of these claims to develop the law in this area, establish precedent, or discourage similar litigation in the future. Assuming the decision is made to use some form of ADR, Larry will need to draft guidelines for FSMA staff and attorneys, as well as for investors, that describe the type of ADR available and the procedures for its use.

PRINCIPLE 2: Tailor the ADR process to the particular problem.

Aside from the organizational fit, there should also be a process fit: the ADR process should be appropriate for the particular problem at hand. Choosing mediation as the ADR process when in fact the nuances of a particular case and the interests of the disputants indicate that neutral expert fact finding would be more appropriate (and possibly more successful) can lead to a conclusion by disputants and organizational leadership that ADR does not make sense. For example, in a dispute involving technical or quantitative issues—the value of a real estate parcel, the amount of soil to fill a hole, or the average life expectancy of certain insureds—fact-finding or advisory methods may in some instances be more useful than facilitative methods. In a dispute involving how certain franchisee disputes will be resolved, it may be more appropriate to use a form of joint problem solving, which improves the ongoing business relationship, as opposed to a more imposed method of resolution such as arbitration, which may have a chilling effect on the ongoing relationship, reducing it to a matter of winners and losers.

Tailoring the process to the problem will depend on a variety of factors, including the goals of the disputants, their tolerance for risk and invasiveness, and the relationship among the disputants. Several useful matrices are available to assist disputants in selecting ADR methods (Sander and Goldberg, 1994). As a general guideline, many practitioners and neutrals recommend that the facilitated methods of ADR, such as mediation, are usually appropriate choices. In fact, mediation has become the preferred or default method of ADR in many settings.

Are there really dangers inherent in selecting an "inappropriate" ADR method? If it fails to work, why not just go back and pick a different method and hope to get it right the second time? The danger in constructing a design built on inappropriate ADR methods is that unsuccessful ADR experiences lead to the impression on the part of managers, resource allocators, disputants, and critics that *all* forms of ADR are unsuccessful or meaningless exercises: "ADR didn't work here, so why should it work somewhere else?"

Thus, experienced design architects often first test their proposed design on experts in the various ADR practices, a version of the "shadow consultation" mentioned in Chapter Five. For example, the design team might ask an experienced mediator, fact finder, or arbitrator whether, based on his or her experience, a particular ADR method would be useful and effective in a particular type of dispute, at this stage of the dispute's life, at escalation, or at maturity.

FSMA, like many other government agencies, will probably decide to use mediation at some early, informal stage of the hostile work environment disputes. This allows the disputants to craft their own solution (assuming that the agency representative at the table has the authority to commit to a resolution or can obtain authority) and also allows both the complainant and the agency to retain their formal remedies if the mediation does not result in resolution. Here, the biggest issue for FSMA will probably be who to use as mediators: in-house personnel, neutrals from other agencies, or outside mediators. With regard to the investor claims, given the agency's mission, its tendency toward more formal conflict resolution, and its desire for closure, arbitration may be most appropriate, although there may be some restrictions on FSMA's ability, because it is a government agency, to enter into "binding" arbitration under the Administrative Dispute Resolution Act of 1990.

When to Use ADR

PRINCIPLE 3: Build in preventive methods of ADR.

Even where an organization decides that ADR is not appropriate in a particular dispute or a cluster of disputes, it may be advisable to build prevention mechanisms into the foundation of the conflict management system. For example, a government agency may decide ADR is not appropriate because the dispute concerns a significant question of public policy, and thus litigation must be used. Consideration could be given, however, to incorporating a reg-neg component into the agency's conflict management system to encourage dialogue among the agency, affected stakeholders, and constituents *before* policies or regulations are promulgated. Reg-neg draws to the surface the interests of stakeholders (who are also potential disputants) during the policy-making process. The reg-neg process gives the agency and its constituents an opportunity to identify their respective interests and to craft modifications to regulations before they are issued. By working together before disputes arise and by experiencing inclusion in interest-based problem-solving and negotiation processes, disagreements may be handled by all involved more effectively when they invariably occur. Many practitioners use the approach of jointly training disputants in interest-based problem-solving skills as a dispute prevention, relationship-building measure, as with labor and management parties.

It may be useful to think of developing a range of preventive methods of ADR that are applicable in a variety of contexts, such as the individual, group, organization, community, and global environments. Table 7.1 demonstrates the sort of matrix that can be developed to illustrate the range of ADR methods and their applications in these diverse contexts. The matrix can be a stimulus to creative thinking about how to apply the spectrum of ADR options to these different arenas. For example, methods of prevention at the individual level may include increasing one's tolerance for and acceptance of conflict or improving interpersonal communication and active listening skills; prevention methods at the level of the group may involve practicing consensus decision making, engaging in team building, and generating problem resolution options through brainstorming; prevention methods at the level of the organization could entail circulating ongoing employee feedback surveys, developing strategic visions collectively (search conferences), and involving constituents in change processes on an ongoing basis; prevention methods at the level of the community might include creating multicultural educational programs and forums, as well as conducting search conferences to establish a community vision and direction; prevention methods at the level of nations could include offering assistance, training, and support to emerging nations in the development of institutional dispute resolution processes as well as in training dispute resolvers. As many of our practitioner colleagues are already engaged in the above efforts in their own communities, we know we are not saying anything new here. We do hope to generate some "ah-ha's" of recognition, however, with regard to the overlay of conflict management systems, contexts, and activities—all of which are intimately tied to what

Table 7.1. Spectrum of ADR Options in Different Systems.

	Individual	Group	Organization	Community	Global
Preventive ADR					
Facilitated ADR		The spectrum of ADR options can be			
Negotiated ADR		applied creatively in each of these contexts.			
Advisory ADR					
Fact-Finding ADR					
Imposed ADR					

Source: A version of this chart was used by Bill Ury in his presentation at the 1992 SPIDR Conference in Pittsburgh.

Weisbord (1987) calls the building of "dignity, meaning, and community"—on current practitioner efforts to broaden dispute resolution efforts systemically.

To date, not much attention has been focused on preventive methods of ADR. As organizations continue to adopt "best practices" in their day-to-day operations and relationships—to compete, to control costs, and to maximize resources—dispute prevention becomes increasingly important. Furthermore, organizations will come to expect design architects to be familiar with ADR methods of prevention and to include them in their recommendations for the furtherance of the systemic management of conflict.

At the Chompist Company, Anne Logan will have the opportunity to be involved in designing preventive ADR methods. For example, reg-neg is a preventive method of ADR, which allows the interested and affected parties to have a hand in crafting regulations that affect them prior to promulgation. Anne may need to educate Chompist leadership about the use of reg-neg as a conflict management tool and work to engage the participation of other companies concerned about the new regulations in this process. As for Chompist's working conditions dispute, it may also be ripe for preventive methods other than the establishment of a permanent joint safety forum: intensive safety education and training for the workforce, replacing outworn machinery, or even inviting federal and state regulators into the workplace to guide and advise on safety issues. For Chompist's consumer disputes, the ombudsperson's office may be a source of important feedback to the company regarding consumer product preferences as well as their complaints.

PRINCIPLE 4: Make sure that disputants have the necessary knowledge and skill to choose and use ADR.

Determining when to use ADR depends in large measure on whether the affected disputants have the necessary knowledge to choose ADR and the skills to use it once they have chosen it. People are unlikely to choose a procedure about which they know nothing. Thus, labor and management need to know how to engage in interest-identification processes, brainstorming, and consensus decision making in order to use interest-based negotiation. A dissatisfied customer needs to know what mediation is and how to participate in it before she can choose it and participate as an informed ADR user. An unhappy claimant needs to know what nonbinding arbitration is before he can decide to submit his claim to such a process. Whether and when ADR is used is often determined by the ADR knowledge and skill levels of those choosing the method.

Practitioners know that disputants, more often than not, are only ready to resolve disputes in their own time. Disputants have to be assured that they have standing and that their complaint has been heard. Further, they need information about their dispute before they can consider possible choices for resolution, especially the more unfamiliar forms of ADR. For example, it may be difficult for claimants to choose early neutral evaluation or a mini-trial if they have not assessed their case or they do not have a basic understanding of the facts to be presented to a neutral. It would be hard for claimants to use the services of an ombudsperson without first identifying the issue or being able to articulate the particular grievance. Some practitioners have seen ADR fail because disputants were unfamiliar or uncomfortable with the facts of their case or had not yet assessed their options; they were thus not only unable to commit to a solution but also unable to commit to a process. Conversely, sometimes practitioners see disputants and organizations delay ADR use to the point where the dollars and time already expended in overdeveloping the facts require them to justify such use of resources to the point of litigation. In this way, the optimal time for the use of ADR in a particular dispute is intimately tied to the organization's culture of dispute development and its tolerance of conflict and risk.

In addition, disputants need to know how to be informed consumers and competent participants. Often, this can be taught and modeled through ADR training and education, a topic discussed in Chapter Eight.

At the Chompist Company, as noted above, Anne will probably have to assess the ADR knowledge and skill levels of management, employees, and consumers in order to determine whether further education and training in conflict management is needed. She needs to ensure that ADR participants have the knowledge and skills to make informed choices about the handling of their disputes.

How to Use ADR

PRINCIPLE 5: Create ADR systems that are simple to use and easy to access and that resolve disputes early, at the lowest organizational level, with the least bureaucracy.

Effective design architects embrace the KISS principle ("keep it simple, stupid"). They make ADR simple to use, easy to access, and readily available, with a minimum of delay.

In order for disputants to actually choose ADR, it must be easier to use than the current dispute resolution system. If ADR becomes too complicated to use or is too frustrating to access, disputants will default to the status quo, the current dispute resolution mechanism (usually litigation or another rights-based method), although in some instances the default mechanism may be for the disputants to walk away and not deal with the conflict at all (which Ury, Brett, and Goldberg call "lumping it").

As all practitioners have experienced, the introduction of new ideas and processes in organizations tends to generate an almost irresistible tendency to overcontrol. To make ADR *difficult to use* and *impossible to access,* a design architect should do the following: first, require multiple levels of approval to use ADR (more than to file a lawsuit) and make people write numerous memos to justify use of ADR. Then, increase the paperwork (again, more than to file a lawsuit) so that there are numerous forms and reports to complete. Third, make it difficult to get approval to use ADR; have only one or two people in the organization or in a particular division who can commit to using ADR. If you want to make it especially difficult, do not give line personnel authority to commit to use ADR or authority to commit to a settlement. Finally, send messages that make it clear that the organization does not support ADR, that it is to be regarded as an anomaly, and that it is risky behavior to recommend use of ADR in any particular case.

In most instances, resolving disputes as early as possible decreases costs and increases satisfaction. As noted above, early resolution may be impeded by the disputants' own understanding and knowledge (or the lack thereof) of their case. More often, early resolution is impeded by organizational constraints, such as cultural attitudes toward conflict or risk, the need for lengthy review and approval processes, or the failure to make ADR simple to use and easy to access.

Many organizations require the use of multiple levels of the bureaucracy to study, dissect, and review the merits of a dispute before it can be resolved. Thus, although the disputants may want to resolve the dispute as quickly and as early as possible, organizational practices and procedures may constrain them. This is where the principle of "subsidiarity" arises: designing conflict management systems that resolve disputes at the lowest organizational level possible. As an architectural design principle, subsidiarity is often difficult to implement in highly stratified, vertically organized institutions that take pride in their review and approval procedures. Some organizations, for example, bifurcate the review and approval processes: they require review and approval through several chains of command to engage in ADR and then a second review and approval (often through the same chain of command) to commit to a resolution reached through ADR. Giving disputants, including organizational disputants, maximum authority to resolve disputes as quickly as possible and at the lowest organizational level feasible creates conflict management systems that are less costly, more timely, and increasingly satisfactory. We recognize the reality that "bucking the bureaucracy" is not always possible in organizations, particularly those that are tied tightly to their policies, procedures, and practices. However, some practitioners have found it helpful to work with such an organization's leadership to point out the benefit and wisdom of designing more streamlined approval procedures for particular divisions, offices, or clusters of cases.

Minimizing the bureaucracy and paperwork necessary to use ADR is a lofty (and often idealistic) goal of any design architecture effort. As noted above, the default mechanism is usually the status quo. Thus, if the paperwork requirements of the new conflict management system are more onerous than the current dispute resolution system or if participants must learn complicated new procedures and adhere to excessive reporting requirements, disputants will in all probability default to the current system. Thus, effective design architecture starts from where the organization is and works with the system's leadership to create approval processes and procedures that are *less* cumbersome than the current system.

At Hopevale, our hypothetical hospital, Jeff Linton and the design team need to craft several dispute resolution approaches: one to deal with doctor-nurse conflict, one to handle pending lawsuits, and one to deal with community dissatisfaction regarding the decision not to expand the Cardiac Care Unit and Emergency Department. An approach to managing the doctor-nurse conflict might be to assemble a highly credible joint practice committee authorized to design an interprofessional conflict resolution process characterized by accessibility, confidentiality, and self-management. In this way, the professionals themselves would be in charge of identifying and resolving issues of concern. Of necessity, such a practice committee would have to be educated in ADR approaches, trained in facilitation and mediation techniques, and provided with broad authority to determine appropriate resolutions with some minimal hospital-set parameters. The practice committee would need to design its resolution process in such a manner that complainants could exit the committee's purview to seek other remedies if the dispute was not resolved satisfactorily through its efforts.

Hopevale's design team might approach the challenge of introducing ADR procedures into the pending lawsuits by encouraging the hospital, the attorneys for both parties, and the complainants to submit to ADR counseling, where the current status of the disputes could be assessed and possible alternative resolution strategies suggested. If the parties are interested, they might find a mini-trial useful, provided the parties believe sufficient information about their cases has been generated. On the other hand, an early neutral evaluation process might be preferred if the case is at a more preliminary stage so that an opinion can be obtained regarding the merits of the cases. If these ADR processes uncovered a mutual interest in pursuing settlement options, engaging a mediator with specialized knowledge of medical issues might be the next step for the medical malpractice case, and a mediator experienced in the settlement of commercial disputes might be appropriate for the vendor case.

Hopevale's design team might approach the dispute with the community by attempting to transform the issue from the micro (expanding specific hospital services and facilities) to the macro (delivering health care services in the community). If those affected were interested in this broader issue, Hopevale might take the lead in designing and facilitating a community search conference that would include the whole health care system, including other providers (and competitors); health care professionals and educators; patients, families, and schools; and local, state, and federal health care regulatory bodies. As Weisbord (1992) and others have shown us, search processes can transform relationships among stakeholders by gathering committed people together to create a collective vision of the future. This truly "whole system" approach transforms understanding into mobilization for action toward important goals. In this manner, Hopevale's ADR design team could introduce a completely new approach to conflict systems management, a search conference, which would take into account the total system within which the hospital operates. Sponsoring such a conference for the community would demonstrate the seriousness of Hopevale's concern for such matters, reinforce its reputation in the community, and in all probability clarify some of the thorny economic issues of its continued viability as a deliverer of health care to the community.

PRINCIPLE 6: Allow disputants to retain maximum control over choice of ADR method and selection of neutral wherever possible.

Not surprisingly, practitioners have found that disputants are likely to be more resistant to an ADR process if they are not involved in selecting it and even more resistant if they have little or no voice in determining who the neutral will be. Consistently attempting to build on the values of participation, openness, and feedback requires that selection of ADR methods be derived rather than imposed. Practitioners have discovered, however, that when an organization makes the conscious decision to impose a particular type of ADR on certain stakeholders or constituents, disputants are somewhat less resistant as long as they retain a degree of control over the selection of a neutral. For example, even in court-ordered and other mandated mediation programs, disputants are often allowed to select a neutral from a panel or to veto several names on a list. The need to observe this principle of "most control over process" and "most control over selection of neutral" was expressed clearly in the Society of Professionals in Dispute Resolution's (SPIDR) first report of the Commission on Qualifications (1989). To encourage dialogue among stakeholders, SPIDR's second Commission on Qualifications' published report (1995) examines the most current analysis and makes recommendations with regard to the provision, selection, training, and competency of neutrals in dispute resolution processes.

In light of this principle, the design team at Hopevale is well advised to leave the actual selection of the ADR method and of the neutral to the parties to the pending lawsuits. Support and information would of course be available with respect to what organizations maintain rosters of suitable neutrals, the average cost of such neutrals, the criteria to use in the selection of a neutral, and the average time the ADR process might take.

Thus, the task of design architecture focuses on *whether, when,* and *how* to incorporate ADR practices and processes into the conflict management system. Relying once again on the principles of participation, openness, and feedback, the design team works collaboratively with stakeholders and organizational leadership to facilitate informed choices about appropriate ADR processes. To assist organizations and stakeholders in making these informed choices, we turn now to one of the six design principles in particular: building the knowledge and skill necessary to choose and use ADR through training and education.

Chapter Eight

Training and Education
Building the Knowledge and Skill Base

Stakeholders need to have a sound skill and knowledge foundation to use new dispute resolution practices such as alternative dispute resolution (ADR). Whether stakeholders are internal or external, they need to know how to access the system, to understand the ADR options available to them, and to have some level of confidence in using the ADR processes they choose. Such skill and knowledge can be learned in a variety of settings and from a variety of sources, both formal and informal. Again, we emphasize that this may be an incremental effort, with the external consultant or internal specialist initially asked by organizational leadership to do some ADR training and education that eventually grows into a more systemic design intervention.

Training and education do not occur in a vacuum; similar to other aspects of conflict management, they are but one integral component of a comprehensive system. Once again, the principles and values of interest-based design (participation, openness, and feedback) are at the core of effective training and education interventions. As those who train know so well, involving stakeholders at the outset of developing an ADR training and education strategy allows them the opportunity to identify their concerns, to develop delivery options that address those concerns, and to participate in joint problem solving and decision making about different aspects of the strategy.

Difference Between Training and Education

Although the terms *training* and *education* are often used interchangeably in the literature and in practice, they are not the same.

ADR education provides the contextual background and framework to understand and appreciate the strengths and limitations of ADR: how it furthers institutional and individual goals and where, when, and how to use it. ADR education is a dynamic, ongoing process of increasing awareness about conflict itself, about the typical individual and institutional responses to it, and about potential choices in conflict management. These educational approaches generally take the form of ADR marketing and awareness programs for executives, managers, resource allocators, and end users. ADR education occurs formally at conference, meeting, and luncheon presentations as well as informally at the coffee machine and water cooler.

In contrast, ADR training is more skill based: building competencies to use ADR, improving communication skills, learning mediation practices, and developing negotiation techniques. Training usually involves providing basic dispute resolution skills for users, including communication skills, and advanced technical ADR process skills for potential advocates and neutrals. ADR training is usually competency based and of longer duration than ADR education, as it often involves modification of attitudes, practices, and behaviors.

Despite their difference in purpose, approach, and target audiences, both training and education are necessary components for a successful conflict management system, particularly one that uses ADR. Although not everyone in a particular conflict management system needs to be highly trained, nearly everyone needs to be educated (or reeducated) in some manner about conflict or conflict management. Similar to architectural design, it is important to match the appropriate type of ADR training or education to the particular target audience.

Myths About ADR Training and Education

Several myths about ADR training and education are rife in organizations today:

All stakeholders need identical ADR training and education. Here, the incorrect assumption is usually that everyone (including senior and mid-level management) needs to be "skills trained" as mediators or neutrals of some type. There is little thought given to what specific skills and knowledge different stakeholders actually need and how they can best obtain those skills and that knowledge. Rather, the emphasis is on an off-the-shelf ADR training product advertised to fit all. With the explosion of ADR providers and vendors, it has suddenly become commonplace to have whole divisions or organizational levels of management and employees trained as mediators when in fact they will probably never serve as such. Rather, they will be overseeing ADR programs, selecting cases for mediation, or sitting at the mediation table as consumers or users, not as neutrals. Our experience has shown that if people are trained in skills they have little chance to use, they become frustrated and reluctant to use the system at all. This unfortunate practice affects both use of the system and satisfaction with it. Thus, it is important to target training and education to the particular population, with regard to both content and ultimate utility. As with design architecture, different organizations have different needs, and training approaches suitable in one setting may be inappropriate in another. Institution-specific, appropriate ADR training and education strategies are a collaborative effort among potential trainers, leadership, and stakeholders both within and outside the system.

For example, at our hypothetical hospital, Hopevale, Conflict Consultants will want to survey at least the doctors, nurses, union representatives, in-house attorneys, and community representatives to see what kind of training and education they think they will need to implement any new conflict management procedures. Whereas the doctors and nurses may need some type of training in joint problem-solving or communication skills, they do not need to be trained as mediators. Similarly, the in-house attorneys may need training in how to participate as users in various forms of ADR such as mediation or arbitration, but they do not need to be trained to act as mediators. Training these two groups at Hopevale to be mediators would be costly, probably produce resistance, and increase the frustration level of the doctors, nurses, and lawyers since they will be trained in skills that they will have no opportunity to use.

ADR training and education is best conducted by outside ADR experts and consultants. Not only is this misperception expensive, it can also be a form of rights-based design. That is, the outside vendors, experts, and consultants decide what kind of training and education is best for the organization. If they are more enlightened, the "outsiders" work with organizational stakeholders to figure out what types of training or education they want but then teach *to* the stakeholders rather than *with* them.

We do not mean to criticize outside vendors, providers, or trainers, nor to imply that all training should be conducted by inside personnel. Most outside ADR experts have the subject-matter expertise to conduct ADR training and education and many are good, even excellent, trainers. However, it is potentially disastrous that most vendors, experts, and consultants who do training are often not familiar with the specific organization's culture, structure, and values and cannot afford to take the time to familiarize themselves. As a result, their training design and strategy is often irrelevant or inappropriate for the specific organization. Conversely, if they do have the time (and have taken it) to learn about the organization and its population, they may conduct training to develop particular skills by using examples and role plays that are not specific or relevant to the particular organization and its actual disputes. Using standardized, off-the-shelf ADR training modules can result in executive trainees (who may be expected to negotiate million-dollar settlements) practicing with training problems that have them buying used cars or resolving neighborhood spats, or attorneys who will be mediating multiparty, multi-issue environmental disputes being trained to do so by practicing with equal employment opportunity exercises, which involve different dynamics and considerations than what they will actually experience.

Obviously, not all outside ADR consultants suffer from these deficiencies. In addition, organizations rarely have the training resources or knowledge to rely solely on in-house expertise to conduct ADR training and education. So what is the alternative? Many organizations and practitioners have successfully used team-teaching and "partnering" arrangements that pair an outside consultant with a stakeholder or organizational representative, not just to design the training but actually to *teach* it. The consultant provides the architectural and technical part of the training (subject matter and techniques) and the stakeholder adds the organizational and cultural components (process and context). This increases the likelihood that participants will have most of their questions answered and will leave satisfied and enthusiastic, not frustrated and cynical. In addition, the organizational representative collaborates with the consultant to design institution-specific training problems, examples, and role plays similar to the types of disputes participants will face.

For example, at our hypothetical agency, Federal Securities Management Agency (FSMA), Larry Terrence or other members of the staff can conduct much of the ADR training themselves if they have the necessary ADR expertise (it also helps to have actual experience using ADR), particularly related to the in-house hostile work environment disputes. Having the training delivered by FSMA in-house personnel who are knowledgeable and credible may also increase buy-in by key groups at FSMA. In order to involve employees in the training process and begin to garner support for the revised system, Larry, in conjunction with employee representatives and staff from the Personnel or EEO Office, might want to design a session introducing employees to ADR techniques (especially interest-based negotiation or mediation) and then explain how these procedures will be offered at the agency. FSMA may also be able to conduct in-house training related to the investor claims, again, if the in-house ADR expertise is available. Indeed, more and more federal agencies are conducting ADR training and education with in-house personnel to reduce costs, tailor the training, and use agency-specific materials and hypotheticals. For example, one federal agency used its in-house ADR personnel to design two courses—one two-and-a-half-day ADR course and one three-day advanced negotiation course to be delivered nationwide to personnel working in certain aspects of the agency's operations—and then "trained trainers" to teach the courses. The courses have been team taught at the local level by an agency attorney and a nonattorney and have been highly interactive through use of agency-specific examples and simulations.

Only organizational stakeholders should be trained and educated. Those who are designing ADR training and education often forget that organizational stakeholders are only half the equation; to engage in ADR approaches, one needs *all* the disputants engaged, educated, and in some cases trained. Training and educating only half of those involved in the conflict management system (internal organizational stakeholders) results in ADR underutilization and possible incongruity of knowledge and skills. For this reason, outside disputants and stakeholders need to be trained as well. Such disputants must be aware of the organization's interest in and advocacy of ADR, the applicable ADR system and its available options, and how to access such options.

Many will raise their eyebrows at this suggestion: why train and educate one's "opponents"? The answer is simple: without bilateral (and, ideally, joint) ADR training and education, the program's projected time efficiencies, cost savings, enhancement of satisfaction, and durability of results are unlikely to become a reality. As with the previously stated collateral benefits of buy-in, commitment, and utilization where stakeholders are involved with organizational assessment and architectural design, so too with training and education. Moreover, joint interest-based negotiation, problem-solving, or decision-making training among disputants can often lead to collateral benefits such as improved understanding, communication, and relationships.

At the Chompist Company, for example, one goal of the ombudsperson's office may be to devise strategies to educate consumers about the company's establishment of the office and about ADR options that the company is willing to offer consumers, such as mediation and arbitration. Such efforts may require the development of written materials, videotapes, or anecdotal material to share with consumers about alternative processes, or an explanation of ombudsperson programs at other companies. One goal of the safety and health joint committee may become the inclusion of local, state, and federal regulators in the training and education of the workforce and managers in good safety and health practices.

Once they are trained and educated, stakeholders will use ADR. Just because they have the skill and knowledge to use the system does not mean that stakeholders will do so. If you build it, it is not necessarily true that they will come; they must have a *reason* to come. It is true that disputants cannot use ADR without the necessary skills and knowledge, but these alone are not enough. We are continually amazed (as are many of our colleagues and other practitioners) at the number of organizations that assume that once they provide ADR training and education, people will somehow magically begin to use ADR. In addition to training and education, disputants also need to have incentives to use the system and they must be able to overcome constraints and resistance—topics that are addressed in greater detail in Chapter Eleven ("Incentives and Rewards") and Chapter Twelve ("Resistance and Constraints"). Here, however, it is simply worth noting again that training and education are part of a larger picture—a conflict management system designed, integrated, and reinforced in a variety of ways to enhance the potential for utilization, durability, and growth.

At FSMA, for example, merely educating employees about ADR techniques and explaining how they are available within the agency to resolve employee disputes is not sufficient. Unless FSMA employees believe that the ADR procedures are fair—not "stacked" against the employee or using biased or otherwise unacceptable neutrals from within the agency—and that it is safe to use them—no reprisal or retaliation—the procedures will languish. The training and education of FSMA employees need to be part of a larger, holistic approach that creates the perception—and the reality—that it is more beneficial (cheaper, faster, more satisfactory) to use ADR than to use other forms of dispute resolution.

Assessing ADR Training and Education Needs

In designing training and education, it is important to ask several key questions of organizational leadership and stakeholders in order to have a meeting of the minds on key training and education issues:

1. What is the purpose of the training and/or education? Is it to market ADR? To increase awareness about ADR options? To train consumers in how to use ADR? To train neutrals in how to perform ADR dispute resolution roles?
2. Who is the target audience? Who is being educated: executives, senior management, mid-level staff, customers? Who is being trained: users, neutrals, or individuals involved in the operation and administration of the ADR program?
3. Who will assess ADR training and education needs? What stakeholders, both within and outside the organization, need to be involved in the training and education needs assessment and task analysis? How will it be done?
4. When will ADR training and education be needed? Is there an immediate need to market ADR or to increase awareness about ADR? What long-term sustained training and education efforts

are necessary? How does the timing of training and education affect implementation?

5. Who will conduct ADR training and education? What internal resources and expertise are available? Can ADR education be conducted by internal stakeholders? If an outside expert or consultant is to be used, what joint efforts are necessary to ensure that the training and education will be specific to the organizational culture, mission, and goals?

6. How will participants use ADR training and education? Will participants use their new skills and knowledge to enhance their ability to resolve disputes and manage conflict in day-to-day work life? To decide whether and when to refer disputes to ADR? To serve as ADR neutrals in a third-party process? To administer an ADR program? To evaluate ADR efforts and results?

7. What will help participants use their new ADR skills and knowledge? Will they need ongoing technical assistance to identify when ADR is appropriate and when it is not? Will they need mentoring and coaching in how to use ADR processes, in how to select cases, and in how to choose the most appropriate form of ADR? What guidance will they need in overcoming organizational resistance and constraints and in evaluating ADR efforts and results?

For example, at Hopevale, Conflict Consultants will probably want to do a fairly broad training and education needs assessment. The purpose of the training or education will depend on the particular target audience: the purpose of training the doctors and nurses is to increase their skills in communication and problem-solving areas; the purpose of training the attorneys is to increase their awareness of ADR options and teach them to be informed ADR consumers and users; the purpose of educating the community groups is to increase their awareness of ADR options and to model certain interest-based skills, such as joint problem solving and facilitated communication. To determine the needs of each of these distinct target populations, Conflict Consultants will want to include training and education as one of the topics discussed in the various focus groups and will want to elicit additional ideas from relevant individuals from the union, the management, and the community. The timing will also vary depending upon which Hopevale population is targeted: there may be a need for immediate training and education for the doctor-nurse populations due to the level of hostility and its effect on the workplace environment and provision of health care services; the community groups may also need immediate attention as these are Hopevale's customers. A less urgent time concern may exist with regard to the attorneys, although it would depend on the stage of the current lawsuits and their attendant costs.

With respect to the actual conduct of training and education for the different groups at Hopevale, a team approach may be most appropriate where those interest groups affected join subject-matter experts, such as Conflict Consultants, to deliver the programs. A doctor-nurse-consultant team, an attorney-consultant team, and a community representative–hospital representative–consultant team might be possible. In addition to actually delivering training and education programs, it may also be necessary to deliver follow-up sessions periodically for each of the groups to reinforce the training and to determine whether there are additional needs.

Five Types of ADR Training and Education

Five basic types of ADR training and education target particular audiences and serve different purposes: (1) marketing efforts, (2) awareness education, (3) conflict management and communication training, (4) consumer/user training, and (5) training of third-party neutrals.

Marketing Efforts

Marketing is a form of education. Its purpose is usually to convince the organization's stakeholders and managers to buy in to ADR. Specifically, it addresses the benefits of ADR, its limitations (including when it is not appropriate), and how ADR will further specific institutional or individual goals (or, as we term it, "WII-FM"—what's in it for me?). ADR marketing efforts are usually targeted toward decision makers, representatives, resource allocators, and those who can champion ADR within the larger organizational population. In creating marketing presentations, it is often useful to use success stories from similar organizations or, even better, to use illustrations from within the organization itself. Most important, effective ADR marketing is targeted to the specific audience, anticipates and addresses that audience's particular concerns and reservations about the use of ADR, and seeks to convince it that ADR is in its best interests, as well as in the best interests of the organization. Often, ADR marketing efforts are most effective when presented by someone who is credible and known to the particular audience and when the presentation is limited to one or two hours at most.

At Hopevale, such marketing might include short presentations to the board and key managers by professionals from other hospitals who have used joint problem-solving techniques, ADR methods, and community facilitation processes to deal with conflict, noting the beneficial impact that these programs have had on cost, workplace morale, and community perception and acceptance.

Awareness Education

Awareness efforts educate stakeholders about what ADR is and how it is used in the particular organizational setting. Such efforts can be targeted toward users and consumers who will be using ADR, to those who will be selecting cases for ADR, or to those who will administer ADR programs. It includes what ADR is (and what it is not), an explanation of the various ADR options, when ADR is inappropriate, and how to access ADR in the particular organization. Success stories are useful, as well as examples of how ADR has actually been used. Having peers and colleagues of the target audience conduct the awareness education is often effective—for example, one employee describing his or her experience with mediation to an audience of fellow employees. Panel discussions also work well if they are lively, interactive, well facilitated, and time limited. The emphasis in awareness education is on interaction and information dissemination rather than on providing skills in how to use ADR or how to be a neutral. We have found that half-day awareness sessions that include some interactive components seem to work well.

Awareness training will be particularly critical at FSMA, both for the employees and the investors. These two populations need to know what ADR is and what ADR options are available to them. This could be done through written materials, videotapes, short panel presentations, and brochures. With regard to the investors, this might involve Larry working with some of the trade associations or organizations that represent investors and perhaps making presentations at outside conferences and seminars about FSMA's ADR program.

Conflict Management and Communication Training

This type of training is generic and not geared toward particular forms of ADR. Rather, it is focused on increasing participants' understanding and acceptance of conflict and on improving their communication skills, including active listening and direct communication. The purpose is to introduce skills that can be used in day-to-day life or are the foundation for additional ADR training such as negotiation or mediation. In addition, this type of training is critical to the improvement of the organization's management of conflict. We have found that conflict and communication training is most effective when it is interactive and takes place for no more than a full day.

The training at Hopevale with doctors and nurses falls into this category—targeted, interactive skills training in problem-solving techniques and communication. Anne Logan might also suggest that the Chompist Company use a similar joint training approach with the joint labor-management safety committee to enhance its work.

Consumer/User Training

Aimed at the organizational stakeholders who will actually be using ADR procedures, this training targets those who will be sitting at the table negotiating or participating in mediation. It is practical, focusing on what to expect in an ADR proceeding, how to select a neutral, how to prepare for ADR, how the process progresses, how to identify interests, and how to develop strategies and options. It is often useful to include a demonstration or videotape showing an actual ADR proceeding, such as mediation or a mini-trial. In addition, we believe it is essential to allow participants an opportunity to prepare for and take part in the simulation of a relevant ADR proceeding during the course of the training. The exercise should be similar in nature and content to the types of disputes the participants will be handling. For example, consumer/user training could be conducted for at least one full day and usually no more than two days.

At Hopevale, in-house attorneys (assuming the lawsuits are being handled in-house) will need to learn to be effective advocates for Hopevale during a mediation or arbitration. This will involve using mock mediations where the Hopevale attorneys actually play the role of the attorney at the table (not the mediator), deal with questions of confidentiality and impasse, and devise strategies for participating in a mediation. Viewing a mock mediation (either a live demonstration or a videotape) may also be useful here.

Training of Third-Party Neutrals

Intensive skills training is targeted only for those individuals who will actually serve as neutrals: mediators, arbitrators, facilitators, and fact finders. It is usually of longer duration than other ADR training and educational efforts and is more intensive and interactive. Such courses are conducted best in small groups—perhaps no more than eight to twelve students per instructor—as direct participation, active and constructive feedback, and role playing are crucial to the successful training of neutrals. Problems, hypotheticals, and role plays should be similar to the types of disputes that the participants will be engaged in resolving. In addition, skills training of neutrals includes a dedication to follow-up and reinforcement measures such as mentoring, clinics, and advanced training sessions, so that participants can ask questions, pose ethical dilemmas, and explore more sophisticated techniques as their experience and skill develops. We suggest a minimum three full days of training for most initial third-party skills training.

If FSMA decides to use internal mediators to resolve workplace disputes, they will need to be trained in mediation techniques. Larry may be able to conduct this training if he is a skilled and experienced mediator and has the time to design it; if not, FSMA may want to use other government resources or a team approach with an outside vendor to deliver training, provided that the vendor understands the culture of FSMA and works jointly with FSMA to develop hypotheticals and simulations that are relevant. As noted above, the training will achieve best results by being highly interactive, conducted in small groups, and engaging the participants in a variety of simulations.

Designing Training and Education Programs

Once these key initial questions have been addressed by relevant stakeholders who are asked on an ongoing basis for program revision, attention can turn to task analysis. This involves identifying the core components of the particular ADR training and education, as depicted in Table 8.1.

Identify the purpose of training and/or education. Here, the design team needs to determine the goal of the training or education effort: marketing ADR, increasing ADR awareness, explaining ADR policies and procedures, building skills, or developing joint problem-solving skills. Such goals identify the training course objectives, which can be measured later to ascertain whether they have been met.

Identify the target audience. Who is being trained or educated: executives, managers, supervisors, disputants, administrative per-

Table 8.1. Task Analysis/Results for ADR Training and Education.

Task	Result
Identify purpose of training and/or education	Determine course objectives
Identify target audience	Determine learning goals
Identify subject matter	Determine course outline
Identify required expertise	Determine instructors (internal or external)
Identify program format	Determine agenda
Identify logistics	Determine administrative, resource, and operational needs

sonnel, evaluators, or neutrals? Ideally, the training or education is specifically tailored to the target audience, anticipating their specific questions, concerns, and needs. Such analysis determines the goals of the education or training effort.

Identify the subject matter. Is the subject matter tailored to the target audience and does it further the purpose of the training? For example, a short demonstration of an ADR technique such as mediation may be appropriate during an awareness training session; it may be unnecessary and poorly received during a marketing session with senior executives. Subject matter will determine course outline accordingly.

Identify the required expertise. The subject matter and process skills being presented will determine what skill and knowledge the instructor must have and whether that skill and knowledge is available internally or whether outside expertise is necessary.

Identify the program format. A key decision is whether the training and education will use interactive exercises, discussion, lecture, panel presentation, visual aids, and how the sessions will be structured. Such determinations derive from *who* is being trained in *what.* The result determines the schedule, including the number of training days involved, and an appropriate agenda.

Identify logistics. The design team needs to focus on what handouts, materials, equipment, and classrooms (including breakout rooms) will be needed for a successful program. These administrative and operational needs directly affect the resources necessary for the training and education effort.

At the hypothetical Chompist Company, key personnel will need training in reg-neg (negotiated rule making) if the state agrees to use this ADR method to promulgate the new food production regulations. The target population for this training will probably include those who will actually represent Chompist during the reg-neg, management officials who will oversee the effort, and possibly representatives from other companies who will participate in the reg-neg. The goals will be to introduce these participants to the concept of reg-neg, explain basic interest-based principles, and build the necessary skill to ensure that Chompist's concerns are adequately identified and addressed during the reg-neg. It may be appropriate for Anne Logan to get someone to speak to the training group who has actually participated in a reg-neg and to explain how it differs from more traditional methods of negotiation or regulation promulgation. In addition, that speaker could identify the preparation necessary to participate successfully in a reg-neg (including prenegotiation with other parties) and possible pitfalls. Anne might also want to design a mock reg-neg so the participants can try out their strategies in advance of the actual reg-neg. Moreover, it may be useful to have a speaker come in from the sponsoring state agency to talk about previous reg-neg efforts.

Implementing ADR Training and Education Programs

What if you are an instructor? What can you do to make the training or education lively and engaging? When delivering ADR training and education programs, we suggest that instructors do the following:

1. Use examples and problems applicable to the culture and mission of the specific organization and of the particular ADR program application.
2. Highlight internal organizational expertise whenever possible.
3. Use experienced ADR neutrals and participants for demonstrations.
4. Keep the course focused and fast paced.
5. Make the course highly interactive and experiential.
6. Vary presentation techniques to appeal to visual, auditory, verbal, and interactive learners.
7. Allow time for questions, discussion, and the sharing of ideas.
8. Conclude by developing a list of next steps or ideas for "where do we go from here?"
9. Solicit and record evaluative feedback on the course and ideas for follow-up activity.

These last two suggestions—developing a list of next steps and providing for feedback and follow-up—are essential. Once the training or education has taken place, it is useful to conduct personal interviews with a representative sample of the participants to follow up and solicit their views on the effectiveness of the course. This step is beyond the normal end-of-course written evaluations. Questions during such interviews might include the following:

What did they like best? What did they like least? What would they do differently? Similar to other interest-based design stages, training and education is constantly assessed and modified in response to feedback and changing circumstances.

In the early stages of redesign, educational and training efforts are one of the key methods by which the revisions to the conflict management system can be understood and can gain acceptability. Careful attention to feedback about ADR in general as well as training and education efforts in particular can also yield valuable information to assist in the process of modifying and improving the overall implementation of the conflict management system's ADR strategy.

Chapter Nine

Implementation
Introducing the New System

At last, the actual implementation phase begins! The previous work of entry and contracting, organizational assessment, design architecture, and training and education pave the way for the implementation of the conflict management system. This stage of the intervention can be truly exciting and rewarding—for the alternative dispute resolution (ADR) design team, for the stakeholders, for organizational leadership. As with previous stages of the design intervention, the prevailing attitudes and practices of participation, openness, and feedback continue. However, even more important, the organization development (OD) perspective and practices of a sociotechnical approach and an experimental frame of mind are added to the mix.

Sociotechnical Approach

The OD practice of a sociotechnical strategy can guide practitioners significantly in the implementation stage. A sociotech strategy is a useful way of identifying in advance the key elements to be included in the implementation effort. In the process of designing and implementing change in a conflict management system with organizational leadership and stakeholder participation, issues, events, and decisions occur rapidly and often simultaneously. During implementation—the testing and doing of an ADR approach—a sociotech strategy helps keep the effort focused and on target. Given the highly charged and ever changing nature of any conflict management system, attention to both the people

(socio) and   nical) aspects of ADR implementation are c

    With re   implementation of conflict management sys-
tems, the "socio" aspects include the following:

- Top-level permission, notice, and publication of the
  intent and opportunity to use ADR in certain programs
- Clear information about possible incentives that may
  motivate people to use the new program
- Assignment of specific individuals to the operational
  aspects of the ADR program
- Reassurance that the ADR approaches to be used are
  fair and equitable
- Education about the ADR program and training in the
  skills necessary to use it successfully
- Ongoing solicitation of evaluation and feedback so that
  individuals see that they have a hand in shaping the program
  to meet their concerns and needs

    At Chompist, our hypothetical company, the socio aspects of
the implementation include the president, Daniel Teznicki, buying into the use of ADR with the state, production workers, and
consumers. It would be advisable for him to publicly signal,
through word and action, his support for the ADR initiatives and
to assign a management leader at Chompist to champion these
ADR efforts as well, working alongside Anne Logan acting as the
external consultant. In addition, Anne will need to tap into the
opinions of the stakeholders, particularly the employees and consumers, on whether they believe the procedures will be regarded
as fair and useful. Finally, appropriate training, education, and
feedback approaches will need to be designed so that people will
be able to take advantage of the processes and to communicate the
nature of their experience in doing so.

    The "technical" aspects of ADR implementation address the
following:

- The actual construction of the design architecture
- The identification and appropriate use of a supply of
  trained neutrals and other technical experts

- Reallocation or designation of material and personnel resources to support ADR implementation
- The administrative and logistical arrangements needed to support the ADR program
- The evaluative components of ADR implementation, such as design and process feedback, as well as performance measures for those charged with administrative and dispute resolution responsibilities
- The decision to introduce ADR systemwide or through a more limited test project or pilot approach

At Chompist, the technical aspects of implementation will include creating the joint labor-management safety committee, the ADR options for consumers, and the establishment of an ombudsperson's office. In addition, Anne will need to address the issue of where to obtain qualified neutrals to use in any instances of consumer mediation. Will Chompist contract with a particular dispute resolution service to provide neutrals, maintain a roster of outside neutrals, and let consumers select one, or allow consumers themselves to suggest individual neutrals? Chompist will also need to determine what resources it is willing to commit to an ombudsperson's office, who will staff the reg-neg (negotiated rulemaking) effort, and how participants for the joint committee will be selected. Finally, an evaluation methodology will need to be developed to measure the following: the effectiveness of the reg-neg in terms of both results and cost savings; the impact of the joint safety committee on workplace safety compliance, workforce education, and workforce injuries; and whether ADR is "cheaper, faster, better" in resolving consumer disputes with the establishment of a company ombudsperson.

Starting a Pilot Program

After organizational assessment and design, and the start-up of training and educational efforts, the organization's leadership and ADR design team now face a choice: should they introduce ADR broadly on a large scale and permanent basis in multiple programs or should they test an experimental design in a given dispute arena? Our preference and that of many other practitioners is the latter—to "think big and act small." Limited testing or a pilot project approach helps to accomplish the following tasks:

- Determine the willingness of disputants to change dispute resolution methods.
- Make it safer for individuals with a stake in the old system to experiment with new behaviors and rewards.
- Test the suitability of the design, its fit with the organization and its members.
- Uncover previously unknown costs, expectations, attitudes, practices, or other restraints to any wide-scale ADR program initiatives.

Pilot testing, where ADR is introduced on a limited, experimental basis in particular programs, affords the design team, the organization's leadership, and its participant stakeholders with the opportunity to test out the reliability of their information, their design, and their planning—with relatively low cost and low risk. The results of a pilot program illuminate how well ADR works (or does not work) in a particular conflict arena. Problems are uncovered in pilots, "bugs" can be worked out, people get motivated.

Further, it is better to discover now rather than later that ADR does *not* work with a particular population or type of dispute. As a pilot program will often be the first experience for many with ADR, starting with a pilot approach creates the potential for intra-organizational success. This first experience will often determine whether ADR is viewed as beneficial by the rest of the organization and its constituents in terms of cost, time, satisfaction, and durability. Successful pilots can give ADR early, favorable publicity resulting in added credibility within the organization, rather than the reputation of being a mistake, inadequate, or "just another gimmick."

Top-level organizational leadership and support is important in the launching of an ADR pilot. Such support can be garnered in the assessment phase when the ADR strategy is developed or through later educational awareness efforts for executives and top managers. The interest and commitment of top management can be gleaned through the questions asked: "What is ADR? How have other organizations benefited from its use? Where in our organization is there an opportunity to try it?" Invariably, some top managers will see the possibilities for using ADR in their part of the organization or for particularly troubling classes of disputes. These same managers will often pursue the opportunity to be the first to use ADR. These are the pioneers and the design team should identify, support, and encourage them, for they often become ongoing champions for change in the organization's conflict management system. The degree to which such champions exist or come forward often determines whether the initial pilot effort is modest or ambitious.

A great deal is usually riding on the results of the pilot, regardless of the notion that it is only a test. It is thus crucial to optimize the possibility for success. We offer the following "how to" suggestions for getting started and selecting a pilot target:

Select individual(s) to be responsible for the pilot. The organization has to make certain resource commitments even when the ADR effort is experimental and limited in scope. One of the key commitments is to identify and reassign an individual who will take charge of the coordination of the pilot program and be responsible for all aspects of its implementation. This individual directs, coordinates, and provides information to others participating in the pilot's design, implementation, and evaluation. This person is the point of contact for information, inquiries, and status of the pilot at any given time. It is a definite plus if this coordinator is from within the organization itself, even if he or she uses outside experts as needed. In this way, the organization starts to build its own ADR human resources from the beginning. This is beneficial when ADR goes systemwide, and it enhances ownership of the program by the employee and internal stakeholder population. Once the pilot's scope is identified and its design finalized, the ADR coordinator can be joined by others, as human resource use and leadership permits, who are interested in being a part of the ADR pilot staff and who can assist through their skills, relationships, and attitudes.

Look to external experience, expertise, and success stories. Even with internal staff to identify, select, and coordinate the pilot, outside experience and expertise may also be appropriate. "Outside experience" here means looking at other similarly situated organizations with relevant ADR programs. Such examination can yield tips and techniques for successful pilot testing. "Expertise" means external designers or neutrals who have skills in the substance or process area of the planned pilot. Contacting these outside resources may generate information about technical, substantive, or procedural details that have been overlooked or that need strengthening. Consultation is usually adequate for this purpose, for it is unwise to introduce any new external designers into the organization at the implementation phase. Fortunately, today's ADR literature is abundant with case studies and other useful information that can provide leads to both outside experience and expertise.

Identify stakeholders who will be affected by the pilot. Once the arena for the pilot is targeted, one of the first tasks of responsible leadership is to identify those persons in various roles (line and program managers, employees, past disputants, legal counsel, internal neutrals) who have a variety of interests (fairness, cost, time, durability of resolutions, access, workability) in the pilot and in the ultimate approach adopted. If outside disputants, customers, or regulators are involved in the targeted dispute resolution process to be changed, they are also included in the notice of the design intent, the design process, and, if appropriate, in the pilot itself. These people will also play a critical role in encouraging others to participate in the pilot and ideally will receive public credit for their involvement, especially in any written documentation.

Choose a pilot linked to organizational goals. If the assessment process has been well conceived and implemented, the selection of an appropriate ADR pilot should be natural. As stated in Chapter Six, "Organizational Assessment," the problems and opportunities in the current dispute resolution system are usually apparent at this point. Which of these arenas to select for a pilot project, however, depends on political, economic, and human resource analyses—always conditioned by the drive for a success. What are the most pressing organizational needs and objectives? The following are organizational goals for the ADR design team and leadership to examine for linkage to possible pilot projects:

- Enhance public image with clients, constituents, employees, and other stakeholders.
- Resolve disputes before they accelerate and escalate.
- Reduce the costs of litigation.
- Eliminate case backlogs.
- Reduce appeals.
- Increase capacity to address a broader range of disputes.
- Increase employee morale and customer satisfaction.

Identifying clear objectives for the pilot effort not only increases the organizational perception of its utility and assures congruity but also helps in the evaluation of the pilot.

Select the site of the pilot with success in mind. Look for a site that offers multiple opportunities for success—in other words, where most stakeholders involved believe that the disputants are just waiting for the opportunity to do things differently. Choose a site where disputants have expended enormous resources of dollars and time to resolve disputes and have been repeatedly discouraged by unresponsive and unsatisfying results—the "sick and tired of being sick and tired" arena. Alternatively, pick a "green field" site where everyone from employees to customers are new and do not have the baggage of an already existing culture of rights-based dispute resolution; this means fewer individuals who need to make a decision to change "the way we do things around here." Another option is to choose a site because customer demand or other environmental forces, such as regulators, have demanded a change and the organization *must* respond. Ideally, link one of these factors with an office, program, or geographical site where people are ready to change and are willing to experiment.

Having linked organizational goals and objectives with broad readiness factors, some practical considerations need to be addressed about the potential pilot:

- Are there sufficient numbers of disputes to test success?
- Are there sufficient resources (time, staff, money) to allocate to the pilot?
- Are the results of the pilot measurable and easily evaluated?
- Is the area of the pilot important to the rest of the organization?

If the answers to most of these questions are affirmative, the critical factors for a successful pilot have probably been met.

In light of the above criteria, if the potential for more than one successful pilot exists, the ADR design team and organizational leadership may want to consider multiple pilot programs, which affords several opportunities for success and significant ADR experiences in a relatively short period of time. This can be especially beneficial if the pilot programs are conducted simultaneously in several "hot spots" in the organization, such as internal disputes (labor-management), external disputes (customer complaints), and preventive/preemptive efforts (reg-neg). The only caution in conducting multiple pilot projects is ensuring that sufficient resources (time, attention, staff, and money) are available, as well as the readiness and support of the organization and its stakeholders to engage in multiple efforts.

Federal Securities Management Agency (FSMA), our hypothetical agency, will probably want to conduct a pilot project using mediation to resolve internal workplace disputes such as the hostile work environment allegations. Someone at the agency will need to be given responsibility for the administration and oversight of the pilot; this should probably be someone other than Larry Terrence who is familiar with EEO procedures, has credibility with both management and employees, and is knowledgeable about ADR. If there is no one with this substantive background who is ADR-knowledgeable, it may be necessary to have someone at FSMA who has substantive EEO knowledge trained in basic ADR techniques and concepts.

One of the first things the FSMA ADR pilot project coordinator will want to do is look to other agencies who have used ADR in similar disputes. Given recent federal legislation and regulations, many agencies are using ADR in employee disputes, including the Department of Health and Human Services, the Department of Labor, the Defense Logistics Agency, the Department of Agriculture, and the Library of Congress. The FSMA ADR pilot project coordinator will also want to determine which stakeholders need to be involved in the pilot design: employees, supervisors, managers, representatives from the EEO Office.

Next, the FSMA pilot project coordinator will need to determine the purpose of the pilot, whether it is to reduce litigation, decrease cost, speed resolution, eliminate backlogs, or increase employee morale. Whether one or all of these goals is chosen for the pilot focus, they will determine how success is measured and how progress is charted throughout the pilot. Selecting the site is also important; here, FSMA will probably want to choose one of the offices where there are a large number of hostile work environment complaints. If management at these offices is resistant, an alternative would be to conduct the pilot at headquarters (Washington, D.C.); the problem in this site selection is that the culture, mission, and operation of a home office such as the Washington office of a federal agency can be quite different from any field office, causing problems ("It'll never work out here") during the eventual rollout of the pilot.

Implementing a Pilot Program

With the selection of the target, the actual details of the pilot design and attendant implementation now begin. Here, the details of how the pilot will actually work get fleshed out. Questions include the following:

- How will disputants be notified that the pilot exists?
- How will disputants actually access the program?
- How will cases be selected for the pilot, by whom, and on what basis?
- What ADR processes will be offered and at what stage of the dispute?
- Who will be the neutrals (internal/external) and how will they be selected?
- What training will participants need to use ADR?
- What will be the measures of success and how will the process be evaluated?
- What is the time frame of the pilot?
- What form of reporting will occur at the conclusion of the pilot and to whom will such reports be given?

All of the above questions (and probably others) need to be answered by the ADR pilot project coordinator and the design team. We offer some general guidelines to steer the actual implementation of the pilot:

Look at similar programs in similar organizations. This can often provide information, ideas, and pitfalls in implementing a pilot.

Design according to the problem. A major overhaul of the entire dispute resolution process is rarely needed, even in a pilot. The introduction of interest-based ADR processes is an effort to *expand* the organization's ability to deal with a variety of disputes; these processes are thus introduced at a stage in dispute escalation where they can do the most for resolution and relationship preservation. Where in the current process does it make good sense to introduce such interest-based processes? Usually, it will be at the beginning of the dispute rather than at the end point. What multiplicity of processes could be applied to the disputes? Often, a design team focuses on the introduction of mediation alone; however, combining mediation with other efforts such as early facilitative communication, willing exchange of information, joint problem solving, and involvement by top leadership can help achieve a comprehensive resolution that is more satisfactory and durable. Thus, the pilot is more than the mere insertion of a singular process; rather, it builds a series of actions and communications that signal early concern for the interests underlying the dispute and a commitment to discover an appropriate dispute resolution method through a variety of options and interventions.

Check the design with experienced neutrals. It takes time to run the key elements of the pilot design past some objective neutral practitioners (for example, mediators, facilitators, arbitrators), but as many design teams have discovered, this is often time well spent. These practitioners can tell whether the construct makes sense to them, whether the pilot offers ADR processes that are likely to be effective for the types of disputes involved, whether the ADR options are arranged in a natural order or progression (from voluntary to rights-based settlement), and whether there are design factors that will work against the process (for example, choosing a dispute arena for the pilot where disputants need a precedent, leading to gravitation toward a rights-based or imposed resolution process).

Determine case selection criteria. How will cases be chosen for inclusion in the ADR pilot? The organization and ADR design team, in collaboration with potential disputants, need to create criteria for selecting cases for inclusion in the pilot, which might include the amount of money involved in the dispute (above or below a certain figure); certain types of disputes (as identified in the assessment); cases filed within a "window" time period, or before or after a certain date; and cases in a given geographical area. Cases can be selected based on the presence of one of these characteristics, or a matrix of characteristics, depending on the population of potential cases and the time frame of the pilot.

Identifying cases whose characteristics make them inappropriate for ADR pilot testing is also wise. For example, cases involving major policy issues might be specifically excluded from the pilot. When notice of the opportunity to engage in ADR is given to potential users, it is useful to include the anticipated organizational criteria for selection as well as for nonselection of cases.

Identify goals and process for evaluating results. Chapter Ten is devoted to a much more detailed discussion and analysis of evaluation philosophy and methodology. The most important task at the implementation stage, however, is to identify the goals of the pilot and the "baseline" or point from which the progress and success of the ADR pilot will be measured. In other words, what component of the conflict management system is being targeted for improvement: is the goal to resolve disputes faster, cheaper, in a more satisfactory manner, or with less publicity? The goals of the pilot, both qualitative and quantitative, need to be clearly identified before the pilot begins. In addition, baseline information against which the results of the pilot will be compared is identified at this point. Measurement of progress toward these goals is an ongoing process throughout the pilot, not merely an analysis conducted at the conclusion of the pilot. Ideally, documents and forms, as well as case tracking systems, are designed to capture the required data from the beginning. In addition, the pilot project design team needs to ensure that information about the progress of the pilot is acquired from all relevant stakeholders, including disputants from both within and outside the organization.

Notify, prepare, and educate participants. Potential pilot participants need to receive adequate information and notice that the opportunity to use ADR exists; they cannot use what they do not know about. Moreover, once selected for inclusion in the pilot, the disputants and organizational participants need to be educated about the ADR processes and procedures they will be using. With the diversity of roles played by individuals in the ADR pilot project, it is important to determine who needs what type of training and to tailor efforts and expend resources accordingly (see the preceding chapter on "Training and Education").

Acquire neutral practitioners. One of the toughest challenges in implementing ADR pilot projects is the acquisition of sufficient numbers of qualified third-party neutrals to help settle the disputes. The issue of whether to use internal or external neutrals raises questions of competence, experience, and perceived "true neutrality." We are aware of several large organizations that successfully use internal neutrals to resolve internal disputes (for example EEO or personnel disputes). We have found that this is not only possible but sometimes preferable where the internal neutrals have credibility within the organization and are perceived as fair and objective. Such use of internal neutrals allows the organization to develop in-house expertise, save costs, and ensure a cadre of neutrals who are familiar with the mission, philosophy, and operation of the organization. On the other hand, outside disputants often have a difficult time accepting an internal neutral as fair and objective and may see the use of internal neutrals as an attempt by the organization to "stack the deck." Other concerns tied to the question of who serves as neutrals, regardless of source, include the need to orient them about the ADR pilot, to ensure that they are qualified and competent, to determine whether they are ready and available to perform as neutrals, and to ensure performance feedback.

Determine how costs will be met. Who will pay the costs, if any, of the neutral provider? Whether the loser pays, the parties split the cost, or the organization always picks up the tab, each method has an effect on the utilization of the ADR procedure. Payment procedures tend to create both incentives and disincentives to use the program or the process. A balancing of such forces is usually the wisest course. For example, as an incentive, the organization may pay the cost of settlement services, including administrative overhead and neutral practitioner services, if the dispute is kept at a certain stage or is settled in a predetermined time period. After that point, all parties to the dispute might split the cost of the neutral evenly. Arrangements such as these can act as incentives to use the system early and to do so with energy, commitment, and speed.

In addition, the question of internal accounting needs to be addressed. Out of whose budget or which organizational department will the costs of dispute resolution come? If all such costs, for example, come out of the legal department's budget, it is crucial that that department be involved in the planning and implementation of the pilot.

Identify incentives to use ADR. Payment of resolution costs is but one incentive that can be used to encourage the use of an ADR approach to settling disputes. Combining a series of such incentives can enhance participation and satisfaction with the ADR pilot approach. For example, some type of merit bonus might be offered to employees who use ADR to resolve particularly difficult or problematic cases; offices or divisions who use ADR regularly can be recognized publicly with awards or through organizational publicity; customers who agree, in advance, to use ADR to resolve any potential disputes may be given preferential terms. These motivators and incentives are explored in more detail in Chapter Eleven, "Incentives and Rewards."

Develop information exchange and case procedures. Depending on the type of ADR proceeding, there may be a need to examine information about the other side's case or to obtain information about how the other side views the organization's case. The design team needs to anticipate whether such an information exchange will be required by the particular ADR process and, if so, develop guidance and procedures on how the exchange will occur, including any documents or forms. For example, the organization may be willing to share information in the interest of settlement but may have concerns about confidentiality, use of documents in subsequent litigation, or disclosure of information to third parties.

In addition, the ADR design team and ADR pilot project coordinator need to identify the information necessary to close a dispute (whether it settles or not) and to develop any necessary evaluation documents. The forms to be completed upon the resolution of the dispute or to signal a dispute's exit out of the ADR process are prepared in advance of the pilot's start-up. This facilitates case tracking and the ongoing measurement of the progress of the cases in the pilot, a subject addressed in more detail in the following chapter.

The Chompist Corporation, for example, may decide to do a

mediation pilot project for consumer complaints. It will need to decide if mediation will be offered in all consumer complaints, in certain categories of disputes, for disputes claiming over a certain dollar amount, in disputes arising out of a particular geographic region, or in disputes at a certain stage. One possibility is for Chompist to engage in good-faith negotiation with the consumer and, if this does not resolve the dispute within a certain period of time, to offer mediation. In addition, Chompist will have to decide whether to offer mediation to both retail and wholesale customers and to develop procedures, brochures, and materials to notify consumers that mediation is available to them. As noted previously, the question of how to obtain mediators will have to be addressed (use of a roster or an outside dispute resolution firm are probably the most viable options for Chompist) as will how these neutrals will be paid (the company and the consumer might split the cost, or to increase the consumers' incentives to use mediation, Chompist might decide instead to offer to pay the entire cost of any mediation services). Chompist will probably want to run the pilot for a short period of time (six to nine months) and then evaluate the results. To facilitate that evaluation, Chompist will need to decide up front what measures will be used to determine the success of the pilot—decreased consumer litigation, increased customer satisfaction, or decreased negative publicity.

Expanding the Pilot Organization-Wide

Once the pilot has been completed and evaluated, it is time to roll out the ADR approach on a wider scale, perhaps throughout the entire organization. At this stage, there may be a tendency for the ADR design team to get sloppy and ignore the three core principles: participation, openness, and feedback. Because the pilot has (ideally) gone well and achieved its goals as measured against the baseline data, there is a tendency to simply take the pilot design and graft it onto another section of the organization's conflict management system. This can be a mistake and may result in the new system rejecting the grafted pilot.

The reality of the rollout phase of implementation is likely to be viewed by the ADR design team as boring or "grunt work." The exciting stages of the intervention—assessment, design, training and

education, pilot program—have been completed. We find it helpful to encourage clients to admit this, affirming that this phase of
the implementation is often tedious—which allows the ADR design
team to go forward in coaching the organization and its stakeholders to stay engaged in a principled fashion during the rollout phase.

Indeed, if the rollout organization-wide is sloppy or goes
poorly, the organizational conclusion is likely to be that the pilot
was successful only because it was new or glitzy or that it worked
only in certain cases or certain offices or certain parts of the country. Thus, the ultimate conclusion will be that ADR is just another
gimmick that does not really work. These conclusions can be
avoided by creating a holistic implementation that weaves ADR into
the organizational fabric. After the pilot, it is helpful if the ADR
design team does not go on "automatic pilot." Here, the "4-T's"
approach to organization-wide implementation can help: tout, test,
tailor, and team.

1.   *Tout the pilot.* Report it, highlight it, talk about it, write
about it. Let people know what worked, as well as what did not and
how it will be fixed. Summarize the results of the pilot in an easy-
to-read format, targeted to the individual audience. Give credit and
recognition to those who participated in the pilot; give them
opportunities to share their experiences about the pilot (meetings,
articles in newsletters, seminars) with others who might use ADR.

Encourage people to disclose their WII-FM (what's in it for
me?). Use rewards and public recognition where possible for
employees, managers, and disputants who participated in the pilot.
Perhaps most important, allow a period of time for the news of the
pilot to travel, time to market the results of the pilot, and time for
the results to sink in before implementing an organization-wide
approach.

If, for example, Hopevale, our hypothetical hospital, decides to
use mediation on a pilot basis in one or both of the lawsuits and the
cases are resolved, it may want to consider using mediation earlier
on in the litigation process or prior to litigation in other disputes.
To pave the way for this, the attorneys may want (within the con-
fines of confidentiality and privilege restrictions) to mention the
successful use of mediation to colleagues, write an article, or speak
about the mediations at professional conferences or seminars.

2.   *Test the pilot.* Do not assume that the design that worked

in the pilot project is automatically appropriate for all types of disputes in all components of the organization. There may be different incentives and constraints at work; ADR processes that were appropriate in one type of dispute may not be appropriate in another, budgetary concerns may be different, and there may need to be a different source of neutrals. For this reason, we urge the design team to go through the ten items listed above under "Implementing a Pilot Program" and test each of them against the new program area before rolling out a full-fledged ADR approach. As always, this exploration is done collaboratively with stakeholders, who are often the best judges of how the new program area will differ from the pilot.

If Hopevale does decide to use ADR in other disputes, it will want to go through the architectural design analysis again to make sure that mediation is the most appropriate form of dispute resolution for that particular case. It may be quite easy for Hopevale to make the assumption that mediation is always the appropriate method of ADR in lawsuits, when this is not in fact true.

3. *Tailor the pilot.* As with architectural design, tailor the pilot to the program. It may be necessary to make modifications to the pilot design to ensure that the ADR approach meets the needs and interests of the stakeholders. Because of the lessons learned from the pilot, and the fact that areas to be explored in the new program have been identified, this redesign can usually be done fairly quickly and often somewhat painlessly.

As experienced practitioners know, it is important at this implementation phase to be alert for pockets of resistance. There will be parts of the organization or there will be managers that continue to resist using ADR, despite the touting of the pilot project results. This resistance stems from a variety of sources, but most are unrelated to the subject area or conduct of the pilot itself. We have found it useful not to fight such resistance at this time. We suggest that design teams make conscious efforts *not* to move into this tension, that they avoid trying to break the resistance, convince the managers of the wisdom of ADR, or impose ADR by getting a mandate from top leadership. Rather, simply refrain from rolling out the implementation into a resistant part of the organization at this time (sometimes easier said than done). Usually, the momentum of the rest of the organization will catch up with the resistant sector, or that part of the system will fail and be ripe for change at a later time. In our experience, some design teams spend far too much time, endless effort, and precious resources trying to break pockets of resistance in the early phases of rollout implementation, usually unsuccessfully. Specific strategies for dealing with resistance are discussed in Chapter Twelve, "Resistance and Constraints."

If Hopevale decides to expand and to introduce ADR into different kinds of lawsuits (such as personnel disputes), Conflict Consultants will want to make sure that Hopevale tailors the results of the pilot to the new target population of cases. Using ADR in these new arenas at Hopevale may involve resistance from quarters other than merely the attorneys in the Legal Department. For example, managers in the Personnel or Human Resource Department may feel that their role is being usurped and their power decreased.

4.   *Team the ADR effort.* Usually, there is an ADR team of coordinators conducting the rollout. Such a team approach allows for brainstorming and joint problem solving as issues arise, the exchange of strategies and practices that are successful, and a shared sense of mission for those involved in the effort. Many design teams have found it useful to have an ADR task force or steering committee, with representatives from all stakeholders and all parts of the organization: managers, disputants, unions, customers, employees. Ideally, the representatives on the team must truly come from all parts of the organization, even those parts that continue to resist ADR. In fact, it is often beneficial (and necessary) to have people on the team who are resistant to ADR. This serves as a reality check and ensures that the interests and needs of *all* stakeholders are being heard and recognized. Obviously, having members who are not in favor of ADR will make the work of the team more challenging, but practitioners have long discovered that the ultimate ADR product created by the very tension in such a team is more realistic, responsive, durable, and satisfactory.

The purpose of the ADR design team is to oversee implementation across the organization and to ensure that the necessary reassessment, redesign, and modification occurs. The team may also need to address systemic issues such as qualifications for neutrals, coordination of training and education efforts, and the need for a written ADR policy. This last point is worth additional comment. We have repeatedly been asked whether top organizational leadership should issue a written ADR policy at the very beginning of the design effort, shortly after entry and contracting. In our experience, this is not helpful and indeed in some organizations may be a hindrance. For example, we are aware of several large institutions, with expansive ADR programs, that issued written ADR policies four years after the program was initiated and in place. Early issuance of an ADR mandate can chill accurate assessment and stifle creative design; it can also freeze in place the new ADR program prematurely. Especially in the early phases of conflict management systems design, the approach to ADR needs to be fluid and flexible, allowing for maximum creativity and learning by the whole organizational system about this subsystem of conflict management. In any case, recognizing that there may be pressure from leadership to issue an ADR mandate, we recommend that the ADR design team hold off issuing one until the organization-wide implementation phase has begun. When issued, the policy needs to emphasize the linkage between ADR and the organization's mission, articulate a vision that appropriate ADR is the responsibility of all employees at all levels of the organization, and clarify that the policy is meant to guide, not limit, the ADR process.

Implementation efforts alone are not enough to assure the use of and satisfaction with the revised conflict management system. Once the system is implemented, the next stage, and the last one of the organization's first pass through the ADR design cycle, is evaluation. The purpose of the evaluation stage is to determine whether the revised system is working and if it is addressing the issues raised in the organization-wide assessment. While we have emphasized throughout this text that evaluation and feedback are ongoing processes during every stage of conflict management systems design, the formal evaluation stage takes a determined look at what has actually been learned and achieved so far in the management of conflict by the organization and its members.

Chapter Ten

Evaluation
Measuring Program Effectiveness

A common belief these days is that alternative dispute resolution (ADR) is "better." The obvious questions are "better than what?" and "if it is better, how do you know?" Also, how do you know if the revised conflict management system is doing what it was designed to do? In this chapter, we look at evaluating ADR systems; specifically, we explore measuring program effectiveness, results, and impact, as well as program administration and delivery.

As the primary method of feedback, evaluation is the means by which the system clarifies its goals and measures progress toward and achievement of those goals. The conflict management system changes in response to the evaluation process. Similar to the other aspects of designing a conflict management system, an effective evaluation process relies on participation, openness, and feedback. Evaluation is often viewed as the last step or final phase in the design effort and therefore is sometimes practiced with little enthusiasm. In some organizations, the methodology of conflict management evaluation has traditionally been decided by "experts" or program analysts, with little input from the disputants and stakeholders.

To improve this methodology and to make the evaluation process more interest based and responsive to specific organizational and stakeholder needs, we suggest that the evaluation process be created at the *beginning* of the conflict management design effort, not at the end. Some may see this as eating one's dessert before the main course, but there is a good reason for it. Designing the evaluation methodology at the beginning of the intervention ensures that the evaluation is measuring progress continuously in accordance with the system's defined goals and objectives. One stated goal might be to increase customer satisfaction. Another might be to decrease the costs of dispute resolution. Each of these goals requires a different form of evaluation, one primarily qualitative and the other more quantitative. Because evaluation is objective, it is similar to design architecture in that it needs to be tailored to system and stakeholder needs. Integrating evaluation aspects into the design from the beginning—what needs to be measured, in what manner will data be collected, how will results be used—and continually conducting evaluation throughout the design process increases the likelihood that the design will be adjusted to achieve the stated ADR and organizational goals.

Second, the evaluation goals and methodology must be understood and agreed to by the organization's leadership and the ADR design team. Anything less is likely to result in a failure to achieve the objectives of the effort and, even more important, in confusion and inconsistency in the implementation stage. Such lack of clarity and consensus in identifying ADR objectives will show up in some manner in any evaluation conducted.

Most evaluation models measure whether goals have been achieved at the completion of the program. We suggest that evaluation be used to measure *progress* toward goal achievement as well—a continuous process providing feedback during the conflict management change effort in order to improve the product. In this way, modifications are made as they become necessary. Similar to the benefits of conducting a pilot project, evaluation during the design process allows the system to resolve problems along the way, responding quickly to the need for change and incorporating creative alternatives as they become apparent. Thus, the organization and its conflict management system participants stay in a learning mode throughout the process of change.

The evaluation of a conflict management system, or any system for that matter, creates a logical sequence of processes and tasks that clarify goals and produce consequences, which may then result in a reclarification of the established goals. In this way, evaluation processes can be seen as cyclical in nature (see Figure 10.1).

Each of the components of the evaluation cycle is explored in greater detail below.

Figure 10.1. Evaluation Cycle.

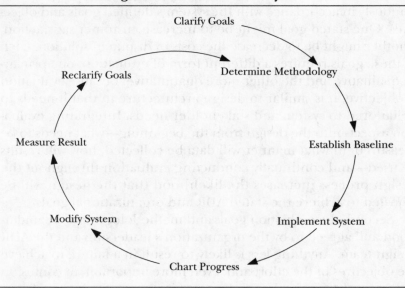

Clarify Goals

Clarity is the key to evaluation. Each type of measure has a different focus, and each produces different evaluation methods. It is possible, for example, to evaluate the *effectiveness or impact* of the conflict management system (whether the system is meeting its goals) or to evaluate the *administration or operation* of the conflict management system (whether the system is operating efficiently). "Impact" measures of effectiveness examine the effect of the program on users and participants, on the accomplishment of the organizational mission, and on results. "Administrative" measures of efficiency examine the structure and delivery of the ADR program and its services.

Early on in their work, ADR design teams need to be clear about how evaluation results will be used. For example, will they be used to modify the system as needed? Will they be used primarily for management, production, or statistical purposes? Will they be used to reward those who have championed and used the new system? Will they be used as a marketing tool to interest other disputants in using the system? Will they be used to allocate future resources for the conflict management system? Discussion among the organization's stakeholders about conflict management system goals increases the likelihood that there will be congruency between such goals and their measurement. This is most easily and naturally done as part of the organizational assessment process discussed in Chapter Six. Almost at the beginning of their efforts, for example, the doctor-nurse practice committee at Hopevale will need to examine how their joint problem-solving efforts, training, and dispute panels are working. One method might be to do a "before" and "after" survey of doctors and nurses from different locations and specialties to ascertain whether the patterns of communication, behavior, and attitudes have changed in any way, and if so, whether the change is attributed to the work of the committee.

Determine Methodology

Once there is a common understanding about the goals of the ADR effort, attention shifts to how the achievement of such goals will be measured and what criteria will be used to measure them. The differences among the goals—effectiveness/impact and administration/operation—supply potential definition to the criteria for measurement. As can be seen in Table 10.1, each criteria of efficiency, effectiveness, and satisfaction can be broken into measurable components. In the following discussion of each component of measurement, an array of questions and brief illustrations

Table 10.1. Measurement of ADR Effectiveness/Impact.

Criteria	Measurement
Efficiency	Change in Cost
	Change in Time
Effectiveness	Nature of Outcome
	Durability of Resolution
	Effect on Environment
Satisfaction	With Process
	With Relationship
	With Outcome

help to elicit information about that component and its relationship to the impact on ADR introduction.

Measurement of Efficiency

Change in Cost: Does the system decrease the cost of conflict management to the organization and its stakeholders? Does it directly decrease dollars spent on conflict management? Does it affect intangible costs such as workforce motivation, lost opportunity, or reputation in the marketplace?

At Federal Securities Management Agency (FSMA), this may require gathering baseline figures on how much time and money the agency currently (pre-ADR) spends on the resolution of hostile work environment disputes and measuring them against the time and dollar costs after the introduction of ADR. At Chompist, it may mean quantifying the costs of resolving consumer disputes before and after the establishment of an ombudsperson. At Hopevale, it may mean comparing the costs of prospective litigation with the costs of mediation.

Change in Time: Does the introduction of ADR in the conflict management system decrease the time that it takes to resolve disputes, that employees devote to managing conflict (rather than to work performance), or that a dispute is "on the books"?

For example, at FSMA, can investor claims be resolved more quickly through arbitration than through the courts? If so, what is the time value of the money saved? At Chompist, does the establishment of a company ombudsperson free the time of other employees from complaint handling? At Hopevale, is it faster to resolve vendor disputes through mediation than through litigation and, if so, what are the savings in time spent?

Measurement of Effectiveness

Nature of Outcome: Does the revised conflict management system increase the number of disputes resolved through nonadversarial means? Does it change the nature of the outcomes? Does it decrease the number of steps or "levels" that a dispute must go through to be resolved?

For example, at FSMA, do fewer employee disputes go to formal processes such as complaints, investigations, and litigation if ADR is an option at the precomplaint stage? Are the awards reached through arbitration of investor claims substantively or quantitatively different than those achieved through litigation? At Chompist, does the use of a labor-management safety committee decrease the number of OSHA complaints filed?

Durability of Resolution: Does having ADR options in the conflict management system increase the experience that, once settled, disputes stay resolved? Does it increase compliance with settlements and resolutions?

At Hopevale, do the resolutions achieved by the doctor-nurse practice committee "stick," or do the same players appear over and over again? Do Chompist's customers return to do business with the company after they have resolved a consumer complaint through mediation or the ombudsperson? At FSMA, is there a decrease in the number of repeat employee complainants when their dispute is resolved through an ADR process?

Effect on Environment: Does the introduction of ADR into the system improve the image or perception of the organization in the marketplace or in the workplace? Does it identify and remedy systemic roots of disputes and therefore enhance the organization's image and acceptability to employees, managers, regulators, and customers? Do the ADR efforts decrease the inventory or backlog of disputes and release human and capital resources for other organizational goals?

For example, is Chompist's reputation in the marketplace improved as a result of its consumer ADR program? Are customers more satisfied? Do they continue to purchase Chompist products? Is Hopevale's reputation in the community improved as a result of the search conference on the nature and direction of health care provision in the community? Is FSMA's reputation in the federal government and the financial marketplace improved as a result of its use of ADR to resolve investor claims?

Measurement of Satisfaction

With Process: Does the introduction of ADR increase satisfaction with conflict management processes—either of customers, clients, employees, or managers? Is the perception of fairness raised? Does

ADR make more sense to system participants—with respect to the appropriateness or utility of alternative dispute resolution in the organizational context? Does it affect stakeholders' views that they have more control over their destiny when dealing with disputes and more active involvement in resolving them?

At FSMA, for example, do employees with disputes feel that they have a greater opportunity to be "heard out" on the complex dynamics that have resulted in their perception that the work environment is hostile? Do the production workers on the line at Chompist feel that they have a credible forum in which to identify safety issues and in which real action will be taken on constructive suggestions? Do the doctors and nurses at Hopevale believe that they now have a credible and action-oriented forum where inter-staff disputes will be examined and relieved?

With Relationship: Does ADR in the system improve or change the perceptions and levels of understanding between and among the parties to a dispute about their differing values, interests, and concerns? Does it increase the disputants' skills and abilities in communication with each other? Does it increase trust and decrease the level of conflict between disputing parties? Does it result in more effective working relationships?

At FSMA, do the affected employees believe that the relationship with supervisors has improved as a result of ADR? Do the production workers and supervisors at Chompist have a more cooperative and problem-solving orientation in their dealings with each other and with issues in the workplace? Have the day-to-day working relationships between doctors and nurses at Hopevale changed in any way as a result of training, education, and dispute resolution efforts?

With Outcome: Does the introduction of ADR in the system result in outcomes that satisfy the disputing parties—in terms of fairness, cost, time, and quality? Does it increase the likelihood that they will use ADR again or recommend its use to others?

At FSMA, are the investors satisfied with the arbitration awards, or do they believe they could have done better in litigation? At Chompist, do consumers believe they got a fair shake? At Hopevale, are the in-house attorneys satisfied that the use of mediation resulted in a credible resolution of the vendor or malpractice lawsuits—that they achieved as good a deal as they could have through litigation?

From criteria by which to measure effectiveness and impact of the ADR processes themselves, we now turn to criteria by which to measure the ADR goals of administration/operation. As can be seen in Table 10.2, the criteria are different when measurement is focused on functional competence. In the following discussion, we again examine an array of questions and brief illustrations to explain how one measures program administration and delivery.

Measurement of Functional Organization

Structure and Procedures: Is the structure of the conflict management system congruent with organizational culture and mission? Are the procedures to use the system made easily understandable to organizational stakeholders and outside disputants? Do the ADR structure and procedures accurately reflect and convey the system's design and its philosophy?

At FSMA, for example, can employees "picture" the structure of complaint processing and see where ADR efforts fit in? Is it clear what they have to do to use ADR procedures prior to filing a formal

Table 10.2. Measurement of ADR Administration/Operation.

Criteria	Measurement
Functional Organization	Structure and Procedures
	Guidelines and Standards
	Lines of Responsibility
	Sufficiency of Resources
	Coordination of Relationships
Service Delivery	Access to System
	Procedures in Use
	Selection of Cases
Program Quality	Training and Education
	Selection of Neutrals
	Competence of Neutrals

complaint? How are FSMA employees informed of the existence of procedures—and does every employee have a copy? At Hopevale, how are the opposing parties in the lawsuits informed and advised of the ADR options? At Chompist, do consumers think that the establishment of a company ombudsperson and of ADR procedures for complaints is a good fit with their view of what the company should be concerned about and how it should act?

Guidelines and Standards: Do the guidelines and standards regarding use and selection of ADR options provide sufficient detail to those who will administer and operate the system? Are the standards written and readily available? Is there a process to modify the standards and guidelines in response to feedback?

At FSMA, are there any types of investor claims where the agency has determined ADR would be inappropriate, and how has this determination been communicated to staff and investors? At Chompist, how is it determined when a consumer complaint will be referred for mediation, and are there cases where the company has determined it will not offer ADR? At Hopevale, are there guidelines to determine whether a lawsuit is appropriate for ADR? Who makes the final decision of whether or not a case is appropriate for ADR?

Lines of Responsibility: Does the delineation of responsibilities for operation and administration of the ADR program make it clear to internal and external constituents who is responsible for what? Does it allow and encourage responsibility for resolution at the earliest possible opportunity and at the lowest organizational level?

At FSMA, who does one call to discuss ADR options in hostile work environment disputes? Is it the same person for employees as well as supervisors? At Chompist, can sales personnel continue to attempt to resolve customer complaints through negotiation? Can they also seek advice and assistance from the ombudsperson's office? At Hopevale, do doctors and nurses always have to take their disputes through the joint practice committee or can they attempt to resolve them informally among themselves?

Sufficiency of Resources: Has the organization allocated sufficient resources (time, money, and people) to the conflict management effort? What procedures are in place to evaluate the sufficiency of resources on an ongoing basis?

For example, at FSMA, how many in-house mediators are available to facilitate resolution of employee disputes? At Chompist, if the number of consumer complaints escalates dramatically, will consumers have to wait to speak to the ombudsperson when he or she gets to them or will the company provide additional trained staff to handle the increased volume? At Hopevale, are there sufficient in-house attorneys with ADR expertise to participate in a meaningful way in mediation or other forms of ADR? If not, will others be trained and educated?

Coordination of Relationships: Is there coordination among the various components of the ADR system internally and between it and the other conflict management system components? Are the working relationships among all functional components of the conflict management system effective and focused on delivering the organization's overall goals in dispute resolution efforts? Is information about disputes, progress on resolution efforts, developing trends, and results achieved shared both within and between the ADR and traditional components of the conflict management system?

For example, at FSMA, how does the ADR pilot project coordinator interact with Larry Terrence, the agency dispute resolution specialist—do they share information readily and act as a team? What is the relationship, both formal and informal, among the ADR pilot project coordinator, Larry Terrence, and the Office of the General Counsel—are they competing or collaborating? At Chompist, how does the ombudsperson interact with the Legal Department—do they respect what the other has to offer in the fulfillment of the company's goals, or are they engaged in a "turf contest" or territorial battle? At Hopevale, how do the members of the doctor-nurse practice committee interact with other dispute resolution components such as the Legal Department and the Personnel Office? Have they isolated themselves or have they reached out for ideas and help on thorny problems?

Measurement of Service Delivery

Access to System: How do stakeholders, both internal and external to the organization, find out about the conflict management system? Are there restrictions on who can use the system, the types of cases that can be brought forward, or the timing of resolutions? What are the perceptions about the accessibility of the system? What impact do these perceptions about accessibility have on system usage?

With respect to FSMA's arbitration option, how do investors find out about it? Are the attorneys who routinely represent investors alerted to the option's existence and offered the same opportunity to explore its benefits? Is there a brochure or videotape that explains the program? At Chompist, do all consumers have an opportunity to use the ombudsperson's services, even if they do not speak English? Are there restrictions at Hopevale about the kinds of disputes that can be presented to the doctor-nurse practice committee—for example, questions concerning ethics, certain medical procedures, or patient abuse?

Procedures in Use: Do users understand how the ADR aspects of the system work? Do they understand its limitations, restrictions, and time frames?

Do employees at FSMA understand the ADR process and know that their complaints will be kept in confidence? Do the consumers at Chompist understand that they retain all of their legal rights, even though mediation is pursued as a method of resolution? Do opposing parties in the vendor dispute understand the settlement authority of Hopevale's in-house attorneys when they engage in mediation?

Selection of Cases: How do disputes get into the ADR component of the conflict management system? At what stage in the dispute is the case considered? Is case selection criteria known, appropriate, and fair? Is there any correlation between the types of disputes, the size of disputes, and/or the stage of disputes and the predicted outcome? Are certain cases more likely to be resolved through the ADR component of the conflict management system than others? What are the characteristics of those cases?

At Chompist, when does a consumer complaint escalate into a dispute and enter the mediation process? At Hopevale, are medical malpractice cases as likely to be resolved through ADR as other types of cases, such as vendor disputes? At FSMA, do employees have the right to "opt out" of the ADR processes attendant to hostile work environment disputes?

Measurement of Program Quality

Training and Education: What training and educational efforts are conducted? Who is trained? Who delivers the training? Was the training and/or education appropriate for the target audience in terms of length, format, and content? Do ADR system participants feel that they received adequate training and education about the ADR program, the options available to them, and the appropriate way to access the system? Do those trained believe that the trainers were knowledgeable and presented the information understandably? Were interactive learning techniques employed appropriately? What impact does the type or amount of training and/or education have on the use of the ADR system and on the outcomes achieved?

For example, did the doctors and nurses at Hopevale find the joint problem-solving, interest-based communication training useful? If not, what would they like to see changed? Do Chompist managers who participated in the reg-neg (negotiated rule making) feel they were adequately prepared through advance training and education efforts? Have FSMA's briefings on ADR and its internal use informed all stakeholders about the basics of ADR, the reasons the agency is establishing such opportunities in its dispute resolution efforts, and where employees can access the system if need be?

Selection of Neutrals: Are participants satisfied with the method by which neutrals are selected? Are participants involved in the selection process and if not, why not? What impact does participant involvement in neutral selection have on outcomes achieved?

Has FSMA established a list of in-house neutrals for employee disputes? Are the individual neutrals considered acceptable, fair, and unbiased by FSMA employees and supervisors? How do consumers at Chompist get involved in the neutral selection process? If they are given a roster from which to select a mediator, are they informed of the differences among mediator qualifications and assisted in making the best selection possible given their interests? How were the mediators selected in the Hopevale lawsuits, and are the other parties satisfied that their involvement in selection was freely sought by the hospital?

Competence of Neutrals: Were participants satisfied with the qualifications and competence of the neutrals? Do they feel the neutrals were sufficiently trained? Do they believe that the neutrals understood the substance of the dispute? Do they believe the neutrals were fair and objective in handling the dispute? Can a relationship be identified between disputants' views of neutral competency and dispute outcomes?

What do FSMA employees and managers using the ADR procedures think about the in-house neutrals with respect to knowledge of the process and of the substance at hand? Did the employees and managers perceive the neutrals, even though they were also FSMA employees, to be fair? Were the mediators in Hopevale's lawsuits efficient and effective in resolving the disputes, as well as sensitive to the relationships among doctors, family, and patient, and between pharmaceutical company and hospital? What did consumers think about their experience with the mediators on the Chompist-provided roster—biased in favor of the company or fair and equitable in the handling of the consumer dispute?

Establish Baseline

Most ADR design teams and relevant stakeholders will need to decide collaboratively which of the above criteria are particularly relevant to their needs and therefore must be measured. With the answers in hand, they will then need to decide what the evaluation results will be compared with in order to determine whether in fact the ADR additions to the conflict management system are an improvement. Will the evaluation data be compared to litigation costs and results? To negotiation costs and results? To the costs and results of failing to resolve the dispute? What baseline data will be needed with which to compare the evaluation results? Where will such baseline information be available—management and annual reports, case studies and statistics? What sources are available for qualitative data, such as satisfaction with outcome and effects on relationships?

In instances where baseline data is not available for comparison, it may be necessary to reconstruct or gather it from a variety of sources. If this is necessary, how will it be done? We have found that this is the most recurrent challenge to ADR evaluations. In more cases than not, there has been no organized past practice of collecting, evaluating, and aggregating current dispute resolution information about cost, time, and satisfaction with results. Such information is often considered one of the "buried costs" of doing business and is therefore information that must be constructed to ascertain the past nature and attendant cost of conflict in the organization.

At FSMA, the ADR pilot project coordinator will need to obtain (or develop if they are not available) baseline statistics on the time and cost of formal dispute resolution of employee disputes. Anne Logan at Chompist will need to come up with a way of measuring the cost and time involved in the company's past handling or failure to handle consumer complaints. At Hopevale, the Legal Department will need to generate data regarding the anticipated cost of litigation (including appeal) in the two pending lawsuits, with contingent liability projections.

Implement System

As discussed in Chapter Nine, the system is usually implemented gradually, perhaps starting with a pilot project or experimental system that can be modified as needed. Although not strictly a part of the evaluation effort, actions taken throughout implementation are integral to the successful performance of the steps in the evaluation cycle. The manner and style of ADR implementation is the bridge to each of the next evaluation steps of charting progress, modifying the system, measuring results, and reclarifying goals. In a sense, without an ongoing partnership between the processes of implementation and of evaluation, insufficient information will be generated with which to compare the status quo of the conflict management system and the results of the introduction of ADR alternatives.

Chart Progress

Many practitioners have found it useful to measure progress *toward* goals, not simply achievement *of* goals. At some point, perhaps three to six months after the system has been implemented or the pilot project started, it is useful to conduct a "reality check." Its purpose is to determine whether the system is doing what it said it would do—whether stakeholders are satisfied, whether goals are being met, whether the system is operating the way it was intended, or whether any noteworthy changes have resulted.

The method of evaluation will vary depending upon the particular characteristics and needs of the system and its stakeholders, but participative, face-to-face feedback is encouraged to ensure accurate and comprehensive data. It is not necessary at this interim stage to compare the preliminary results to the baseline data, although a "snapshot" is possible and can give system evaluators an idea of how well the system is operating and can expose any noticeable shifts. We have found it helpful, however, to ask organizational participants the following basic questions regarding this early stage of implementation of ADR in the conflict management system: (1) What should we *start* doing? (2) What should we *stop* doing? (3) What should we *continue* doing?

At Hopevale, the doctor-nurse practice committee could be encouraged to do a start-stop-continue feedback session at the end of each significant effort to improve interstaff dealings. At Chompist, such stop-start-continue feedback could be an ongoing part of its initiatives with the production workers and with the consumers. At FSMA, the same process would capture early information about how things were going in both the internal employee dispute ADR program and the external investor ADR claims procedures. In all three instances, the goal is to measure progress during the implementation effort and not wait until the end to learn that something is not working or needs to be fixed.

Modify System

Based on the responses to these or similar questions, the ADR initiatives can be modified in an ongoing fashion where necessary and appropriate. Such feedback can be looped back into the design effort, with alterations made to improve utility and responsiveness. Again, ideally, the decision to modify the system at this stage is made in consultation and agreement with other conflict management system stakeholders.

In addition, modifications made as the result of information gained through evaluation can act as real motivators for ADR system use and acceptance: such action signals a willingness to learn by ADR system administrators as well as leadership, and it demonstrates that concerns are taken seriously. Evaluation can also prevent a flawed system from continuing to the point that acceptability is lost, results are disappointing, or scarce resources are wasted.

At Chompist, for example, consumers may be confused about the role of the ombudsperson; they may be frustrated by this individual's lack of real decision-making authority to "fix" their complaint—thus indicating that the ombudsperson needs to be more clear, in writing as well as verbally, about his or her role and function regarding relief of specific complaints. In a similar fashion, there may be misperceptions about the role of Hopevale's doctor-nurse practice committee; some nurses, for example, may view it as a disciplinary board. This misunderstanding could be cleared up by additional informational efforts, in-service training, and town meetings among the professional population, planned and carried out in close collaboration with the nurses' union. At FSMA, some employees may believe that the in-house FSMA mediators report back to higher management and relate the information disclosed to them in the mediation. Correcting this misperception might require a written notice explicitly stating the confidential nature of the mediation process and the steps to follow if complainants believe such confidentiality has been violated by any management official or agency neutral involved in their dispute.

Measure Result

Despite the ongoing learning and self-correction processes encouraged and built into every phase of ADR implementation, there eventually comes a time when the results of the ADR efforts as a whole must be measured to determine whether the organization's conflict management goals are being met.

Ideally, an advance determination is made, usually during the contracting or assessment stage, of when results will be measured—after a certain number of cases have been resolved, after a certain amount of time has passed, or after a certain amount of resources have been spent. It is at this phase of the evaluation cycle that the results of the ADR program are compared to baseline data. Here, the complete picture is drawn of the integration of ADR systems improvement and its impact on the organization's management of conflict.

How this comparison is performed and the shape of it is largely determined by the organizational goals initially identified, the purpose for which the evaluation and comparison data will be used, and the target audience that will receive the evaluation. For example, if the results will be used to market the system to potential users, the format is one that addresses their concerns and is tailored to answer "what's in it for them." If, on the other hand, the purpose of the evaluation is to justify allocation of additional resources for the ADR system, the format will probably need to be more quantitative in nature. As noted previously, just as the conflict management system has multiple goals and stakeholders, so too with the results of evaluation. As always, it is important to address as many of the ADR system's goals as possible and to be responsive to the concerns and needs of a variety of populations in the evaluation.

For example, the time and cost of mediating FSMA employee disputes can be compared with the time and cost of the complaint/investigation/litigation process. At Hopevale, the Legal Division may decide that it wants to hire an attorney to work solely on ADR matters and needs additional resources from the board of directors to do so. Estimating the dollars saved in litigation costs through the use of ADR in the two lawsuits would be useful information for the board's budget committee to have in considering the request. At Chompist, President Teznicki may be interested in knowing what effect use of an ombudsperson and mediation have had on customer relations so that he can include a paragraph on ADR in the annual report.

Reclarify Goals

By using the results of the evaluation, the goals of the ADR component in the conflict management system are then reclarified as needed. This keeps the system responsive to its experience and to its environment. For example, the evaluation may show that stakeholders are not using the system because they do not view it as accessible. Whether this is actually true is less important to system utilization than the perception by disputants that it is true. An evaluation finding to this effect could result in changes to ADR criteria, practices, and priorities relating to accessibility, education, and personnel. If, however, accessibility was never considered to be a goal of ADR efforts, it could become a new one based on the results of the evaluation.

In addition, in a conflict management system where the initial goals were largely quantitative in nature (such as increased usage of system, decreased cost and time to resolve disputes), the goals may gradually change over time to become more qualitative (for example, increased disputant satisfaction or improved relationships). As with all open systems, the organization's conflict management goals and evaluative processes will continually evolve to reflect the impact of a changing environment and of the shifting needs of its stakeholders.

At FSMA, the initial evaluation may reveal that employees and managers are reluctant to use the mediation process because the mediators are FSMA employees; the agency may have to decide to use neutrals from other agencies or outside neutrals to increase the acceptability of the ADR process. At Hopevale, evaluation results may reveal that the doctors and nurses think that the joint practice committee lacks any real authority to make a difference; management there may decide to give them more authority or to seek a more effective method of overcoming interstaff disputes. At Chompist, evaluation results may reveal that the joint labor-management safety committee is very useful and effective at not only resolving safety disputes but in preventing them. As a result, President Teznicki may urge the ADR design team to explore whether to expand the concept into other areas.

As can be seen from all the above, an interest-based ADR system evaluation is thus a process that follows an evolutionary cycle, responsive to user concerns and attentive to the need for measurable results. Such a comprehensive and ongoing approach to evaluation woven into the fabric of the conflict management systems design itself can help identify areas for modification, point out resistance and constraints, and assist in system troubleshooting.

In Part Two, we have identified and explored the "how-to" aspects of interest-based conflict management systems design.

Inevitably, given the ongoing and fluid nature of organizational design work, practitioners will encounter roadblocks and resistance in their change interventions. Therefore, we turn now in Part Three to the motivation, troubleshooting, and acceptance aspects of conflict management systems design.

Part Three

Making the System Work

Chapter Eleven

Incentives and Rewards
Creating Support for the System

Once a conflict management system or an ADR (alternative dispute resolution) program is implemented, how does the organization support its use? As practitioners have seen time and time again, effective contracting, assessing, designing, training, educating, implementing, and evaluating efforts do not necessarily mean that participants wind up actually using the system. If the incentives to use the conflict management system are too weak or the constraints acting against its use are too strong, disputants will probably default to the status quo—the current dispute resolution program—rather than struggle with the revised system.

Where incentives (both individual and organizational) to use new ADR processes and procedures are maximized and constraints are minimized, the likelihood that stakeholders will try out the new system is increased. Applying the basic principles of force field analysis, pushing harder on the forces driving a change (incentives) in the way conflict is managed in the organization does not usually create change by itself; it may in fact simply make organizational members more aware of the need for change without causing any movement in that direction.

We recognize that there are limitations to focusing here on incentives and rewards, especially in light of the dynamic nature of an organization's conflict management system. However, our experience has shown us the unique power of incentives and rewards for answering the "what's in it for me?" (WII-FM) question in conflict management change.

While the terms *incentives* and *rewards* are often used synonymously, we believe they are not the same. They address different needs, promote different sets of behaviors, and serve varying purposes. Incentives look forward, encourage positive future behavior, and are often intangible: accomplishment of the organizational vision and mission, ownership of the conflict resolution process, improvement of products or services, enhanced interactions with customers and employees, or involvement in the "new, different, and unique." At Hopevale, for example, community members may be energized by being part of a search process for the future of health care provision in the community or with the idea of "getting the whole system" in the room, regardless of the topic addressed (Weisbord, 1987).

Rewards on the other hand look backward and recognize past behavior; they are often tangible and may take the form of bonuses or merit raises, performance-based pay, plaques, certificates, or awards. At Hopevale, a decision to recognize those who have been instrumental in enhancing the management of conflict in the hospital might take the form of an annual awards ceremony. The hospital might add an "ADR Advances" column to the hospital's quarterly newsletter, where individual and collective efforts to pursue improved dispute resolution practices are highlighted. In this way, both incentives and rewards activity can produce increased energy and motivation for those who work with and use the conflict management system.

It is also important to be clear about the target audience toward whom incentives and rewards are directed. Middle managers may be motivated by different incentives and rewards than executives, than administrative personnel, than end users. In fact, each different interest and functional grouping of those involved in the organization's conflict management system probably has distinct preferences when it comes to motivators. Many might think that an approach to the question of differing incentives and rewards preferences among these groups deserves a chart representing what appeals to the different groups. We have resisted such a temptation and offer instead a categorization of the potential universe of rewards or incentives that can serve as motivators for a variety of organizational participants in reinforcing and stabilizing the use of the changed conflict management system. In this way, we seek to reinforce one of the core principles of interest-based design: active participation of relevant stakeholders in the design of key aspects of their ADR system—in this case, the voluntary identification of what would be satisfactory incentive and reward components. This is exploration and discovery that we believe is best left to stakeholders and leadership working together. Too many reward systems have been created by "the few" for "the many" with little or no input from those who will be affected. Thus, many organizational leaders have been startled by how "off the mark" and unsatisfactory their selections of incentive and reward systems have been as a result.

What we believe we can contribute to this discussion is a more general focus on the variety of incentives and rewards that serve to energize stakeholders as individuals, both within and outside the organization, to use the ADR system. We wish to stimulate the thinking of all those engaged in developing incentives and rewards for using ADR, as well as to enhance an understanding of how rich and varied motivators in general can be. Therefore, a sampling of distinct incentive and reward categories is illustrated below, which we find suitable for application in the ADR context.

For Organizational Stakeholders

Incentives and rewards for internal users, employees, managers, supervisors, and administrators communicate appreciation for their use of the new ADR components of the conflict management system and for their assumption of responsibilities for its implementation and administration.

Recognition

Some people are motivated by the need or desire to be recognized—to be affirmed for having done a good job and for being part of an effective ADR pilot program or organization-wide implementation effort. They appreciate recognition by their peers and supervisors for taking risks, for being innovative, and for competencies such as knowledge and efficiency. The roles in which these individuals make their contributions might vary, such as providing training or coordinating evaluation efforts. Recognition for such

involvement can take many forms: verbal gratitude, written com-
mendations, specific attribution in organizational newsletters or
publications, and requests to represent the organization's efforts
in ADR publicly through speaking assignments or written articles.

At FSMA, the ADR pilot project coordinator may be an individual who is motivated by recognition; a special performance award
or cameo article about him or her in the agency newsletter may
serve this purpose well.

Being Part of a Team

Some individuals are motivated by being asked to be a part of a
group effort—being involved as a member of an organizational
ADR task force engaged in helping to design the conflict management system initially, solving a particular ADR application problem,
or evaluating and improving the ADR system during the rollout
phase. Such individuals feel honored to be included and consulted
for the ideas they bring to an organizational improvement effort.
Some additional benefits these contributors seek may be the opportunity to "be in the know" about new organizational developments,
the excitement of grass-roots involvement in organization-wide
efforts and change, or the chance to meet and work closely with
other individuals who have a stake in the organization, as part of a
collective effort. At Chompist, some production employees may be
motivated by being asked to join a team effort to meaningfully
improve workplace safety.

Creation of New Initiatives

Some organizational members are natural risk takers; they are
motivated and energized by being seen as responsible innovators
of new ideas and by the application of those ideas to the ongoing
life of the organization. They may like to be involved in cutting-
edge initiatives that will change the organization in a worthy and
progressive direction. More often than not, these individuals are
easily bored with the routine and enjoy direct involvement in projects that stir things up. These individuals often thrive on the new
and on the creation of better organizational systems and methods. They often make valuable and significant contributions as

members of stakeholder teams assisting in the various aspects of interest-based design, especially the architectural construction and evaluation phases.

At FSMA, the agency's dispute resolution specialist, Larry Terrence, may be strongly motivated to create new initiatives and for that reason stepped forward to volunteer for this responsible yet potentially high-risk assignment in the agency.

Achievement of Organizational Mission

Some people are not risk takers; they are most highly motivated by the achievement of the established organizational mission. These individuals often prefer clearly defined goals and predictable outcomes, or they have an interest in creating a secure and stable future within the organization. Regardless of the reason, such individuals get the message when improved conflict management becomes a high organizational priority and they get on board by devoting energy, time, and effort to ensure that the ADR system becomes institutionalized.

At Chompist, some members of the reg-neg (negotiated rule making) team may see this new method of promulgating regulations as a direct benefit to organizational performance and survival; hence, they will work to ensure the reg-neg's success.

Fulfilling Personal Visions and Values

In contrast to those who are externally motivated, other organizational members are driven by personal vision and values, in the hopes of embedding them into the organization itself. Such individuals seek to achieve a greater alignment of the organization's beliefs with their own beliefs and a greater congruency between mission and practice. Seeing themselves as organizational change agents, these individuals look for ways to make the organization more human, more responsive, more receptive, more open. Promotion and advocacy for the ADR system is a natural for them since ADR's values and practices help those engaged in conflict within or outside the organization. Where ADR efforts result in, among other things, more satisfied customers and colleagues, such efforts are perceived by these internally driven individuals as serving a greater good. According to Maslow's hierarchy of needs (1954), some individuals, such as these stakeholders, will be motivated by seeing their work of involvement with the ADR system as a "self-actualizing" activity—making a contribution that is congruent with deeply held personal needs, values, and beliefs.

At Chompist, Jeff Linton of Conflict Consultants may be motivated to do the kind of work he does in the area of conflict management because it is personally congruent with his own values and is part of his personal vision of a more peaceful world where people work together to overcome and resolve conflict.

Increased Efficiency or Effectiveness

In contrast to the motivating forces of personally held values, other individuals are driven by a desire to develop more effective and more efficient systems in the workplace and in the marketplace. They see the conflict management system as needing to be finely tuned so that it operates smoothly and quietly, eliminating disruption of the "real work" of the organization. Such individuals are concerned with logical, predictable, and rational administration of the entire conflict management system as a means to improve overall organizational results. Thus, the efficiency aspects of introducing ADR into the existing conflict management system—less cost, time, disruption—will be strong motivators and incentives for these individuals to work for implementation and use of the system.

The doctors and nurses who serve on Hopevale's joint practice committee may come up with a variety of methods for handling interstaff conflicts because of a drive to create an environment in which the science and delivery of health care may proceed efficiently and effectively.

Economics

Lastly, some organizational members are strongly motivated by pure economics. If they know that they will receive a bonus, pay-for-performance increase, or other tangible economic benefit if they champion or use the ADR program, they will do so. Surprisingly, research has demonstrated that economic incentives are not the powerful workplace motivators they were once thought to be. It appears that people are more strongly motivated by some of the intangible incentives and rewards listed above rather than by pure dollars. In spite of such findings, it may be useful to offer economic rewards in tandem with other incentives to ensure successful ADR implementation.

If, for example, the ADR pilot project coordinator at FSMA knows that he or she is likely to be awarded a within-grade raise under federal pay guidelines for successful administration of the ADR project, the possibility will serve as one more incentive for that individual to put the extra time and effort needed into the project.

For External Stakeholders

Thought needs to be given as well to improving the incentives and rewards for external stakeholders to use the ADR system. In many designs, almost no thought is given to how these stakeholders—mostly suppliers and customers—will be made aware of the opportunity to use the ADR system. Even less attention is often given to identifying and creating appropriate incentives and rewards for external stakeholders to actually use ADR. It makes sense to involve such individuals in brainstorming, either through focus groups or surveys, those motivators that would increase ADR's appeal to external constituents. Listed below are some of the factors that may serve as incentives and rewards for external stakeholders' involvement and use of the ADR system.

Positive Publicity

Like the organization itself, external customers and individuals are often driven by their perception of their image as innovative, cooperative, responsive, public-spirited, and efficient. If they are seen as participating in the resolution of disputes with the values of innovation, responsiveness, and efficiency, their public image as socially conscious and responsible citizens is enhanced. In addition, there may a public relations or competitive advantage gained by being the first customer or client to use a new ADR conflict management system instituted by a public institution—government agency or court system—or by a private company.

In the case of Chompist, for example, state officials may be motivated to offer reg-neg if it can be pointed out that such an action will enhance their reputation for concern about customer-friendly approaches to regulation and for litigation cost savings in the eyes of the public, the regulated community, and the legislature.

Increased Efficiency and Effectiveness

Outside stakeholders may also be driven to use a new ADR system for reasons of cost effectiveness and timeliness. Thus, incentives that reward prompt resolutions (discounts or faster product delivery) and involve less cost to achieve resolution (the organization offering ADR pays the entire cost of the neutral's expenses) can promote increased use of ADR. Given the direct costs of inter-organizational disputes, an ADR system can often create mutual gains in efficiency and cost effectiveness for all parties involved in the dispute.

The investors dealing with FSMA, for example, may be most interested in using arbitration to determine their claims in order to avoid the time, aggravation, and expense of litigation.

Increased Access

Particularly with customers and clients who have ongoing business relationships with the organization or institution, there may be an incentive to use the ADR system as a way to gain access to key organizational leaders or to acquire a voice in organizational operations. Thus, external stakeholders may be motivated to use particular alternative dispute resolution options, such as mini-trials, where the presence of key decision makers is often required. In this fashion, it is possible during the resolution process to communicate about systemic issues that may go to the core of similar or recurring disputes.

In addition, interest-based resolution processes provide increased opportunities for external stakeholders to explore the reasons why products or services are produced or delivered in a particular fashion. A mutual sharing by the organizations involved or the individuals affected, as in consumer disputes, of information about how and why disputes occur between them may result in changes in operations to prevent future occurrences of disagreements.

At Hopevale, for example, community representatives may be anxious to serve on a commission with hospital management to study the issue of expanding only the Emergency Department and not the Cardiac Care Unit (since Mainline has a competitive edge in that practice area) because it gives them access to hospital decision makers. The consumers dealing with Chompist may be motivated to use mediation or the company ombudsperson if they believe it will be less costly and faster than resorting to litigation or state consumer agencies and will result in improved customer service.

Relationship Improvement

A frequently important incentive to use the ADR system is to build and strengthen ongoing relationships. Because interest-based ADR systems are usually less adversarial than traditional methods of dispute resolution, there is an opportunity to practice improved communication and problem-solving techniques and mechanisms that can last beyond the moment of the immediate dispute. Further, there are benefits to the way that interest-based processes often get to the heart of the problem and enhance understanding of the perspectives of those in disagreement. Thus, improvement in the ongoing relationship results from increased understanding of one's counterparts' interests and can be a by-product of ADR.

Hopevale's community representatives may be interested in improving their relationship with hospital management so that they can address other community issues as they arise. The search conference may enhance and deepen both the hospital and the community representatives' recognition of each other's interests. It may also heighten appreciation of the importance of their ability to work together to achieve high-quality, cost-efficient community medical services.

As we have illustrated in all of the foregoing, the appropriate use of incentives and rewards ranging across potentially differing preferences of organizational stakeholders, both internal and external, increases the utilization of and the sense of commitment to the new ADR elements of the conflict management system. We would suggest, however, that none of these incentives or rewards take the place of a high-involvement, high-quality ADR design effort; nor do they take the place of organizations, stakeholders, and practitioners involved in conflict management systems practicing ADR rather than just preaching it, and learning about conflict by using the processes themselves.

Chapter Twelve

Resistance and Constraints
Having Tea with Your Demons

Resistance and constraints happen. Budgets get slashed, turf battles are waged, power is diminished, managers get uncomfortable. Although the concepts of resistance and constraints have been discussed throughout the book, this chapter examines them more deeply from the perspectives of personality, politics, and practice. Many practitioners think of resistance and constraints as the "shadow" side of conflict management systems design. We like to think of them as an ideal opportunity for identifying levers for change in conflict management systems. We see *resistance* as a mostly unconscious social, cultural, and personality-driven phenomenon, and *constraints* as the instrumental aspects of architectural, resource, and systemic impediments.

In this chapter, our approach to the topics of resistance and constraints is to "get *on* the table what is *under* it." In this regard, we acknowledge the work of Judith H. Katz and Robert J. Marshak in their NTL Institute workshop on "Dealing with Covert Processes." To offer an approach and an attitude for dealing with covert processes such as resistance and constraints, they use the following Zen parable, which gives rise to the title of this chapter:

Having Tea with the Demons

A seeker of knowledge was climbing a mountain when hideous Demons appeared. The seeker took refuge in a deep, dark cave. Scared by the Demons, the seeker thought to roll a giant rock in front of the cave to prevent the Demons from entering.

On further reflection, the seeker realized that rolling a rock in front of the cave might keep the Demons out but would also keep the seeker locked in the cave in darkness.

Instead, the seeker of knowledge invited the Demons into the cave to sit and have tea. Scared at first, the seeker slowly became accustomed to the Demons. They no longer appeared as hideous or as powerful. Once this happened, the seeker was free to pursue the journey of knowledge.

The seeker also realized that first having tea with a few of the smaller Demons was easier than immediately having tea with the biggest and most hideous ones.

Some Thoughts on Force Field Analysis

To learn how to have tea with our demons and to understand fully and deal effectively with resistance and constraints, we return once again to the principles of force field analysis. As with many of our colleagues and other practitioners, our practice and experience has constantly revealed that movement toward organizational objectives can be enhanced if particular care is taken to identify and reduce at least some of the factors that prevent change. Reducing the number of restraints often enhances change in a startling fashion. As organizations and their members experience the results of this reduction, they often develop long-term strategies, such as education and training or systems of rewards and incentives, to reduce other sources of resistance and constraints as well. They also discover that successful reduction of restraints requires explicit and periodic identification of the forces that constrain change *and* the intentional targeting of certain restraints for short- and long-term action planning.

Anticipation of Resistance

We have noted repeatedly that conflict is natural, inevitable, and a fact of life. Yet, conflict often generates great fear and anxiety. We suggest that resistance too is a natural phenomenon—to be expected any time change in the status quo conflict management system is proposed. As with the common reaction to conflict, individuals often resist the new and the unknown and thus they reject change. Such resistance is usually seen as "bad" and is often dreaded and resented by stakeholders and leadership, as well as by the ADR design team, intervenors, and change agents.

One analogy we find useful in this regard is the medical practice in organ transplant procedures: scientists and medical doctors anticipate and plan for the fact that the human body will vigorously attempt to reject the new part. Thus, they do everything possible to get a good fit between the cell, antibody, and blood type characteristics of the donor organ and the intended recipient and they condition the recipient's body to be more receptive to the new organ through appropriate preoperative and postoperative drug therapy and observation. The relevance of this analogy for the work of conflict management systems design is obvious: by anticipating resistance every step of the way, design teams and leadership can plan for it and, it is hoped, decrease rejection of the new system.

Sources of Resistance and Types of Constraints

In order to understand what is happening in the organization when barriers to ADR surface, we find it helpful to have a "taxonomy" or chart of change barriers. We believe that if one can name what is happening and identify its source, remedial action can be more easily targeted and can be intentional. Relying on the distinction between resistance (unconscious social, cultural, and personality-driven phenomenon) and constraints (instrumental aspects of design architecture, resource, and systemic impediments), we name and identify below some sources of resistance and constraints and suggest possible actions to overcome them.

Resistance

Fear ("We're afraid to use ADR because . . ."): It is human nature to fear the unknown, and the introduction of any new system, including a conflict management system, encourages this emotion to emerge. Most individuals do not like change, in part because of their fear that it will lead to a loss of some kind (usually of control). Stability and predictability are important to some organizational members, and change is often seen as threatening to perceived stability. As a resistance factor, fear is nearly always present and does not favor women over men nor managers over employees. Rather, fear in its multiple forms is to be expected as part of the social fabric of an organization, particularly a changing one.

At Hopevale, for example, the in-house attorneys (particularly if they are litigators) may be afraid to use ADR because it will result in a reduction of their caseload and their jobs may be eliminated; the nurses' union may be reluctant to use ADR because they fear loss of bargaining power and influence; management may be reluctant to engage in ADR with community groups because they fear loss of control in business decisions.

Possible Actions: One of the most powerful interventions when fear seems to be operating is to name it. Creating processes where individuals have a safe environment to explore their fears can be useful. In addition, it is often helpful if as practitioners we name our own fears—of uncertainty, of loss of reputation, of conflict, of resistance, of failure, or of making a mistake.

At Hopevale, this might involve having the general counsel or vice president for the Legal Department explain why the hospital is using ADR to resolve its lawsuits and to reassure the staff attorneys that they have an important role to play in the ADR process. As for the nurses' union, it may be useful for union representatives to raise these fears with management and to confirm that participation in ADR to resolve some of the doctor-nurse disputes does not diminish in any way the union's obligation to represent nurses and to negotiate on any matters covered by the terms of the collective bargaining agreement. With regard to the conduct of ADR in the community, management may want to discuss exactly what control they feel they will lose—control of the process, control over the agenda of meetings, control of publicity and reports to the press, control over making long-term decisions that are in the best interest of the hospital—and determine what flexibility they can tolerate.

Culture ("ADR won't work in this organization because . . ."): This resistance factor arises from organizational, group, and individual attitudes, practices, and beliefs. As noted in Chapter One, an organization-wide example of cultural resistance might be the predominance of a "warrior-type" belief held by labor leaders or litigators, a belief that any dispute resolution process must have a high degree of advocacy or mandated settlement. An example of an organizational subgroup's cultural resistance might be that of "equity-enforcement," related to the belief that employees are powerless and somehow disadvantaged and hence disputes are an opportunity for them to advocate, to seek empowerment, and to "get back" at the dominant organizational culture. An example of an individual's cultural resistance might involve cultural and religious beliefs with regard to conflict, where turning the other cheek is the response, even within an organizational context. All such cultural resistance factors establish norms, or standards, by which dispute resolution procedures and results are judged.

For example, as a (hypothetical) enforcement agency, Federal Securities Management Agency (FSMA) may be reluctant to use certain facilitated methods of resolution given the larger organizational culture and mission. Often, enforcement and regulation is seen as an area where there is a "right" and a "wrong," with little room for interest-based negotiation or facilitated ADR. In addition, statutes and regulations often prescribe the outcome for certain types of disputes. As a result, FSMA's resolution of the investors' claims by arbitration may be for FSMA a congruent and acceptable form of ADR because it is an "imposed" method and closest on the ADR spectrum to formal, adversarial resolution methods such as litigation or administrative adjudication.

Possible Actions: As practitioners, we can choose to look at the "multiculturalism"—using that term in the broadest sense—in any given system as an adventure in making conflict management systems truly relevant and useful to all stakeholders as well as an opportunity to ensure that a conflict management system fits with the specific organization. If the process of design and involvement is valid, these cultural variables will be incorporated into the final product as a natural phenomenon. The resultant design will be unique to the specific organization, thereby assisting organizational leaders in addressing systemic conflicts, encouraging the system to keep learning about itself and its constituencies' needs, and encouraging the exploration of new ways of managing conflict.

At FSMA, arbitration is probably a good first-step ADR method for the agency to use with outside parties such as investors. It is congruent with the organizational culture and enables the agency to continue to meet it mission and goals. If the arbitration program is satisfactory to both the agency and the investors, it may be that at some point in the future the agency will be willing to try some "advisory" forms of ADR such as neutral expert fact finding or even a version of the mini-trial, depending on the nature of the disputes.

Power ("If we do ADR, I will lose power because . . ."): This resistance factor is often disguised as problems with the structure, operation, or perceived equity of the proposed or revised design. Usually, however, when one looks more closely at the identity of the "resistors" and any change in their level of influence (gains or losses in power) in the revised dispute resolution architecture, a core concern is uncovered: what's *not* in it for me? The power resistance factor may also be about loss of control by managers over their work practices, workforce, or work products. Designing the conflict management system to make it more accessible and responsive to disputes exposes organizational subcomponent operations more readily, making them more vulnerable and open to scrutiny, perhaps calling into question their very existence or utility. Also, having power (or maintaining the perception) is important to many organizational players, particularly as it relates to the win/lose paradigm in traditional dispute resolution. By rationalizing, economizing, and depolarizing conflict and dispute resolution practices, even if only in a small subpart of the system, ADR can literally take the fun out of the dispute resolution game for some who value the rush of the fight or winning the prize. ADR can thus be seen by some as a disempowering event, particularly by those who like to be in control of conflict.

At Chompist, for example, managers in the Customer Service Department may fear that they will lose power and control over customer disputes if an ombudsperson is introduced. In addition, they may fear that the customer will get an unfair advantage and that the ombudsperson will blindside not only the Customer Service Department but perhaps the Legal Department as well. As for the effort to use reg-neg (negotiated rule making), the company's Government Relations Office may fear that they will lose expert power and influence within the company if the more collaborative and expansive reg-neg process is used rather than the traditional comment and protest process of rule making and promulgation.

Possible Actions: System members need to know the costs, both tangible and intangible, of maintaining the current dispute resolution practice and its impact on mission accomplishment. Organizational members who are truly powerful often anticipate the need for change in the conflict management system and are frequently leaders of such change. On the contrary, it is often the people who are not powerful (but who think they are) who generate the greatest resistance. Those who believe that they will lose power in a revised conflict management system need to have the same opportunity as others to examine the need for change and to shape it in such a way that their individual concerns are uncovered and addressed. Astute power players can see or sense shifts in the attitudes and practices of the dominant organizational leadership about the issue of conflict and how it will be handled, and if this includes managing conflict "smarter" and with less cost, such players will usually align with the new coalition or revised system in order to survive. What is important for the ADR design team to do in such cases is to assist in the creation of a visible and committed critical mass of leadership who explore, embrace, and champion alternative directions in conflict management. Others will follow to the extent they are able, or they will exit the system—perhaps not physically but at least psychologically and emotionally—if adjusting is too costly for them personally.

At Chompist, the Customer Service Department, Legal Department, and Office of the Ombudsperson need to work together to determine how consumer complaints will be handled and what their respective roles, responsibilities, and limitations will be when dealing with consumers. Making these determinations may involve achieving a facilitated understanding of how this should be done, written out if need be. In addition, it might help for Anne Logan as the external design consultant to point out to each of the departments the threat to their continued functioning and to the company's viability if consumers cannot access an acceptable method of dispute resolution. With regard to the reg-neg, this may be seen as an opportunity for Chompist to win power and influence by taking the lead with the other companies and the state in addressing concerns about the proposed regulations.

Personality Preferences ("I don't like ADR because . . ."): Individual responses to changes in the conflict management system vary according to personality as well. Some people are comfortable with confrontation and direct dealings; others prefer distant, impersonal forums with representatives rather than with the principals themselves. Further, some individuals are adaptable to change, others are frustrated by it, and still others positively thrive on it. Some people tolerate ambiguity and others want precision; some relish spur-of-the-moment encounters and others value meticulous preparation. While one may like to focus on the rational, analytical, and logical aspects of dispute resolution, another may prefer to focus on the values, people, and "feel" of the dispute. Given these personality preference variations, which we base on the Myers-Briggs Type Indicator (MBTI), finding common ground for acceptable dispute resolution procedures is often difficult (and frustrating) at best.

For example, at Hopevale, there may be doctors who do not want to participate in the joint practice committee because they think it is beneath them or will somehow damage their image as being in charge. In addition, there may be doctors who have more traditional, hierarchical views of how staff conflict should be handled. There may be in-house attorneys at Hopevale who do not want to participate in ADR because they consider it too "soft" or indirect or time consuming.

Possible Actions: It helps to anticipate the diversity of preferences and responses to conflict and to make room in the design process for them. Beyond that, the design team can encourage the identification and acceptance of differences on the part of those charged with administration and implementation of the conflict management system. This can be done through training appropriate system implementers and administrators in team-building and individual awareness tools such as the MBTI. If the ADR team members are sensitized to the differences and preferences among the MBTI's sixteen personality types with regard to information gathering, decision making, and handling conflict, their ability to work together to plan and implement the ADR efforts in the organization will be enhanced. It can also sensitize them to the needs of other system participants in the creation and implementation phases of determining an appropriate approach to ADR. A more ambitious approach (and one that we admit is not practical or realistic in all organizational settings) is to educate the organization's stakeholders as a whole about preferences and MBTI typology in order to improve whole-system understanding of and tolerance for varying styles of managing conflict. This latter approach is a more preemptive or preventive approach to conflict management.

At Hopevale, for example, it makes no sense to "force" doctors to be on the joint practice committee. However, Jeff Linton of Conflict Consultants may want to ensure that there are opportunities for resistant doctors to raise their concerns and channel them to other doctors who will be on the committee. Similarly, attorneys who prefer to handle conflict directly and quickly may be inappropriate choices for Hopevale's legal management to designate initially as participants in a facilitated ADR proceeding. Here too, Jeff will want to design training opportunities to educate these attorneys to the benefits of ADR and reasons for its use, including strategic and tactical issues.

Symbols and Images ("ADR doesn't feel right here because . . ."): Another source of resistance may be the dominant organizational symbols, images, and metaphors, or the failure to adequately communicate the ADR message through their use. Resistance can surface when the ADR image does not match with the more predominant organizational image. Mandating mediation in court programs is a classic example. The ADR process of mediation relies on voluntary participation and decision making by the participants, with the assistance of a third party skilled in negotiation and sensitive to the needs of the parties to the dispute. When people are forced to use such a process at the direction of a judge, the two images—that of voluntary resolution and mandated participation—are not congruent. Symbolic resistance can surface as well when new images are not created to signify, support, and clarify the uncertainty and confusion that usually accompanies a change in the conflict management system. Thus, the use of clasped hands as the logo for many labor-management cooperation initiatives signifies the intent behind the initiatives and symbolically supports the image of cooperation in the eyes of organizational participants; the existence of a troubled labor-management relationship is incongruent with this symbol. Similarly, when the introduction of an ADR process is ill timed with other important organizational events, the image of ADR's interest-based processes as beneficial to both the organization and its stakeholders is often irreparably tarnished. For example, there may likely be skepticism and resistance by employees to the apparent hypocrisy of using a new ADR approach to resolving internal personnel disputes if the program is announced at the same time that the organization is laying off employees. In such a circumstance, the ADR image of "faster, less costly, and more satisfactory dispute resolution" would likely generate the impression that such benefits are intended solely for the organization, so that it can get rid of employees without too much hassle.

At the Chompist Company, the use of an ombudsperson and a joint labor-management safety committee may be in keeping with the image of the organization as a family-run business that resolves its disputes cordially and informally. Although the use of reg-neg may appear to be image-congruent as well, there may be some in the company who balk not at the notion of reg-neg itself but at working with competitors during the process.

Possible Actions: In the ideal world, changes in the conflict management system are aligned with organizational goals, timing, intentions, and their attendant symbols. If the organization is developing a revised mission statement with regard to customer service or employee relations, it helps if any attendant ADR program is congruent with the new mission. An ADR program can be heralded as part of that new focus if the images, symbols, and metaphors match. In addition, the power of symbols can often be used advantageously by organizational leadership. The letter from the company president encouraging use of the ADR program—or better yet the video announcement where top leadership and organizational stakeholders state together their hopes for the ADR program—can be invaluable in disseminating the image of top-level support for and broad involvement in the ADR initiative. In the same way, developing special documents with a new ADR program logo may help promote the importance of the new effort.

In this way, all of the typical promotional and marketing tools and symbols available to organizations are equally applicable to the management of the image of the ADR effort. Here, it is important that design teams increase their ability to sense the metaphors and symbols that exist in the organization and then develop a method for linking the ADR system to them.

At Chompist, such action might involve a statement from President Teznicki about his desire that Chompist work collaboratively with its competitors around the issue of the proposed regulations, or the convening of a management "rally" to kick off the new initiative and encourage input. Conversely, establishing a joint labor-management safety committee to study and gather information about the organization-wide problem of safety would be insufficient symbolically if it is done as the initial response to an employee's death in an accident. In such an event, immediate action is advised to correct the cause of the accident and to intensively signal genuine interest by the organization in preventing any further occurrences.

Constraints

Structural ("ADR doesn't fit here because . . ."): The ADR system itself may be a constraint. Issues of access and design construction are often the culprits here. A structural constraint may exist, for example, if the entry to the ADR system is difficult to access by intended users such as external stakeholders who have disputes with the organization but do not know that ADR is available or do not know how to enter the process. The entry point to the ADR system needs to be visible and free from impediments (such as geographical separation or reprisal) in order for external participants to use it. Another structural constraint may be an ADR system that accelerates or amplifies disputes or devalues a particular resolution technique because of where it is placed in the sequence of resolution processes. For example, squeezing the opportunity for mediation or some other facilitated method between a quasi-judicial hearing on the merits and access to the courts may be an inappropriate construction.

At FSMA, employees may not know that ADR is an option available to them in employee disputes, or they may know about the program but be reluctant to use it if they have to access the system through a formal mechanism such as a case manager or adjudicator rather than an EEO counselor. Conversely, management may choose to make access difficult by deciding to place the ADR option (mediation) *after* the formal complaint stage on the theory that allowing mediation in the informal stages of the dispute will open the floodgates to unmeritorious claims.

Possible Actions: Careful design architecture can overcome most structural constraints, which is why it is important that the architectural design phase not become rote or mechanical. Appropriate architectural constructs and successful implementation are the result of valid assessment and determination of appropriate ADR methods for appropriate ADR cases. Structural constraints can be easily identified and remedied through pilot projects, provided that the organization and the design team stay in a learning mode and open to opportunities for modification and improvement.

Ideally, the pilot project in hostile work environment disputes at FSMA will bring to light any problems with access. Moving the initial access point to the EEO counselors and allowing mediation in the precomplaint stages can alleviate these access problems, although these actions also increase the possibility that more disputes will enter the system. Such an increase in disputes in these types of cases may signal that there are more latent hostile situations in existence than previously thought to be the case. A healthy way of looking at the possible upsurge of disputes is that employees feel more free to raise these issues because the organization has signaled its receptivity to learning of any such potential conditions. As a result, employee morale and retention may improve.

Resources ("We don't have resources to do ADR because . . ."): Probably the most commonly voiced constraint in conflict management systems design is the scarcity of personnel, capital, time, and material resources needed to support a fully functioning ADR effort. "We just don't have the resources" is a frequent excuse given by those who are reluctant to introduce ADR opportunities into the organization's conflict management system. In a sense, the problems of self-limited thinking and self-fulfilling prophecy exist on a broad scale in both organizations and individuals. With individuals, this approach to problem solving sounds like "I don't have the resources to get more education and thus I cannot get a better job." With organizations, it is often stated as "We don't have the resources to do what we are supposed to be doing now, so we cannot possibly start something new." This limited and somewhat circular thinking starts and ends with whether the organization has the functional capability to engage in a new endeavor. In many ways, it is a vestige of the traditional view that organizations are static and stable, with fixed resources that cannot be expanded or leveraged or changed. Lack of resources can be a convenient excuse for an organization's failure to be innovative and to engage in appropriate and necessary change, particularly as more and more organizations use resource reallocation and customer satisfaction as the keys to staying afloat and competitive in their environments.

The Chompist Company, for example, may decide that it simply cannot devote any more internal resources to dealing with consumer complaints and that because the Customer Service Department already addresses these disputes, an ombudsperson would merely be "window dressing."

Possible Actions: The ADR design team would do well to anticipate that most organizations have a substantial element of resource conservatism. To overcome this, marketing strategies are useful: what will we as an organization get if we reallocate our limited resources to ADR? Will customers be more satisfied, will costs be reduced, will our reputation in the marketplace be improved? What will happen if we do *not* reallocate our resources to address conflict management issues? Quantitative motivators such as cost reduction can be useful here, since the ADR elements of a conflict management system often have a stated objective of reducing the costs of litigation and other dispute resolution practices. In some cases, the assessment process engages organizational leadership for the first time in the open practice of dispute cost analysis (looking at intangible as well as tangible costs). In addition, the evaluation process takes the achievement of cost objectives into account as part of its ongoing measure of success. Eventually, organizational resource allocators, leaders, and participants begin to see that ADR initiatives are less costly and more responsive to resource concerns and as a result additional resources and/or the reallocation of existing ones are provided to ADR efforts. For this to happen, however, assessment and evaluation data must be thorough and valid.

At Chompist, this process might involve Anne Logan engaging management in a "worst case" analysis—pointing out what might happen if it chooses not to have an ombudsperson. She might go further and note areas where Chompist might leverage existing resources (for example, filling the slot of ombudsperson with an employee or manager already working in the Customer Service Department) as a way of meeting both needs.

Leadership ("I can't support ADR because . . ."): Absence of organizational leadership support for ADR efforts can be a constraint. If commitment from the top is missing for the ADR effort, it is an uphill climb for the design team and the system to engage in many of the design processes outlined in this book. Indeed, although conflict management systems may be designed, implementation will be difficult (and in many organizations impossible) without buy-in and support from senior management and executives. Such leaderless ADR efforts often look and feel like guerilla tactics, covert and quiet efforts to win small battles to improve organizational responses to conflict. Unless top-level support can be obtained and sustained, the ADR effort may be doomed to marginality and obscurity.

In our experience, lack of mid-management support can also be a constraint. Middle management is usually the most heavily invested in the status quo—maintaining and defending the current dispute resolution methods—and therefore the possibility of a change in such methods is seen as threatening. In addition, it is often hard for middle managers to answer the WII-FM question (what's in it for me?) to their own satisfaction, given time and resource constraints on developing anything new. Thus, ADR education and training are an imperative here, as well as involvement of middle managers in every aspect of ADR design and implementation.

At FSMA, certain mid-level managers in the Legal Division may be reluctant to use ADR to resolve the Red River investor claims. They may fear that they will lose control over the caseload or that if the results do not favor the agency, there will be repercussions from senior management, the board of directors, or perhaps Congress in the next round of oversight or budget hearings.

Possible Actions: Our suggestion here is to "start small and think big." There will usually be some organizational manager, even at a subunit level, who is having difficulty managing disputes efficiently or effectively or who has a large backlog of cases and thus is looking for some assistance. Targeting these managers in need is the logical place to pursue small but successful ADR efforts. Here, it is critical to protect (to the extent possible) the manager's interests so that he or she does not lose face as a result of engaging in ADR efforts. Providing quality design and ADR services to such a manager can yield a harvest of ADR acceptability. Then, once the ADR effort is successful, such a middle manager will probably support the introduction of ADR through participating actively in publicizing the success of the ADR pilot as well as through quietly being available to discuss how it really worked with his or her peer middle managers.

FSMA may want to house the arbitration project in a particular section of the Legal Division—one that is headed by an attorney who is open to ADR, is looking to reduce the backlog in his or her unit, or is interested in having the unit be on the cutting edge of a new initiative.

Orchestration ("We cannot manage all of the details of introducing an ADR system because . . ."): This last major area of constraint addresses the difficulty of managing the transition from traditional dispute resolution practices to more interest-based conflict management systems. Keeping in mind that the default mechanism in any conflict management system is the status quo dispute resolution mechanism, people will not use the new system if it is perceived as too cumbersome, too confusing, or too costly. Active leadership in managing and coordinating the various elements of the change effort is therefore an imperative. We use the term *orchestration* here intentionally to suggest the image of the symphony conductor who must be attuned to the instrumentation of the entire orchestra in order to facilitate the creation of music. Likewise, managing diverse and simultaneous conflict management design activities is a challenge for the ADR coordinator, administrator, or design team because it requires maintaining a "whole systems" perspective and an ability to work on discrete problems while the organization continues to conduct its ongoing daily business. Design teams and organizational leaders discover quickly that "it is what you are *not* looking at that usually comes up and bites you," causing confusion, discord, and new challenges.

Orchestration of the community-wide search conference could be a political and logistical nightmare for Hopevale. For example, the design team will need to determine who to invite from the community and from other health care providers to be involved in planning such an effort. Planning committee members will then need to educate themselves and other potential participants about the search process at the same time that the logistics of a meeting place, administrative support, and other details are pursued. Multiple political, economic, and logistical dynamics and decisions will occur up to and indeed even during the search event, while at the same time the planning committee will need to deal with any resistance or sabotage that arises from the complex mix of interest groups involved—the community, other institutional health care providers, state and local officials, patients and their families, and health care professionals.

Possible Actions: Design teams that include representative stakeholders can help here because they can reach back to work with various segments of the organization. These individuals become the "sensing agents" for what is occurring in the ADR implementation phase. They can caution and caucus with other design team members about perceived constraints, needed action, and appropriate responses. In addition, this is where an ADR steering committee, task force, or coordinating council composed of representatives and managers from various divisions and offices across the organization can be invaluable as a way to keep track of both the logistics and dynamics at work. Organizational leadership will rely on such groups for valid feedback and information about the status of the change effort. Managing the political dynamics of the ADR change effort is primarily a leadership task, and the design team has a responsibility to keep the organizational leadership apprised of when and where there is a need for intervention. For example, organizational leaders need to be made aware of the fact that the public image of their adversarial labor relations practices flies in the face of the stated organizational goal of being a star in the universe of ADR-friendly organizations. As a result of increased awareness, organizational leadership may choose to realign this element of their organizational practice in order to achieve congruency with their conflict management objectives.

At Hopevale, the ADR team may want to brainstorm with management some of the potential pitfalls of the community-wide search conference. They may also want to enlist the personal commitment and support of members of the board of directors who are active in the community, and they may want to work closely with Hopevale's Public Affairs Office to produce appropriate "shaping" of the publicity surrounding the event. Education about the goals of the search conference will need to be targeted to all of the varying constituencies involved. Also, along with orchestrating the place, time, and other logistics, the ADR team will need to acquire the advice and assistance of other consultants, organization development (OD) practitioners, conflict intervenors, and public participation practitioners who are knowledgeable about search conferences to optimize the success of the event.

Personality, Politics, and Practice

As a way of summarizing, we find it useful to group the sources of resistance and types of constraints into three broad categories: personality, politics, and practice. The following chart (Table 12.1) produces in an abbreviated form an initial collection of the manifestations of resistance and constraints that we have uncovered in our practice, and our thoughts on potential actions to begin to address them. Our hope is that the chart and this chapter's discussion will stimulate dialogue among our fellow practitioners on the differing forms in which resistance and constraints in conflict management systems design efforts can appear and be addressed.

In all of the above, what is most important is the ability of the ADR design team to be open to data and to the more subtle hints and guesses about what is truly going on organizationally when the team senses resistance and constraints. The ability to anticipate and perceive what system members are reacting to and what they are really saying is a gift rather than a skill. Is it a question of appropriate ADR design and access (a constraint)? Or is it rather a question of the perceived loss of power or control (resistance)? In addition, ADR design team members need to be aware of their own "stuff"—discomfort, resentment, or defensiveness when resistance emerges, which can block important signals about the need for action.

By anticipating resistance and constraints as organizational responses to change in the conflict management system, planning for them, and naming these behaviors, the ADR design team can

Table 12.1. Resistance and Constraints in ADR Systems Implementation.

Type of Resistance or Constraint	Manifestation	Possible Actions
Personality	• Fear • Personal preferences	• Educate about conflict • Increase MBTI awareness • Involve in early assessment • Name behavior • Build teams • Answer WII-FM question • Develop appropriate rewards and incentives • Give support and acceptance
Politics	• Organizational culture • Power	• Increase awareness of choices and costs • Increase buy-in through involvement and valid data • Seek committed leaders, managers, and stakeholders • Ensure congruency in all aspects of design • Market and campaign • Link ADR images to organizational culture and goals • Address WII-FM
Practice	• Organizational structure • Resources • Leadership • Orchestration	• Adopt experimental mode • Provide valid feedback • Focus on learning • Ensure accurate assessment • Work together across functions • Design appropriate architecture • Ensure resource innovation and commitment • Create multiple levels of support • Publicize success • Create ADR coordination

move into the tension and work with these concerns rather than block them or deny their existence. By having tea with their demons, ADR design teams can ensure that the introduction of ADR into the system has an optimal chance of acceptance, which is the focus of the final chapter.

Chapter Thirteen

Changing the Culture
Accepting Conflict and Encouraging Choice

Conflict is woven deeply into the very fabric of our lives, from our thoughts to our relationships with co-workers, friends, acquaintances, and family members to our interaction with groups and organizations. Throughout this text and our efforts to marry the principles, practices, and values of alternate dispute resolution (ADR), dispute systems design (DSD), and organization development (OD), we have attempted to make conflict accessible to analysis and exploration, with suggestions for enhancing the perceptions, choices, and actions that conflict generates. We believe that managing the turbulence of conflict requires nurturance, special skills, and improved practices on the part of individuals, groups, organizations, and nations. It also requires an attitude of acceptance—not of fighting, fleeing, denying, avoiding—and an understanding of the power of choices, not either/or, right/wrong polarities.

It is not enough to continue to tinker at the edges of conflict, with interventions that are limited, slow, and unintentional. With the increasing experimentation of practitioners in large group interventions, where design and application share Weisbord's vision of "getting the whole system in the room" (Weisbord, 1987), practitioners need to continue to enhance their understanding of conflict management as a system. The once-dominant image of individuals and small exclusive groups unilaterally determining the future and direction of their organizations is fading. Instead, organizations are turning to collaborative efforts with stakeholders and organizational participants, because these groups have the innovative ideas—and the energy to carry them out—so key to organizational survival, effectiveness, and growth. Allied with this shift is the belief that systems as a whole—be they families, organizations, or even nations—need to continue educating, informing, and empowering their members to more fully understand and accept conflict.

We think that the increasingly interdependent nature of our world cries out for an increased effort to accept conflict and to learn the skills and processes of conflict management and teach them to each other. We suggest that one way to make progress in this challenge is by creating changed cultures of choice and acceptance of conflict, initially at least in our organizational systems. Our hope is that by doing so, learning and increased awareness of conflict will permeate to a deeper level of every aspect of human interaction and change. One way to begin this voyage is to move beyond questions of why someone or some organization prefers to deal with conflict in a certain way (even though we have spent time discussing the topic in this book) toward an approach that accepts conflict and validates choices. This last chapter, then, focuses on the changed culture of choice and acceptance of conflict—on the part of the organization, its stakeholders, and its practitioners.

The Organization

In most instances throughout our examination of the design of conflict management systems in organizations, we have raised "what if" questions. What if the organizational leadership is unwilling to assess the current state of its total complex of dispute handling and results? What if the organizational leadership is unwilling to have organizational participant and stakeholder involvement throughout every phase of the design process? What if the organizational leadership is determined to only "insert" ADR offerings into its ongoing dispute resolution mechanisms? In other words, what if the organization does not want to examine the way it handles conflict within its boundaries and the attendant costs—dollars, time, satisfaction with results, and durability of resolutions? Should the practitioner walk away and wait until the organization experiences a crisis that increases its willingness to examine how it manages conflict? These are the dilemmas of working with organizational conflict management systems development, and such dilemmas are not uncommon in any change process. Rarely, if ever, is the "ideal" approach realized by the practitioner or the "ideal" response made by the organization. Given the importance of this arena of inquiry and action in the life of the organization, we offer some suggestions for moving forward in view of these challenges.

First, when one is dealing with one of the most sensitive aspects of human interaction—that of conflict—and advocating that the system and its members move into the tension of conflict, we suggest that there needs to be a conscious recognition that this is advocacy of courage beyond what is often possible or even realistic for the organization. We have a good friend and colleague, John Settle, who frequently addresses audiences after we have laid out the "best and ideal" approach to "doing it right" in conflict management systems design—and his message is to "just do it." In many ways, our friend is right, for there is never an ideal organization, ideal leadership, ideal time, or ideal method to improve a conflict management system. As practitioners, we all take the organization as we find it and if we wait until tomorrow—for more buy-in, for more resources, for more data—tomorrow never comes and the system never changes.

In addition, the real beauty and gift of interest-based processes is in using them, not talking about them. The mediation process in particular can be an amazingly empowering and energizing one for disputants enmeshed in conflict—a freeing of human need and desire in the midst of our more common expectation that we will win if only we can hide our pain, vulnerabilities, and weaknesses. Actually participating in interest-based alternatives to dispute resolution often leads to the deepest understanding on the part of organizational participants that they have and want a choice in the manner in which conflict will be resolved. The choice among diverse conflict management paths is organizational self-determination in action. But if organizations offer no range of choice in conflict management processes—structuring the resolution process as a polarity between all or nothing—they lose the opportunity to experience interest-based processes and perhaps more durable, satisfactory results at lower cost. In addition, they can become inelastic and inflexible in their response to disagreement, which can be increasingly dangerous and self-defeating in an age of vigorous demands for organizational adaptability and responsiveness.

Second, in the study of group dynamics, a frequent caution is that any group is doing the best it can at any given point in time. We would urge that the same perspective be adopted when practitioners, managers, and other organizational stakeholders are pursuing improvement of the organization's system of managing conflict. Therefore, in doing design work, we have found it useful to constantly remind ourselves that the organization is doing the best it can right then. The core task, it seems to us, is to encourage the organization to be open to making discoveries through questioning, assessment, and learning processes about the nature of conflict in its midst. From such inquiries, a key discovery is for the organization to learn that it does in fact have an existing system for managing conflict. Another key discovery is for the organization to learn the nature of the costs of conflict—in time, dollars, satisfaction, relationships, and results, and in lawsuits, settlements, ongoing disputes, and damaged relationships. Here, a key discovery is learning that there is an incredible array of possibilities open and available to the organization and its conflict management system.

Third, we would encourage experimentation by organizations as an ongoing part of learning about conflict and its management. This allows the organization to constantly reevaluate the proper fit between the dispute arena and the appropriate method of resolution, as well as to ensure congruency between the conflict management system and organizational mission and culture. Stakeholders and practitioners can assist the organization in adopting such an approach of experimentation by signaling that it is OK with them to reassess, redesign, and reevaluate the conflict management system.

The Stakeholders

Usually, little is said about the role and responsibilities of stakeholders as part of an organization's efforts to change its conflict management system. As we have repeatedly emphasized, we believe that those who have a stake in the organization, whether from the inside or from the outside, need to be involved in bringing issues to the surface, suggesting options, offering feedback, and reacting to revisions. If such individuals are excluded from the design process, they will face the choice of whether or not to protest and seek inclusion. Our focus here, however, is limited to reflecting briefly on what stakeholders can contribute to a changed culture of choice and acceptance of conflict in the organizations in which they have a stake.

Most stakeholders are no less than startled when they are first invited to become part of a survey or assessment focus group reflecting on an organization's current conflict management practices. This is the result of having a valued voice and a respected "place at the table," often for the first time. In this respect, the initial behavior of stakeholders may often appear subdued and in some cases awed—most likely a result of being thrust into the role of advising, guiding, and participating from one of advocating, reacting, and complaining. This can be particularly true when the organization has a regulatory or other directive role with its stakeholders. Moreover, because of the past history and pattern of dealings, it is not uncommon for stakeholders to have a low level of trust at this initial stage: "They never cared what we thought before, so why should we believe they want our ideas now?" In the face of such uncertainty, stakeholder involvement is rarely freewheeling, creative, and open in the early stages of interest-based design—a state that needs to be accepted and respected by both organizational leadership and practitioners.

What can change this lukewarm commitment by stakeholders to the process and the product of interest-based conflict management systems design? One method we suggest is ongoing stakeholder involvement as members of the ADR design team. As a member of an ongoing team, the role of the stakeholder changes significantly from sporadic, uncertain "consultant" to highly informed, involved, responsible, and committed team member. High-quality involvement really requires a new sense of responsibility, accountability, and stewardship on the part of stakeholder participants, as well as a tremendous commitment and reallocation of their time and energy. The costs are high in truly becoming a part of the solution, not just part of the problem. If such a high degree of involvement and commitment is not possible for stakeholders or not feasible in a particular organization, we have some observations about acceptance and choice regarding the manner in which stakeholders pursue their roles and responsibilities in conflict management change processes. These are intimately tied to each of the key areas of discovery discussed in the previous section about organizations: openness, systems thinking, cost assessment, possibilities, and experimentation.

Just as Funches (1989) noted the "three gifts" of the practitioner, heart, discernment, and presence, in dealing with client organizations, so too with the gifts stakeholders can bring to the process of conflict management systems design. In the case of stakeholders, the gifts may well need to change to those of willingness, forgiveness, and participation. The gift of *willingness* reaches to the core of stakeholder involvement—to willingly set aside reservations, to openly share information about the organization's current conflict management system, to meaningfully engage in the ongoing process we call conflict management systems design. The gift of *forgiveness* that stakeholders can bring to the process goes to the possible past failures of the organization and its leadership to include and involve stakeholders in decisions affecting their vital interests and concerns, as well as the possible failure to explore and respond to the causes, costs, and consequences of conflict. Lastly, the gift of *participation*—not superficial presence but deeply involved and engaged partnership—runs through all of the key processes of discovery for organizations in conflict management systems design, yet most particularly on the part of stakeholders. Without high-quality, responsible, and committed stakeholder participation, the organization is no better off for its efforts to involve those with an interest in the outcomes of the design process. With these three stakeholder gifts, the entire dynamic of interchange and involvement contributes to a changed culture of organizational conflict—again, to one of choice and acceptance.

The Practitioners

Much of this book has been devoted to the multiplicity of roles the practitioner plays in conflict management systems design. Here, we emphasize in particular that the practitioner's guidance and orchestration of organizational learning about conflict management systems is, as identified in Chapter Four, an interest-based intervention akin to the mediation of an entire system. When the tasks of a mediator (introduction, clarify issues, gather information, identify interests, develop options, narrow options, and closure) are wedded with the spirit embodied in Funches' three gifts of the OD practitioner, a whole picture of a practitioner's role in the delicate process of conflict management systems design emerges.

In light of these multiple tasks and gifts, we believe that as practitioners we have a very different burden from organizations and stakeholders in the process of changing the culture of conflict and honoring acceptance and choice. Even with deep knowledge of and experience with interest-based principles and processes, we cannot force systems to be open, to offer choices, or to change. Rather, as practitioners, we must constantly remind ourselves (and each other) to respect organizational and stakeholder self-determination. This can be personally frustrating, for we know in our heads that a failure of the organization to be open or a failure to change in response to valid feedback may affect the very survival of the organization or its continued viability. Moreover, and particularly with past histories of bitter disputes, organizations are often unwilling to include all aspects of their system in the discovery and change process—and thus fail to act as an integrated whole. As a result, the remaining process of identifying the costs of conflict, uncovering choices for action and remedy, and experimenting to learn the best fit of ADR processes becomes flawed and incomplete. As practitioners, it is easy for us to feel responsible for such perceived failures.

We find it useful at such times to remember that our role in interest-based conflict management systems design is that of a guide and a resource, with the organization and its stakeholders maintaining the control and responsibility for results. After we have applied whatever skill, knowledge, and influence we bring as gifts to the change intervention, we find it helpful and comforting to adopt an attitude of humility and acceptance: humility that the process and the results are "owned" by the organization and the stakeholders, not us, and acceptance of the choices that have been made or not made. It is the courage to accept that which *we* cannot change.

We also find it useful to remember the initial tenet of the Hippocratic oath: "First, do no harm." If we have avoided harm—that is, have not increased the level of conflict and blame in the system—then we have remained true to our clients. If we have also honored and enacted the values of openness, feedback, and participation in the design process, then we have remained true to ourselves. It is perhaps this personal congruency—walking the talk, so to speak—that is both the greatest gift *and* the greatest burden for the practitioner.

Mirroring

How does one synthesize the various "gifts" and roles of organizations, stakeholders, and practitioners with regard to acceptance and choice? The "mirror exchange" (as it is called in OD) or "reflecting back" (in ADR parlance) is a time-tested tool used by mediators and other neutrals that can be adapted for use in the design arena. The mirror exchange has been used to improve intergroup relations (such as between labor and management in the workplace) and to de-escalate hostilities in the international community; it can also be insightful in the conflict management design process.

"Mirroring" in the design context involves the stakeholders holding up a figurative looking glass to organizational leadership and asking questions such as "What can the organization do to improve its management of conflict with respect to stakeholders?" This exercise requires the organization to be willing to look at itself and articulate what it sees. This elicits a "to-do" list of possible action items. The magic of the exchange occurs when the question is reflected back to the stakeholders (who must also be willing to look and to share insights): "What can stakeholders do to improve management of conflict with the organization?" This exchange can also be done by practitioners (both internal design specialists and external design consultants), particularly in the entry and contracting phases. Such mirroring leads to a wealth of information as well as to an increased awareness that conflict management is *everyone's* responsibility.

We suggest that the ultimate breakthroughs in effective conflict management systems design and in the creation of changed cultures of choice and acceptance of conflict can occur with the use of such mirrors but most particularly when we are willing to hold them up for our own reflection—as organizations, as stakeholders, as practitioners. Only through such self-examination can we recognize that we all contribute to and help sustain present levels of conflict in the world around us and that we can all contribute to changing the way we manage conflict.

Epilogue
Implications for Improving Conflict Management Systems

And so we return to the water, which is where we began. As we mentioned at the beginning of this book, conflict is like water: it is everywhere—within individuals, within groups, within communities, within nations, within the global village. As with water, conflict presents unlimited opportunities for growth and healing as well as for damage and destruction. What we do with these opportunities is our choice as practitioners and as stakeholders. There is a saying: "If you want peace, work for justice." Perhaps if we want peace, we should learn, create, build, practice, manage, teach, and design interest-based conflict management systems.

The basic question seems to be, "Why should *I* (or he, she, we, they, or it) care about systemic conflict management? Why should I as a practitioner, as a stakeholder, strive to create interest-based conflict management processes?" The answer lies in whether we aspire to be stewards of the many systems within which we live or whether we settle for being mere spectators. Stewardship involves more participation, more energy, and more work than spectatorship, but the rewards can be far greater.

An effective organizational conflict management system can have multiple implications for many groups of people. Some parts of the system will reflect back on the individuals within the organization—by serving as a model of communication and problem-solving techniques that can be used in daily life with co-workers, spouses, partners, children, parents, and friends. Other parts will bounce back to groups within the organization—by setting up processes for joint problem solving that engage people of all types, preferences, and backgrounds in working together toward a common goal. Some aspects of the conflict management system will shine within the local community as organizations work hand in hand with the partners with whom they share land, resources, and responsibilities. One can hope that parts of the system will reach out to the nation, changing how the governed and the governing conduct business and how they reach resolution on issues of public policy and national identity. Finally, some parts may spread out to the larger world in which we live, changing in some small way the values underlying our management of international conflict.

What can we do as individuals? First, we can give ourselves permission to be comfortable with conflict, to be tolerant of it, to be more accepting about the way it presents itself in our lives. We can teach ourselves to stop trying to control conflict and to start trying to communicate about it. Perhaps that means speaking our mind, voicing our complaints with requests for change, setting limits or boundaries, or allowing ourselves to live peacefully with discomfort about unresolved issues. As practitioners, we can practice what we preach and be personally congruent—we can model the behaviors we advocate, incorporating ADR values into every part of our lives.

What specifically can we do as members of groups—in our workplace, in our families, in our friendships and social interactions? We can move away from hierarchical or dictatorial decision making and toward consensus building and joint problem solving. We can learn to voice differences and be comfortable with ways of resolving problems that look and feel different from those that we have previously witnessed, modeled, or mirrored. We can teach our children that participation, openness, and feedback about conflict are important and useful values to put into practice.

What can we do as members of communities? We can promote participative conflict management processes in our schools as they struggle with violence, anger, and polarity; in our churches as they grapple with leadership, doctrine, and ministry issues; in our communities as they address crime, drugs, environmental pollution, and unemployment. We can promote peer mediation and counseling programs in schools; we can promote open dialogue about

Kelly Hunter

822-9774 -

C# 868-0829

hunterk@sympatico.ca

the role of the church and the clergy; we can support neighborhood justice mediation centers.

What can we do as citizens of the nation? As government is downsized, right-sized, and reinvented, what is our role as citizens who are stakeholders in that system? We can advocate interest-based methods of dispute resolution that save the government and thus the taxpayer time and money—negotiated rule making, mediation, early neutral evaluation. We can promote participative public-private partnerships that improve both the process and the product of government.

Finally, what can we do as members of the global village? We can continue to promote mediated or facilitated resolutions of international disputes, to assist emerging nations in setting up conflict management systems, to support multinational dispute resolution organizations and efforts.

There are many other opportunities and possibilities to incorporate systemic conflict management into our lives and into our world. If we do—if we choose to become stewards instead of spectators, if we channel the waters of conflict instead of trying to dam them—we will free ourselves to be the instruments of peace.

Resources

Conflict Management Organizations

Administrative Conference of the United States (ACUS)
2120 L Street N.W., Suite 500
Washington, D.C. 20037
(202) 254–7020

American Arbitration Association (AAA)
140 West 51st Street
New York, N.Y. 10020–1203
(212) 484–4000

American Bar Association (ABA) Section on Dispute Resolution
740 15th Street N.W.
Washington, D.C. 20005–1009
(202) 662–1680

Center for Public Resources, Inc. (CPR)
366 Madison Avenue
New York, N.Y. 10017
(212) 949–6490

Federal Mediation and Conciliation Service (FMCS)
2100 K Street N.W.
Washington, D.C. 20427
(202) 606–5445

Harvard Program on Negotiation (PON)
Harvard Law School
516 Pound Hall
Cambridge, Mass. 02138
(617) 495–1684

NTL Institute
1240 North Pitt Street, Suite 100
Alexandria, Va. 22314–1403
(703) 548–1500

National Institute for Dispute Resolution (NIDR)
1726 M Street N.W., Suite 500
Washington, D.C 20036–4502
(202) 466–4764

Organization Development Network (ODN)
P.O. Box 69329
Portland, Oreg. 97201
(503) 246–0148

Society of Professionals in Dispute Resolution (SPIDR)
815 15th Street N.W., Suite 530
Washington, D.C. 20005
(202) 783–7277

Additional Reading

Alternative Dispute Resolution

Administrative Conference of the United States. *Sourcebook: Federal Agency Use of Alternative Means of Dispute Resolution.* Washington, D.C.: Administrative Conference of the United States, 1987.

Administrative Conference of the United States. *Negotiated Rulemaking Sourcebook.* Washington, D.C.: Administrative Conference of the United States, 1990.

Administrative Conference of the United States. *Implementing the ADR Act: Guidance for Dispute Resolution Specialists.* Washington, D.C.: Administrative Conference of the United States, 1992.

Anderson, D. R., and Hill, L. B. *The Ombudsman: A Primer for Federal Agencies.* Washington, D.C.: Administrative Conference of the United States, Resource Papers in Administrative Law, 1991.

Bush, R., and Folger, J. *The Promise of Mediation: Responding to Conflict Through Empowerment and Recognition.* San Francisco: Jossey-Bass, 1994.

Carver, T. H., and Vondar, A. A. "Alternative Dispute Resolution: Why It Doesn't Work and Why It Does." *Harvard Business Review,* May/June 1994, pp. 120–130.

Colosi, T. R., and Colosi, C. B. *Mediation: A Primer for Federal Agencies.* Washington, D.C.: Administrative Conference of the United States, Resource Papers in Administrative Law, 1993.

Costantino, C. A. "FDIC Favors Use of ADR." *World Arbitration and Mediation Report,* 1992, *3*(10), 256–258.

Costantino, C. A. "FDIC Uses Spectrum of ADR Options to Resolve Disputes." *Federal Bar News and Journal,* 1992, *39*(9), 524–527.

Costantino, C. A. "Can Private Parties Get to the Government?" *Alternatives to the High Cost of Litigation,* 1993, *11*(10), 135–136.

Costantino, C. A. "Commentary: Resolving Disputes." *Harvard Business Review,* July/Aug. 1994, p. 144.

Costantino, C. A., and Kaplow, C. M. "FDIC Criteria for Neutrals Depends on Experience." *Alternatives to the High Cost of Litigation,* 1994, *12*(7), 85–95.

Costantino, C. A., and McClellan, M. M. "Scoring with ADR: The FDIC and RTC." *Probate and Property,* July/Aug. 1993, pp. 52–55.

Dauer, E. *Manual for Dispute Resolution: ADR Law and Practice.* New York: McGraw-Hill, 1994.

Davis, A. "Mediation: The Field of Dreams? If We Build It, They Will Come." *Negotiation Journal,* 1993, *9*(1), 5–11.

DeLeon, L. "Using Mediation to Resolve Personnel Disputes in a State Bureaucracy." *Negotiation Journal,* 1994, *10*(1), 69–86.

Drake, W. R. "Statewide Offices of Mediation." *Negotiation Journal,* 1989, *5*(4).

Feuille, P., and Kolb, D. "Waiting in the Wings: Mediation's Role in Grievance Resolution." *Negotiation Journal,* 1994, *10*(3), 249–264.

Fisher, R., and Brown, S. *Getting Together.* Boston: Houghton Mifflin, 1988.

Fisher, R., and Ury, W. *Getting to Yes.* New York: Houghton Mifflin, 1981.

Folberg, J., and Taylor, A. *Mediation: A Comprehensive Guide to Resolving Conflicts Without Litigation.* San Francisco: Jossey-Bass, 1984.

Folger, J., and Jones, T. S. *New Directions for Mediation: Communication Research and Perspectives.* Newbury Park, Calif.: Sage, 1994.

Goldberg, S. B., Sander, F.E.A., and Rogers, N. H. *Dispute Resolution.* (2nd ed.) Boston: Little, Brown, 1992.

Hall, L. *Negotiation Strategies for Mutual Gain.* Newbury Park, Calif.: Sage, 1993.

Keltner, J. W. *The Management of Struggle.* Cresskill, N.J.: Hampton Press, 1994.

Kolb, D. M. "Her Place at the Table: A Consideration of Gender Issues in Negotiation." *Program on Negotiation Working Paper Series* (revised). Cambridge, Mass.: Program on Negotiation, Oct. 1988.

Kolb, D. M., and Kolb, J. E. "All the Mediators in the Garden." *Negotiation Journal,* 1993, *9*(4), 335–339.

Kressel, K., Pruitt, D. G., and Associates. *Mediation Research: The Process and Effectiveness of Third-Party Intervention.* San Francisco: Jossey-Bass, 1989.

Moore, C. *The Mediation Process: Practical Strategies for Resolving Conflict.* San Francisco: Jossey-Bass, 1986.

Rogers, N., and McEwen, C. *Mediation: Law, Policy and Practice.* (2nd ed.) Deerfield, Ill.: Clark, Boardman, Callaghan, 1994.

Rosenberg, J., and Folberg, J. "Alternative Dispute Resolution: An Empirical Analysis." *Stanford Law Review,* 1994, *46,* 1487.

Singer, L. R. *Settling Disputes: Conflict Resolution in Business, Families and the Legal System.* (2nd ed.) Boulder, Colo.: Westview Press, 1994.

Stevens, C., Donnelly, L., and Grove, S. *Court-Ordered Mediation in North Carolina: An Evaluation of Its Effects*. Chapel Hill: Institute of Government, University of North Carolina Press, 1989.

Susskind, L. E., Babbitt, E. F., and Segal, P. N. "When ADR Becomes the Law: A Review of Federal Practice." *Negotiation Journal*, 1993, *9*(1), 59–75.

True, J. M., III. "Commentary: Employment ADR: Leveling the Playing Field." *Alternatives to the High Cost of Litigation*, 1994, *12*(11), 140–143.

Ury, W. L. *Getting Past No*. New York: Bantam Books, 1991.

Wilkinson, J. H. (ed). *Donovan Leisure Newton & Irving ADR Practice Book*. New York: Wiley, 1990 (and supplements).

Dispute Systems Design

Brett, J. M., Goldberg, S. B., and Ury, W. L. *Managing Conflict: The Strategy of Dispute Systems Design*. New York: Business Week Executive Briefing Service, 1994.

Cloke, K. "Conflict Resolution Systems Design, the United Nations and the New World Order." *Mediation Quarterly*, 1991, *8*(4), 343–347.

Costantino, C. A. "How to Set Up an ADR Program." *Government Executive*, 1994, *26*(7), 44–45.

Costantino, C. A., Merchant, C. S., and Administrative Conference of the United States, Dispute Systems Design Working Group. "Introduction: Disputes System Design in the Federal Government." *World Arbitration and Mediation Report*, 1993, *4*(7), 169–173.

Ertel, D. "How to Design a Conflict Management Procedure That Fits Your Dispute." *Sloan Management Review*, 1991, *32*(4), 39–42.

Goldberg, S. B., and Brett, J. M. "Disputants' Perspectives on the Differences between Mediation and Arbitration." *Negotiation Journal*, 1990, *6*(3), 249.

Goldberg, S. B., and Brett, J. M. "Getting, Spending, and Losing Power in Dispute Systems Design." *Negotiation Journal*, 1991, *7*(2), 119–121.

Goldberg, S. B., Brett, J. M., and Ury, W. L. "Designing an Effective Dispute Resolution System." *Negotiation Journal*, 1988, *4*(4), 413–431.

Goldberg, S. B., Green, E., and Sander, F.E.A. "Litigation, Arbitration or Mediation: A Dialogue." *American Bar Association Journal*, June 1989.

Kelly, J. B. "Dispute Systems Design: A Family Case Study." *Negotiation Journal*, 1989, *5*(4), 373.

Kolb, D. M. "How Existing Procedures Shape Alternatives." *Journal of Dispute Resolution*, 1989.

Lesser, D., and others, Administrative Conference of the United States, Dispute Systems Design Working Group. "Performance Indicators for ADR Program Evaluation." *World Arbitration and Mediation Report,* 1994, *5*(2), 41–44.

Manring, N. J. "Dispute System Design and the U.S. Forest Service." *Negotiation Journal,* 1993, *9*(1), 13–21.

Murray, J. S. "Designing a Disputing System for Central City and Its Schools." *Negotiation Journal,* 1989, *3*(4), 365–372.

Murray, J. S. "Dispute Systems Design, Power and Prevention." *Negotiation Journal,* 1990, *4*(1), 105–108.

Rowe, M. P. "The Ombudsman's Role in a Dispute Resolution System." *Negotiation Journal,* 1991, *7,* 353–361.

Rowe, M. P. "Options, Functions, and Skills." *Negotiation Journal,* 1995, *11*(1), 103–114.

Rowe, M. P. "The Post-Tailhook Navy Designs: An Integrated Dispute Resolution System." *Negotiation Journal,* 1993, *9*(3), 207–213.

Sander, F.E.A., and Goldberg, S. B. "Fitting the Forum to the Fuss: A User-Friendly Guide to Selecting an ADR Procedure." *Negotiation Journal,* 1994, *10*(1), 49–68.

Simons, T. "Practitioners of a New Profession." *Negotiation Journal,* 1989, *3*(4), 401–405.

Slaikeu, K. A. "Designing Dispute Resolution Systems in the Health Care Industry." *Negotiation Journal,* 1989, *3*(4), 395–400.

Slaikeu, K. A., and Hasson, R. H. "Not Necessarily Mediation: The Use of Convening Clauses in Dispute Systems Design." *Negotiation Journal,* 1992, *8*(4), 331–337.

Ury, W. L., Brett, J. M., and Goldberg, S. B. *Getting Disputes Resolved: Designing Systems to Cut the Cost of Conflict.* San Francisco: Jossey-Bass, 1988.

Weise, R. H. "The ADR Program at Motorola." *Negotiation Journal,* 1989, *5*(5), 381–394.

Weise, R. H. *Representing the Corporate Client: Designs for Quality.* Englewood Cliffs, N.J.: Prentice-Hall, 1991.

Organization Development

Argyris, C. *Personality and Organization.* New York: HarperCollins, 1957.

Argyris, C. *Integrating the Individual and the Organization.* New York: Wiley, 1964.

Argyris, C. *Intervention Theory and Methods: A Behavioral Science View.* Reading, Mass.: Addison-Wesley, 1970.

Argyris, C., and Schön, D. A. *Organizational Learning: A Theory of Action Perspective.* Reading, Mass.: Addison-Wesley, 1978.

Argyris, C., and Schön, D. A. *Theory in Practice: Increasing Professional Effectiveness.* San Francisco: Jossey-Bass, 1992.

Barker, J. *The Business of Rediscovering the Future.* New York: HarperCollins, 1992.

Beckhard, R. *Organization Development: Strategies and Models.* Cambridge, Mass.: MIT Press, 1969.

Beckhard, R., and Harris, R. T. *Organizational Transitions: Managing Complex Change.* Reading, Mass.: Addison-Wesley, 1977.

Beckhard, R., and Pritchard, W. *Changing the Essence: The Art of Creating and Leading Fundamental Change in Organizations.* San Francisco: Jossey-Bass, 1992.

Benne, K. "The Processes of Re-Education: An Assessment of Kurt Lewin's Views." *Group and Organization Studies,* 1976, *1*(1), 26–42.

Bennis, W. G. *Changing Organizations.* New York: McGraw-Hill, 1966.

Bennis, W. G. *Why Leaders Can't Lead: The Unconscious Conspiracy Continues.* San Francisco: Jossey-Bass, 1990.

Bennis, W. G., Benne, K., and Chin, R. (eds.). *The Planning of Change.* (4th ed.) New York: Holt, Rinehart & Winston, 1985.

Bennis, W. G., and Nanus, B. *Leaders: The Strategies for Taking Charge.* New York: HarperCollins, 1985.

Bion, W. R. *Experience in Groups.* New York: Basic Books, 1959.

Blake, R. R., and Mouton, J. S. *Consultation: A Handbook for Individual and Organization Development.* (2nd ed.) Reading, Mass.: Addison-Wesley, 1983.

Block, P. *Flawless Consulting.* Austin, Tex.: Learning Concepts, 1981.

Block, P. *The Empowered Manager: Positive Political Skills at Work.* San Francisco: Jossey-Bass, 1991.

Block, P. *Stewardship: Choosing Service over Self-Interest.* San Francisco: Berrett-Koehler, 1993.

Bolman, L. G., and Deal, T. E. *Modern Approaches to Understanding and Managing Organizations.* San Francisco: Jossey-Bass, 1984.

Bunker, B. B., and Alban, B. T. "Large Group Interventions." *Journal of Applied Behavioral Science,* 1992, *28*(4), 471–591.

Burke, W. W. *Organization Development: Principles and Practices.* Boston: Little, Brown, 1982.

Cohen, A., and Bradford, D. *Influence Without Authority.* New York: Wiley, 1991.

Connor, D. *Managing at the Speed of Change.* New York: Random House, 1992.

Covey, S. *Principle-Centered Leadership.* New York: Simon & Schuster, 1992.

Cross, E., Katz, J., Miller, F., and Seashore, E. *The Promise of Diversity.* New York: Irwin and NTL Institute, 1994.

DePree, M. *Leadership Jazz.* New York: Dell, 1992.

Eisenstadt, S. N., and Ben-Ari, E. *Japanese Models of Conflict Resolution.* New York: Routledge & Kegan Paul, 1990.

Emery, F. E. *The Emergence of a New Paradigm of Work.* Canberra: Centre for Continuing Education, Australian National University, 1978.

Emery, F. E., and Trist, E. L. "The Causal Texture of Organizational Environments." *Human Relations,* 1965, *18*(1), 21–32.

Emery, F. E., and Trist, E. L. *Towards a Social Ecology.* New York: Plenum, 1972.

Emery, M. *Searching for New Directions, in New Ways for New Times.* Canberra: Centre for Continuing Education, Australian National University, 1982.

Festinger, L. "The Motivating Effect of Cognitive Dissonance." In G. Lindsey (ed.), *Assessment of Human Motives.* New York: Holt, Rinehart & Winston, 1958.

French, W. L., Bell, C. H., Jr., and Zawacki, R. A. *Organization Development: Theory, Practice, and Research.* (3rd ed.) Homewood, Ill.: BPI-Irwin, 1989.

Fritz, R. *The Path of Least Resistance.* Salem, Mass.: DMA, 1984.

Funches, D. "Three Gifts of the Organization Development Practitioner." In W. Sikes, A. Drexler, and J. Gant (eds.), *The Emerging Practice of Organization Development.* Alexandria, Va. and San Diego, Calif.: NTL Institute and University Associates, 1989.

Hackman, R. J., and Oldman, G. R. *Work Redesign.* Reading, Mass.: Addison-Wesley, 1980.

Hammer, M., and Champy, J. *Reengineering the Corporation: A Manifesto for Business Revolution.* New York: HarperCollins, 1993.

Handy, C. *The Age of Paradox.* Boston: Harvard Business Review Press, 1994.

Hanna, D. P. *Designing Organizations for High Performance.* Reading, Mass.: Addison-Wesley, 1988.

Johansen, R., and Swigart, R. *Upsizing the Individual in the Downsized Organization.* Reading, Mass.: Addison-Wesley, 1994.

Kanter, R. M. *The Change Masters.* New York: Simon & Schuster, 1983.

Kolb, D. M., and Bartunek, J. M. *Hidden Conflict in Organizations: Uncovering Behind-the-Scenes Disputes.* Newbury Park, Calif.: Sage, 1992.

Kolb, D. M., and Silbey, S. S. Enhancing the Capacity of Organizations to Deal with Disputes. *Negotiation Journal,* 1990, *4.*

Kotter, J. P., and Heskett, J. L. *Corporate Culture and Performance.* New York: Free Press, 1992.

Kroeger, O., and Thuesen, J. M. *Type Talk.* New York: Dell, 1988.

Kroeger, O., and Thuesen, J. M. *Type Talk at Work.* New York: Dell, 1992.

Lawler, E. E., III. *High-Involvement Management: Participative Strategies for Improving Organizational Performance*. San Francisco: Jossey-Bass, 1991.

Lawrence, P. R., and Lorsch, J. W. *Organization and Environment*. Boston: Harvard University Press, 1967.

Lewin, K. *Dynamic Theory of Personality*. New York: McGraw-Hill, 1935.

Lewin, K. *Field Theory in Social Science: Selected Theoretical Papers* (D. Cartwright, ed.). New York: HarperCollins, 1951.

Lippitt, G. L., Langseth, P., and Mossop, J. *Implementing Organizational Change: A Practical Guide to Managing Change Efforts*. San Francisco: Jossey-Bass, 1985.

Lippitt, R. "Future Before You Plan." In *NTL Managers' Handbook*. Arlington, Va.: NTL Institute, 1983.

McGregor, D. *The Human Side of Enterprise*. New York: McGraw-Hill, 1960.

Marrow, A. F. *The Practical Theorist*. New York: Basic Books, 1969.

Maslow, A. H. "A Theory of Human Motivation." *Psychological Review*, 1943, *50*(3), 370–396.

Maslow, A. H., and Murphy, G. (eds.). *Motivation and Personality*. New York: HarperCollins, 1954.

Mayer, R. J. *Conflict Management: The Courage to Confront*. Columbus, Ohio: Battelle Press, 1990.

Metcalf, H. C., and Urwick, L. (eds.). *Dynamic Administration: The Collected Works of Mary Parker Follett*. New York: HarperCollins, 1940.

Mohrman, A. M., and others. *Large-Scale Organizational Change*. San Francisco: Jossey-Bass, 1989.

Morgan, G. *Images of Organization*. Newbury Park, Calif.: Sage, 1986.

Moss-Kanter, R., Stein, B. A., and Jick, T. *The Challenge of Organizational Change*. New York: Free Press, 1992.

Myers, I. B., and Myers, P. B. *Gifts Differing: Understanding Personality Type*. Palo Alto, Calif.: CPP Books, 1980.

Nadler, D., Gerstein, M. S., and Shaw, R. B. *Organizational Architecture: Designs for Changing Organizations*. San Francisco: Jossey-Bass, 1992.

Natemeyer, W. E. (ed.). *Classics of Organizational Behavior*. Oak Park, Ill: Moore, 1978.

Owen, H. *Open Space Technology: A User's Guide*. Potomac, Md.: Abbott, 1992.

Pascale, R. T. *Managing on the Edge: How the Smartest Companies Use Conflict to Stay Ahead*. New York: Simon & Schuster, 1990.

Pasmore, W., and others. "Sociotechnical Systems: A North American Reflection on Empirical Studies of the Seventies." *Human Relations*, 1982, *35*(12).

Peters, T. J. *Liberation Management: Necessary Disorganization for the Nanosecond Nineties.* New York: Fawcett Columbine, 1992.

Peters, T. J., and Waterman, R. H. *In Search of Excellence.* New York: HarperCollins, 1982.

Rahim, M. A. *Managing Conflict in Organizations.* New York: Praeger, 1992.

Ritvo, R., Litwin, A., and Butler, L. *Managing in the Age of Change: Essential Skills to Manage in Today's Diverse Workforce.* New York: Irwin and NTL Institute, 1995.

Ritvo, R., and Sargent, A. (eds.). *The NTL Managers' Handbook.* Arlington, Va.: NTL Institute, 1983.

Schein, E. H. *Organizational Culture and Leadership.* (2nd ed.) San Francisco: Jossey-Bass, 1992.

Schindler-Rainman, E., and Lippitt, R. *Building the Collaborative Community: Mobilizing Citizens for Action.* Riverside: University of California Press, 1980.

Schwarz, R. M. *The Skilled Facilitator: Practical Wisdom for Developing Effective Groups.* San Francisco: Jossey-Bass, 1993.

Senge, P. M. *The Fifth Discipline: The Art and Practice of the Learning Organization.* New York: Doubleday, 1990.

Sikes, W., Drexler, A., and Gant, J. (eds.). *The Emerging Practice of Organization Development.* Alexandria, Va.: NTL Institute and University Associates, 1989.

Sitkin, S. B., and Bis, R. J. *The Legalistic Organization.* Newbury Park, Calif.: Sage, 1994.

Tannenbaum, R., and Hanna, R. W. "Holding On, Letting Go, and Moving On: Understanding a Neglected Perspective on Change." In R. Tannenbaum, N. Margulies, F. Massarik, and Associates (eds.), *Human Systems Development: New Perspectives on People and Organizations.* San Francisco: Jossey-Bass, 1985.

Tichy, N. M. *Managing Strategic Change: Technical, Political, and Cultural Dynamics.* New York: Wiley, 1983.

Trist, E. L. "On Socio-Technical Systems." In W. G. Bennis, K. D. Benne, and R. Chin (eds.), *The Planning of Change.* (2nd ed.) Troy, Mo.: Holt, Rinehart & Winston, 1969.

Trist, E. L., and Dwyer, C. *The Innovative Organization.* Elmsford, N.Y.: Pergamon Press, 1982.

Vaill, P. B. *Managing as a Performing Art: New Ideas for a World of Chaotic Change.* San Francisco: Jossey-Bass, 1989.

Varoufakis, Y. *Rational Conflict.* Cambridge, Mass.: Blackwell, 1991.

Vayrynen, R. *New Directions in Conflict Theory; Conflict Resolution and Conflict Transformation.* Newbury Park, Calif.: Sage, 1991.

Weisbord, M. R. *Organizational Diagnosis*. Reading, Mass.: Addison-Wesley, 1978.

Weisbord, M. R. *Productive Workplaces: Organizing and Managing for Dignity, Meaning, and Community*. San Francisco: Jossey-Bass, 1987.

Weisbord, M. R. *Discovering Common Ground*. San Francisco: Berrett-Koehler, 1992.

Wheatley, M. *Leadership and the New Science: Learning About Organization from an Orderly Universe*. San Francisco: Berrett-Koehler, 1992.

Wright, S., and Morley, D. (eds.). *Learning Works: Searching for Organizational Futures*. Toronto, Canada: York University Press, 1989.

Ziegenfuss, J. T., Jr. *Organizational Troubleshooters: Resolving Problems with Customers and Employees*. San Francisco: Jossey-Bass, 1988.

References

Argyris, C. *Intervention Theory and Methods: A Behavioral Science View*. Reading, Mass.: Addison-Wesley, 1970.

Emery, F. E. *The Emergence of a New Paradigm of Work*. Canberra: Centre for Continuing Education, Australian National University, 1978.

Emery, F. E., and Trist, E. L. "The Causal Texture of Organizational Environments." Paper presented to the International Psychology Congress, Washington, D.C., 1963. Reprinted in *Human Relations,* 1965, *18*(1), 21–32.

Emery, F. E., and Trist, E. L. *Towards a Social Ecology*. New York: Plenum, 1972.

Fisher, R., and Ury, W. L. *Getting to Yes*. Boston: Houghton-Mifflin, 1981.

Funches, D. "Three Gifts of the Organization Development Practitioner." In W. Sikes, A. Drexler, and J. Gant (eds.), *The Emerging Practice of Organization Development*. Alexandria, Va. and San Diego, Calif.: NTL Institute and University Associates, 1989.

Gore, A. *Report of the National Performance Review: Creating Government That Works Better and Costs Less*. Washington, D.C.: U.S. Government Printing Office, 1993.

Lewin, K. *Dynamic Theory of Personality*. New York: McGraw-Hill, 1935.

Lewin, K. *Field Theory in Social Science: Selected Theoretical Papers*. New York: HarperCollins, 1951.

Lewin, K. "Quasi-Stationary Social Equilibria and the Problem of Permanent Change." In W. G. Bennis, K. D. Benne, and R. Chin (eds.), *The Planning of Change*. New York: Holt, Rinehart, Winston, 1969, pp. 235–238.

Marrow, A. F. *The Practical Theorist*. New York: Basic Books, 1969.

Maslow, A. H. "A Theory of Human Motivation." *Psychological Review,* July 1943, *50*(3), 370–396.

Maslow, A. H., and Murphy, G. (eds.). *Motivation and Personality*. New York: HarperCollins, 1954.

Myers, I. B., and Myers, P. B. *Gifts Differing: Understanding Personality Type*. Palo Alto, Calif.: CPP Books, 1980.

Sander, F.E.A., and Goldberg, S. B. "Fitting the Forum to the Fuss: A User-Friendly Guide to Selecting an ADR Procedure." *Negotiation Journal,* 1994, *10*(1), 49–68.

Senge, P. M. *The Fifth Discipline: The Art and Practice of the Learning Organization.* New York: Doubleday, 1990.

Society of Professionals in Dispute Resolution. *Qualifying Neutrals: The Basic Principles.* Report of the Commission on Qualifications, April 1989.

Society of Professionals in Dispute Resolution. *Ensuring Competence and Quality in Dispute Resolution Practice.* Report of the Second Commission on Qualifications, April 1995.

Trist, E. L. "On Socio-Technical Systems." In W. G. Bennis, K. D. Benne, and R. Chin (eds.), *The Planning of Change.* (2nd ed.) Troy, Mo.: Holt, Rinehart & Winston, 1969.

Ury, W. L. *Getting Past No.* New York: Bantam Books, 1991.

Ury, W. L., Brett, J. M., and Goldberg, B. *Getting Disputes Resolved: Designing Systems to Cut the Cost of Conflict.* San Francisco: Jossey-Bass, 1988.

Weisbord, M. R. *Productive Workplaces: Organizing and Managing for Dignity, Meaning, and Community.* San Francisco: Jossey-Bass, 1987.

Weisbord, M. R. *Discovering Common Ground.* San Francisco: Berrett-Koehler, 1992.

Weise, R. H. "The ADR Program at Motorola." *Negotiation Journal,* 1989, *5*(5), 381–394.

Vaill, P. B. *Managing as a Performing Art: New Ideas for a World of Chaotic Change.* San Francisco: Jossey-Bass, 1989.

Index

A

Acceptance, attitude of, 9–10, 56

Access: as incentive, 196–197; measuring, 177–178

Accommodation, attitude of, 9, 55–56

Administration/operation, evaluation of, 175–177

Administrative Dispute Resolution Act of 1990, 35, 71, 122, 125

Aetna, ADR at, 34

Alternative dispute resolution (ADR): advisory methods of, 40; as appropriate, 41, 121–124; architectural issues for, 117–133; aspects of, 33–48; at assessment stage, 112–113; continued evolution of, 48; dark side of, 41–44; dispute systems design for, 44–48; dynamics of, 38; ease and simplicity of, 129–132; emergence of, 33–34; at entry stage, 72, 73–74, 80, 83, 93–94; evaluation of, 168–186; facilitated methods of, 39; fact-finding methods of, 39–40; force field analysis for, 28–29; and identity of designer, 55; implementing, 150–167; imposed methods of, 40–41; as inappropriate, 122–123, 124–125; incentives and rewards for, 189–198; interest in, 34–37; knowledge and skills for, 128–129, 134–149; mandated, 52, 167; negotiated methods of, 39, 119–120, 125–126; options in, 37–41, 119–120, 126–127; practices of, 65–66; preventive methods of, 38–39, 125–128; process fit for, 124–125; reading list on, 235–237; resistance and constraints for, 199–217; and stakeholder control, 132–133; teaming for, 166–167; using, 139–140

American Arbitration Association, 38, 233

Architecture: aspects of designing, 117–133; background on, 117–118; how to use, 119–120, 129–133; principles of, 120–133; when to use, 118–119, 125–129; whether to use, 118, 121–125

Argyris, C., 28, 30, 92, 105, 108, 111, 238

Army Corps of Engineers, ADR at, 34

Arrogance: as conflict response, 8; and participation, 63

Assessment: and architecture, 121–122; aspects of, 96–116; background on, 96–97; and decision to act, 115–116; diagnosis distinct from, 97; of disputes, 100–102; issues in, 96–97; of needs for training, 140–142; of organization, 97–100; process of, 105–111; proposal from, 111–115; of resolution methods, 102–105; of results, 104–105

Avoidance, attitude of, 8–9, 55

Awareness, training for, 143–144

Aztec Corporation, 62–64

B

Boundaries, in conflict management systems, 24

Brett, J. M., 44, 129, 238

C

Center for Public Resources, and ADR, 36, 233

Change: conflict management for, 26–30; continual, and interest-based systems, 65; cultural, 218–226

Chompist Company: architectural design for, 119–120, 127–128, 129; at assessment stage, 99–100; at entry stage, 86–92; evaluation at, 172–174, 176–185; implementation at, 151, 152, 162–163; incentives and rewards at,